GLOBAL
Security Consulting

Overwhelming Praise for **Global Security Consulting**

"It's rare that a book delivers on its title, but *Global Security Consulting* really goes above and beyond what's advertised."

—P.T. Mikolashek, Lieutenant General, U.S. Army (Retired),
former Inspector General of the U.S. Army;
former Commanding General, Third Army, Operation Enduring Freedom

"Luke Bencie has written a very fine book on how to operate an international security firm. Working with Luke for several years, I can attest that he is a consultant who knows how to deliver."

—Major General Yousef Mansour, Kingdom of Saudi Arabia (Retired)

"This book provides insightful advice that is helpful for anyone looking to start a new endeavor – whether in the security management field or any other entrepreneurial venture. Luke Bencie's no-nonsense, how-to guide is infused with healthy doses of reality, encouragement and humor but packs a punch with keen insight and lessons learned based on years of field [and] high-level management experience."

—Mary Beth Goodman, former diplomat and
senior adviser to the U.S. Department of State

"Luke Bencie's *Global Security Consulting* provides a beacon of light to the profession of security management. His work represents his many years of experience in this difficult and risk-laden field of endeavor and will be the seminal how-to treatise on the security field for years to come."

—Guy Wyser-Pratte, CEO, Wyser-Pratte Management Company, Inc.

"As a former guerrilla fighter, intelligence operative, special ops practitioner and instructor, I have had the opportunity to work in some of the world's most dangerous environments. I promise that no matter what your experience and background in security, Luke's book will offer you something new to add to your global consulting toolkit. He writes from real-world experience, and the result is both useful and entertaining."

—Remy Mauduit, former FLN leader, French Intelligence Operative,
Special Forces counterinsurgency instructor

"Navigating the unique business environment of the Middle East can be difficult for outsiders. From cultural aspects to day-to-day practices, it is not a place where you can simply show up and expect business as usual. Luke Bencie has not only found success there as a security consultant, he has also thrived . This book gives away the secret to his success. If you're looking to become an international security consultant – or want to build on your existing practice – [it] is a wise investment."

—Majd Hosn, CEO, Saucal, Inc., an international business development firm

Global Security Consulting provides indispensable planning advice for worldwide security consultants. For perhaps the first time in security management history, you, the reader, can access invaluable insights and knowledge from a leader in the field to create maximum value for your company."

—Robert Bradshaw, President, Central Asset Management, Inc.

"Luke Bencie provides a clear roadmap on how to navigate the challenging arena of international security consulting. Don't attempt to transition into this field without first reading this book."
—Edward Leacock, Major General, U.S. Army (Retired)

"As the FBI's former lead international kidnapping negotiator and now an international consultant myself, I am impressed by the tips offered in Luke's book."
—Christopher Voss, CEO, The Black Swan Group

"I have had the opportunity to work with Luke Bencie in other parts of the world. After reading *Global Security Consulting*, I can honestly say he does live up to the mantra, Practice What You Preach. This is a great book for any type of international consultant – not just security professionals."
—Rigoberto De Castro, Global Events Manager, IIF

"Luke provides a practical guide to starting a global consulting firm, addressing best practices, common mistakes and challenges from his 'real world' experience in the intelligence community and founder of one of the leading security consulting companies in the industry. *Global Security Consulting* offers an unfiltered and in-depth view of the security consulting market that should be on the top of the reading list for individuals considering starting their own practice or moving into the field after careers in the government or military, as well as current consultants that are expanding their practice overseas."
—Michael Southworth, CEO, Contact Solutions

"From my personal experience, being believable is a product of having lived the actual life you write about. That makes Luke Bencie an expert, because he has experienced, firsthand, the value of good security management practices, and he continues to provide critical guidance to international high-profile clients. What makes this one-of-a-kind book worth reading? Luke gives the nuts and bolts of setting up a security company and then supplies hardcore practical guidance about managing clients and serious security issues. He also personalizes his work, including often unflattering, difficult experiences while highlighting some of his savored moments. And he couches everything in his down-to-earth sense of humor and realism. He helps you make certain you are meeting both your client's needs and the challenges of the profession. His book can help you become successful as well as personally satisfied."
—Martha D. Peterson, author of *The Widow Spy:*
My CIA Journey from the Jungles of Laos to Prison in Moscow

Global Security Consulting is the ultimate guidebook for professionals wishing to launch their own security consulting business. Bencie reaches deep inside himself and his own practice to show how to be a success, from the smile and handshake to the contract and process. Based on my 25+ years as a technology journalist, author and publishing consultant, I can safely say *Global Security Consulting* has no peer."
—Jack B. Rochester, author of *The Naked Computer*
and *Pirates of the Digital Millennium*

GLOBAL

Security Consulting

How to Build a Thriving International Practice

Luke Bencie

Mountain Lake Press
Mountain Lake Park, Maryland

GLOBAL SECURITY CONSULTING
How to Build a Thriving International Practice

© 2014 Luke Bencie – All Rights Reserved
Published in the United States of America by Mountain Lake Press
Library of Congress Control Number 2014945084
ISBN 978-0-9908089-0-9

Design by Michael Hentges

Printed in the United States of America

All statements of fact, opinion or analysis expressed are those of the author and do not reflect the official positions or views of the Central Intelligence Agency or any other U.S. Government agency. Nothing in the contents should be construed as asserting or implying U.S. Government authentication of the information or agency endorsement of the author's views. This material has been reviewed by the CIA to prevent the disclosure of classified information.

To all those entrepreneurs who recognize
that without risk there is no reward

Also by Luke Bencie

AMONG ENEMIES:
Counter-Espionage
for the Business Traveler

Contents

Foreword

PROVIDING SECURITY TO THE COMMERCIAL SECTOR has skyrocketed as a business in the 21st century because of the global spread of terrorism and organized crime, the increasing use of espionage against American companies, and the newly evolving threats of cyber theft and cyber warfare. The security components of multinational corporations no longer deal just with gates, guards, locks and ID badges. Today they fulfill a vast array of tasks, from risk mitigation, crisis management and intelligence analysis to due diligence and protecting information systems. No question, top-flight security now is essential to commercial success.

The situation has opened a new world of consulting opportunities, both here in the United States and overseas, for experienced and capable individuals in law enforcement, intelligence and the military. But the commercial environment differs drastically from the military or public service, in which so many seasoned professionals have spent all or most of their working lives. As independent security professionals, they must handle even the most mundane tasks themselves, lacking the usual support from government agencies or specialized personnel.

Likewise, the security professional's income depends entirely on his or her effectiveness in serving clients – no more doing the job routinely and receiving a government paycheck every two weeks. Earning income results from meticulous planning, successful marketing and delivering on promises negotiated in contracts. The rewards of global security consulting can be great, but the challenges can seem daunting, particularly to those lacking a background in the private sector.

Fortunately, Luke Bencie's *Global Security Consulting: How to Build a Thriving International Practice* provides a comprehensive guide for anyone considering making the leap from the government or corporate sectors to independent business. The book is easy to read and written for the layman, and it encompasses the gamut of requirements for building a successful security consulting business – everything from conducting sensitive negotiations overseas to procuring business cards and office supplies.

When I retired from the CIA, I decided to form my own consulting practice specializing in security and intelligence-related issues. During my career, I had spent years working and living overseas. I also was stationed in the United States, where I logged more years dealing with other government agencies and Congress. But like many of my colleagues, I felt lost wandering through the strange and dark forest of the commercial world. I pored over countless how-to books and articles about establishing a small business. Some were more helpful than others, but none dealt with the unique field of security. As Luke stresses in his book, security professionals operate in a rarefied atmosphere, where the risks are high and lives could be on the line. As one who learned on his own both the advantages and pitfalls of security consulting, I wish I had Luke's guide at the time. It certainly would have made it easier to establish my business.

Global Security Consulting is an especially useful resource, not only because it is comprehensive, but also because Luke has based it on his own experiences starting and building an extremely successful consultancy from the ground up. When he left the intelligence community and made the leap into private business, he quickly expanded beyond working out of his home to an international practice with offices on three continents.

I collaborated with Luke on a project and was impressed with his – and his company's – meticulous attention to the smallest detail of every aspect of the endeavor. Luke brings that same attention to detail to each topic in this book, whether the complicated world of financial management or preparing for a simple meeting with a prospective client. The topics represent not a mere checklist of requirements for the fledgling global security consultant. They include practical do's and don'ts often drawn from Luke's own business encounters, both good and bad, and they provide insights into all of the areas a budding security consultant will encounter.

Two aspects of the book impress me in particular. One involves conducting security consulting overseas; the other covers dealing with foreigners in a business setting. As I mentioned, there are now great opportunities overseas to work as a security specialist – but those opportunities are fraught with many potential pitfalls from legal and cultural standpoints. Luke explains those pitfalls convincingly and provides specific preparations and solutions to avoid them, often illustrating them with personal anecdotes from his own commercial dealings abroad.

Luke's advice not only educates aspiring security consultants but also helps them gain the confidence needed to build a global business. Although the commercial sector might seem a bewildering maze for newcomers accustomed to life in the government, Luke illustrates by example how security professionals have already acquired many of the skills required to succeed in the business environment. The secret is learning how to apply those skills and experience in the most effective ways, and Luke describes the best ways to do so.

Perhaps Luke's most valuable advice is how to sharpen your "BS detector" to spot potential problems and prevent missteps in business. That advice – and the tips he provides – applies to consultants in any business, not only security. I've honed my own detector over the years, and I can promise that *Global Security Consulting* will be a valuable reference for anyone interested in building a new career in this field. Read it, study it and absorb its lessons.

Michael J. Sulick
Former Director
National Clandestine Service,
Central Intelligence Agency

Introduction

Far better it is to dare mighty things, to win glorious triumphs,
even though checkered by failure … than to rank with those poor
spirits who neither enjoy nor suffer much, because they live in a
gray twilight that knows not victory nor defeat.

—Theodore Roosevelt

IT'S A FUNNY THING ABOUT STARTING A BUSINESS. Sometimes it can result from an Aha! moment, one that inspires you to strike out on your own. Or, it can happen much more innocuously. For me, it was the latter – and I'll never forget how it all began.

One fateful morning, I was driving my treasured silver Jaguar XK coupe along the picturesque George Washington Memorial Parkway from Rosslyn, Virginia, just across Francis Scott Key Bridge from the Georgetown section of Washington, D.C., to Central Intelligence Agency headquarters in Langley, Virginia. The 15-minute drive along the bluffs above the Potomac River was usually the most enjoyable part of my day.

I had been working for the CIA for over a decade, primarily as a contractor, and I had enjoyed the exciting lifestyle provided by the cool training, the exotic travel and, most of all, the excitement of conducting operations overseas. I had been to more than 100 countries, including numerous trips to Iraq, Afghanistan and throughout Africa. But as I approached my forties, I realized it probably was time to settle down and live a more normal life.

Although I was grateful for all that I had been part of the previous decade, most notably being able to serve my country after the terror attacks of September 11, 2001, I was starting to find my strengths better suited to the business world. In addition to working within the intelligence community, I had also spent three years with a major defense contractor, traveling the world developing business in several emerging markets, such as Brazil, Lebanon and India.

Surprising enough, it was during my time with this big Beltway bandit, as these firms are called, that I realized I was capable of opening my own consulting practice.

I had just returned from another two-month temporary duty, or TDY, in Afghanistan, and my fiancée was getting tired of my long absences. Back in the States, I was stuck in the hospital-like atmosphere at CIA headquarters. Unlike the movies, where high-tech computer screens hang on every wall of HQ, streaming images from around the globe, I worked in a cubicle with a couple of flat-screen TVs showing CNN and Fox News. Whenever a snowstorm approached the Washington area, instead of keeping tabs on live feeds from satellites peering down on terrorist training camps or adversarial military facilities, little by little the people would switch to the Weather Channel – again, contrary to the movie portrayals, agency employees are normal people.

Often on my drives to HQ, I'd share a cell phone call with my brother, a successful entrepreneur who employed nearly 300 people at his two marketing firms. Plus, he owned a French bakery. That particular morning, I informed him I wanted to start a security company as just "something to do … a hobby." My aim was to incorporate a small business using LegalZoom.com that could bring in maybe a thousand dollars a month or so. I would name it Security Management International, or SMI, in honor of late CIA legend Mick Donahue, the man who had first hired me at his own private consulting firm of the same name.

Little did I know that my dabbling into private consulting would become my new career within just a few months.

Now, nearly five years later, SMI has three offices – two of them international, in Brazil and Dubai. I employ more than a dozen people, I've written two books (with a third on the way), I speak monthly at business schools and at security organizations, and I'm regularly interviewed in magazines and on television. I recently spoke at the Pentagon. My clients include U.S. agencies and foreign governments, several Fortune 500 companies, law firms and universities, and a Hollywood studio, as well as non-profits. Most important, I earn a living doing something I truly enjoy. I still travel quite a bit, but I have more time to pursue my interests and be with my family. I've come to realize that although my life was always interesting, it's now more fulfilled.

What does this mean to you?
My experiences have allowed me to write a book that provides step-by-step guidance on how to build a global security consulting practice. Naturally, that doesn't mean if you quit your government job tomorrow you will experience the same success. But if you have recently retired from the military, law enforcement or the intelligence community, and if you are looking for a blueprint for establishing your own security consultancy, I can help you – including full disclosure about my mistakes.

Yes, I made a ton of mistakes getting to where I am now. They all cost me time, money, a few fights with my wife – which she always won – and a lot of sleepless nights. Starting any business, especially security consulting, isn't easy. But despite the hardships, I persevered and got things on track.

The good news – in a sense – is that opportunities for starting a global security consultancy have never been better. The explosive growth in technology over the past few decades has allowed global consulting to go from the privilege of the rich to the purview of the many. Just in time, too. The proliferation of computer and telecommunications technologies has not only made working internationally easier, it has also upended the playing field on which the geopolitical world is based. Consequently, reliable security services are at a premium.

Consider the turmoil that emerged with the so-called Arab Spring of 2010. All across North Africa and the Middle East, demonstrators voiced their discontent with living conditions and the governments that imposed them. Nearly every country in that region experienced upheavals. In the aftermath, tensions across the Middle East have frequently boiled over. At this writing, brutal Islamic extremists are running amok across Iraq and Syria, the Libyan government seems on the verge of collapse, Egypt's future remains unknown, and Iran's push for nuclear capability remains unchecked.

Meanwhile, in the Far East, China is flexing its military muscles to intimidate its neighbors; likewise North Korea continues its saber rattling. Islamic extremists are active in the Philippines, Malaysia, Indonesia and Thailand. Drug cartels in Latin America exert a murderous influence as jihadists wreak havoc in Nigeria, Somalia and Kenya. Taliban and al-Qaida operatives threaten the delicate political balances in Afghanistan and Pakistan. And of course, Russia is on the rise again. All these cases present urgent security concerns. Government officials and businesspeople alike desperately need the type of help experienced security consultants can provide.

There's also been an explosion of economic and industrial espionage around the globe pursued both officially and privately. It's become a multibillion dollar activity. Intellectual property and business secrets are being stolen daily from traveling executives, while cyber criminals and hacktivists routinely hit government and corporate targets in their offices. Counterfeit luxury goods and knock-off electronic equipment cost manufacturers substantially. Email scams, identity theft and bank fraud are proliferating. With the expansion of international investment opportunities by U.S. companies, the need for security firms to conduct due diligence on foreign business partners has become the new norm.

As mentioned, many governments have gotten in on the action of economic espionage. Pierre Marion, director of France's intelligence service, DGSE, once famously explained France's relationship with the United States – and why France is repeatedly accused of stealing U.S. business secrets: *In economics, we are competitors, not allies.*

Perhaps the largest demonstration of the need for global security consulting occurred on 9/11. Following that horrific day over a decade ago, the number of such firms within the United States experienced a thousand-percent increase. The number of individual consultants has grown even faster. Universities now offer degree programs in security management, national security studies, counterterrorism and related subjects. Twenty years ago you would be hard pressed to find a handful of schools with these curricula. Now, their proliferation represents the times in which we live.

If you want to add your knowledge and experience to the global security industry, this book can help. It will show you how to establish a security consulting business from the ground up. Whether you're new to the world of entrepreneurship or just looking for tips to expand your already successful firm, I'm convinced you will find the following chapters full of useful information.

For example, you'll learn the best way to form and organize your business, how to land clients and, most important, how to make a comfortable living. I have included anecdotes from my own experiences as a security consultant on six continents. I recount the good, the bad and ugly, including everything from the successful deals and how they were won to the hard lessons learned at the hands of conmen and corrupt government officials. For this and other reasons, I hope *Global Security Consulting* will become a frequent and reliable reference.

That said, please know that my results aren't typical, and I certainly can't guarantee you'll enjoy similar success in the same amount of time. I will promise, however, that the following pages contain the same practical advice I used to build my own firm.

Many of my friends, colleagues and even competitors have asked me, "Why would you write a book that explains how you run your business? You're just giving away valuable intellectual property." I respond as someone who wrote extensively about the threat of economic and industrial espionage in my last book, *Among Enemies: Counter-Espionage for the Business Traveler*. I have come to realize that any advantage contained in such property is fleeting. Perhaps Bill Gates put it best when he said, "Intellectual property has the shelf-life of a banana."

As an international security consultant, I'm constantly reinventing and upgrading my services – and you should be, too. Don't stress too much about the competition. Instead, focus on improving your clients' security conditions.

A word to the wise: Even if you're only working part-time, consider global security consulting a career, not a hobby. If you're only interested in earning extra income or just looking to keep in the game, consider teaching a class on security or starting a blog. But if you want to earn a six- or even seven-figure income in global security consulting, then you'll need to understand the tasks and strategies – and sacrifices – involved. Believe me, it isn't easy. Starting any business requires a strong stomach, thick skin and a high tolerance for risk. Most of all, it requires perseverance.

If you think you have what it takes, let the journey begin.

Luke Bencie

FALLS CHURCH, VIRGINIA

AUGUST 2014

PART I

Establishing Your

Global Security Consultancy

Note from the Field
Undisclosed Location, Afghanistan
0515 hours local time

It's an early morning in Afghanistan. I'm writing this from inside my pod – essentially a shipping container with a bunk bed – along the Pakistan border. I will be meeting one of my colleagues at 0600 to go for a short mountain hike inside the fence line while it's still relatively quiet. Like many Americans, my work has brought me to this part of the world several times over the years, both as a government representative and on behalf of the large defense companies operating under lucrative U.S. government security contracts.

When you work inside the Beltway encircling Washington, D.C., you quickly discover that opportunities to travel to Iraq, Afghanistan and the like are quite the norm. Some people take on these assignments for the substantial hazard pay. But the majority of us do it for patriotism and support of the mission. SMI, my company, keeps me busy, but I try to do an occasional TDY, or temporary duty, to a war zone. I believe it's important to contribute whenever I can, especially when so many brave men and women in uniform are making much greater sacrifices every single day.

1. What Is a Global Security Consultant?

Economic results are earned only by leadership,
not by mere competence.

—Peter Drucker

SO, YOU'VE MADE THE DECISION TO PARLAY your international security experience into a revenue-generating business venture. You want to sell your skills to those who need it, and you're fully committed to becoming the next big thing in the security industry. But before you start thinking about how you can cash in on your anticipated success, let's examine this particular discipline in detail. There's much more to security consulting than hanging out a shingle.

The first question you'll need to answer is: What type of security consulting are you going to offer?

Webster's Dictionary defines "consultant" as "one who gives professional advice or service." It also defines "security" as "measures taken to guard against espionage or sabotage, crime, attack or escape."

In other words, the discipline contains important distinctions, so you'd be well advised to choose a specialty. I advise you not to attempt to be a universal security expert, as many vain consultants essentially claim.

Even the word "consulting" can mean numerous activities. For many Harvard MBA types, for example, a consultant means someone who works for McKinsey & Company and dispenses advice to Fortune 500 CEOs. Equally prominent names such as Boston Consulting Group, Deloitte, and Bain also conjure up images of young, strategic management experts wearing expensive Tom Ford suits, crisscrossing the globe in business class while racking up outrageous hourly fees. These companies have constituted the gold standard in consulting firms over the past hundred years, but global security consulting is a different endeavor altogether – different even from what's known as strategic management consulting. This isn't to say that the business management models employed by the top firms aren't applicable – on the contrary. I encourage you to study these organizations and incorporate their best ideas into your daily operations. That's what we've done at SMI, and I've found many of the business methodologies from these traditional management firms to be valuable. For readers with a military background, you might have encountered the strategic teachings of Sun Tzu, Clausewitz, Machiavelli, Thucydides and other great masters of war. These studies will serve you well in your new business venture.

But before you try to transform yourself from police officer to strategic visionary for new product development at GE, remember Clint Eastwood's self-advice from the movie *Magnum Force*: *A man's got to know his limitations.* In other words, stick to what you know best in the field of security and make your mark there. Companies such as Kroll, Control Risks and G4S have grown from security startups into major global brands by sticking to what they know best: security. Avoid trying to do it all. There are riches in niches.

What are the niches?

In my experience, the global security consulting business can encompass the following services:

+ **Physical security:** The traditional gates/guards/guns analogy associated with perimeter security, monitoring of CCTV cameras and access control systems

+ **Physical security assessments:** Conducting security surveys to determine risks and vulnerabilities of a physical infrastructure and associated assets, as well as providing response guidelines in the event of emergency

+ **Information technology security:** Performing tests to ensure that an individual's or organization's computer network is secure from cyber intrusions such as hacking, malicious software or viruses

+ **Investigations:** Making systematic inquiries of a person, product or organization to determine or expose potential risks or uncover background information

+ **Risk management and due diligence:** Slightly different from investigations, risk management and due diligence involving financial and investment assessments

+ **Training:** Delivering security-related information sessions or materials to prepare clients for avoiding and responding to threats

+ **Emergency preparedness and crisis-response planning:** Reviewing, revising and creating all-hazards response, business continuity or mitigation response and recovery plans

+ **Executive protection:** Providing physical security such as bodyguards or protected transport (e.g., armored vehicles)

+ **Security products:** Creating and distributing security-related equipment or materials for resale

+ **General security consulting:** Offering advice for various security situations or potential security situations that might present themselves to an individual or organization

Many professionals pay their annual membership fees to security-based organizations and get certified in every possible security field they can. It never ceases to amaze me how IT professionals can take a three-day continuing-education course in, say, Terrorism 101 and suddenly feel compelled to market themselves as counterterrorism experts. Every time someone tells me they're in counterterrorism, my first question is always, "Really? So how many terrorists have you actually been face-to-face with in your life?" In my experience, less than 10 percent of these experts have ever amassed real operational or analytical experience with counterterrorism. Some think following cable news on the subject, coupled with taking a few classes, qualifies them as an authority. Such people are a liability to the profession and can become dangerous to their clients.

The way to separate yourself from this crowd, and make money as a security consultant, is to plow a niche and develop as much expertise in it as you can. Better yet, create a new market altogether. For this, I recommend reading the book *Blue Ocean Strategy* by W. Chan Kim and Renée Mauborgne. Only when you have created a solid company, with employees possessing an array of critical skills, should you present your security services as all-encompassing.

You might argue, "Why can't I just claim to do everything and subcontract out all of the work to someone else when necessary?"

It might be a common approach in other fields, but in the security business, again, you must consider whether you're creating a danger to your client. This isn't like construction, where it might not matter if you've never used a hammer, as long as you hire someone who knows what to do with one. Never forget that in this business a lack of skills or experience could cost lives.

If you maintain a Rolodex of skilled security colleagues, my advice is to refer prospective clients to trusted professionals whenever you or your company can't furnish the required skills. You can always request a finder's fee from those you refer, and if your colleagues are ethical and legitimate, they'll no doubt return the favor.

Moreover, by being straight with prospective clients, you can gain their trust and respect, which no doubt will lead to keeping the job and receiving future business. If you find that you don't have the expertise requested by a prospective client, try this:

Mr. (Prospective Client), I appreciate your considering me to perform this task for you. Although I am familiar with this service, my real expertise lies in (another service). So, to ensure that you will receive exactly what you are looking for, I refer you to (Company X), run by a colleague who is a top professional in this field.

Please keep in mind it would be easy for me to say yes, I can do what you are asking, subcontract the work to my colleague then add my markup. But I am committed to maintaining an ethical reputation. If cost is important to you, I want to make sure you get the best service for the lowest price. If cost is not an immediate concern, and you would like me to oversee the project, I would be happy to subcontract the service to my colleague while continuing to be your primary point of contact and ensuring quality control, but with your full knowledge and consent.

I know such a response flies in the face of that entrepreneurial mantra Fake It Till You Make It, but in my experience, playing it straight has allowed me to keep about half of the jobs I've been offered. Of the half I didn't win, I typically received, about half of the time, some form of compensation, either a finder's fee from the client or reciprocal work from the contractor. So, by maintaining my ethics, I've lost money only on 25 percent of the jobs I wasn't fully qualified to perform.

Again, you might say, "Good contracts are hard to come by, so you should never turn anything away." Maybe so, but I'd rather decline to take on clients I can't serve properly and maintain my reputation than have a client label me incompetent or endangering someone.

Never forget: In this line of work, life-and-death situations can appear with frightening speed. Only top-of-the-line training and experience can handle them properly.

Here's another possibility: If you're adept at project management, meaning you're highly organized, you fully understand the client's needs, and you understand how the job will get done, you could label yourself as a security consultant who specializes in project management. This could be even more marketable if you focus on a particular region of the world and maintain a high level of language skills, cultural understanding and up-to-the-minute knowledge of the local situation.

Thinking Ahead

You must constantly be looking to the future in terms of geopolitical realities, trends and opportunities. Many security consultants fail to understand this simple rule. They repeatedly bog down trying to recycle old security assessment reports or training courses they utilized years before, during their law-enforcement, military or intelligence careers, naively assuming if it worked in Country X in 1994 then it surely will work in Country Y now.

This type of business model is weak and will inevitably cost your client money. Moreover, boilerplate reports are obvious and amateurish. Neglecting the future and ignoring specific geographical or regional concerns will prevent your company's growth. If you can identify threats and vulnerabilities as they are unfolding – or, better still, before they happen – you'll greatly increase your chances for success.

How, then, do you think ahead and prepare yourself to catch the next great business opportunity? As management guru Peter Drucker once stated:

Before an executive can think of tackling the future, he must be able … to dispose of the challenges of today in less time and with great impact and permanence. For this he needs a systematic approach.

Drucker's point was that you can't allow yourself to become trapped in the day-to-day administrivia – paperwork and pointless meetings – that saps the energy of so many consultants. Likewise, try not to dwell on the problems of yesterday, unless those problems can provide insight into current or future challenges. Don't confuse activity with productivity. If you want to be paid to look busy, work for the government. But if you want to improve your client's security and make money in the process, then produce results – and produce them now. The best way to accomplish this is through an established, written process intended to allow your business to run efficiently without you – at least temporarily.

Numerous business books, from the *E-Myth* series to the controversial *Rich Dad* series, can help you automate your business, so your money works for you instead of you working for your money. This is much harder than it sounds, however. Streamlining your day-to-day activities so you can walk away for a month or more without the business missing a step is, for most, a daunting challenge – possibly even an unrealistic expectation. Most consultants, particularly one-man shops, are forced to shut down their operations when they go on even a brief holiday. But such a capacity is essential if you want to generate multiple streams of income simultaneously and if you want to be able to sell your business in the future.

Producing Results Is What Produces Income

In global security consulting, as in similar professions, you make your money by persuading clients to pay you for advice. Therefore, your clients determine how much money you'll make each year – not the other way around. Many consultants think they'll make a certain amount, boasting, "This year, I'm going to make US$650,000 in salary." To which I always respond, "Why $650,000 and not $750,000? Why not $1.65 million?"

There's nothing wrong with setting a goal; I'm a big believer in goal setting. Just recognize that a goal is only a starting point. This is particularly true when you consult in the global arena. You're not selling widgets at a fixed price to a targeted demographic. In this field, you'll be dealing with persistent and pervasive uncertainties. Your revenue will often be uncertain at the start of the year. But it's also virtually unlimited. You need to believe that.

You obtain financial results by exploiting the problems your clients bring to you, not by solving their problems. Now before you criticize that statement, please hear me out. Resources, to produce results, must be allocated to opportunities rather than to problems. Your real value to your clients is neither your security methodology nor the years of experience you have. More often than not, real value means asking the question: What is it worth to my clients to make their headaches go away quickly? That should be your key methodology as a global consultant, not your trademarked theory on "Assessing Political risk in Africa during Unfair Elections," or your "10-Step Process to Ensure Perimeter Security."

When the stuff hits the fan, I want my clients to say, "Get me Luke Bencie on the phone right now!" Because, let's face it, nobody will be saying, "Get me a consultant who specializes in the geopolitical security theory of Africa!" or "Quick, I need a process to ensure that the perimeter around my house is safe!" You must become the top-of-mind consultant, the one who will bring fast-acting relief.

It isn't the number of clients you have that will make you rich. It's their quality and how much they rely on you. To achieve this status, you'll need to make your services invaluable. This is even more difficult than it sounds, although if you can achieve it – and bear it mind it's an ongoing process – you'll be on your way to growing a successful consultancy.

Lessons from Brazil

When I first opened my company, I received a request from a prospective client to provide recommendations for secure transportation in Brazil. The client was traveling to Rio de Janeiro and wanted to hire an armored car with an experienced bilingual driver to take his people around for the week for business meetings, meals and sightseeing.

My wife, who is from São Paulo and had previously worked as both an officer in the Civil Police and as a regional security director for a Fortune 500 company, had compiled a Rolodex of such service providers. She sent off a few emails and made some calls on my behalf to her contacts. In short order, we had lined up an armored sedan with an experienced driver.

Based on that information, I informed my client we would be happy to act as their security facilitator and make all the logistical arrangements with the armored car company in Brazil for a nominal service fee. I also communicated with the company (they had minimal English speakers and poor phone lines) to ensure everything was provided on time, and I handled the invoicing (which included currency conversion and wire transfer of payments).

As I mentioned earlier, it's always important to inform your client when you're using subcontractors and incorporate that detail into your written agreement. You never want to claim that the vehicles or personnel you're outsourcing are your own. One reason: If there's an accident, it's better the client recognizes that liability will be held by the company providing the direct service and owning the vehicles. A smart lawyer will ensure that you – the facilitator – are protected.

In my example above, everything went smoothly. The client's needs were met, and they were impressed and grateful for the service we provided. Just as important, I had created a new market for my startup security consultancy. Since that time, we have provided dozens of security services a year in Brazil for high-profile clientele. We also were heavily involved with security for the 2014 FIFA World Cup, and we'll be helping with security for the 2016 Olympic Games in Rio. With a full-time office in São Paulo since 2011, the SMI Brazil Security Division is now a recognized brand name there as well as in the United States among corporate security directors. It shows that you never know how your business will evolve.

Traditional Global Security Consulting
vs. The Future of Global Security Consulting
Traditional forms of global security consulting include providing investigations or vulnerability/risk assessments. I have always been amazed at how many risk-assessment and vulnerability-assessment experts are out there. I have come to discover, however, that most of them perform such assessments using a basic checklist of security requirements. Items such as, "How high is the fence?" "Is there a redundant generator system?" "Is the Continuity of Operations Plan up to date?" and so forth make a good frame of reference, but they aren't useful if you have no practical security experience.

Sad, but many security consultants have never received effective training, never accumulated real-life experience or are even licensed or insured to perform such assessments. They might have been asked to conduct one when they served in the military or law enforcement. But chances are they did so based on their own judgment and common sense. Their experience might have been limited and their assessment process flimsy. Likewise, their report-writing skills might not have been strong enough to serve a client in the globalized, post 9/11 era.

The point is we live in a world that's more dangerous than ever. Where retired small-town sheriffs or career military men once transitioned easily into the role of company security directors, the field has grown into a multibillion-dollar industry. Students at universities now prepare for careers as chief security officers (CSOs) or geopolitical analysts the same way their classmates prepare to work on Wall Street. Top schools such as Harvard, Georgetown and George Washington offer degrees in security studies. Exchange programs between European, Asian and Middle Eastern countries are widely prevalent. There's good money to be earned in the field, and the travel opportunities are extensive. Jobs can be thrilling, and security is no longer associated with so-called knuckle draggers – people who provide only brute force. Moreover, given the current state of the world, the need won't be slowing anytime soon.

Prepare for Competition

Anyone can call himself or herself a "consultant." Even more troubling, someone with slick brochures and a fancy website can claim to be a global security consultant, even with subpar or weak experience in the area.

Recently, a colleague sent me a link to a website for a European security firm. It looked high quality for sure, but what shocked me were its layout, text and even videos. They all essentially copied information I had posted on my own site. Things were changed just enough not to infringe on copyright laws. But when viewed side by side, it was obvious the owners were riding on the coattails of my intellectual property. I thought, "How dare these ham-and-egger consultants steal my content? I spent a lot of time and money coming up with all of this stuff!"

As I wrote in my other book, *Among Enemies: Counter-Espionage for the Business Traveler*, the best you can hope for is to stay six months ahead of your competition in terms of content. Now more than ever, everything is on the Internet, and good ideas are up for grabs. It fulfills the prophesy by Stewart Brand, author of *The Media Lab*, who said:

On the one hand information wants to be expensive, because it's so valuable. The right information in the right place just changes your life. On the other hand, information wants to be free, because the cost of getting it out is getting lower and lower all the time.

It's in line with what the late Steve Jobs famously remarked:

Picasso had a saying: 'Good artists copy; great artists steal.' And we (Apple) have always been shameless about stealing great ideas.

This wasn't the first time I've had my materials ripped off. One gentleman took our training courses only to turn around a month later and market a similar course under his own company's name. In fact, it wasn't just similar; it offered exactly the same training materials but under his company logo and a thousand dollars cheaper. We were lucky. The guy lacked the experience to teach an advanced group of military professionals. This is what we call being one question deep. His company folded like an old lawn chair.

Remember the ancient saying that imitation is the sincerest form of flattery? If your content is good, be prepared to have it stolen.

As in any industry, there are bound to be quick-buck artists who will employ unethical tactics to steal business away. In my 15 years-plus in this industry, I have learned my craft from some of the greatest patriots and most talented professionals in the field. But I have also encountered my share of scoundrels. As one of my mentors reminded me, when I was back in my twenties, "In our profession, we don't exactly work with the Boy Scouts." If you want to be a global security consultant, you'll need to grow some thick skin. The competition is fierce, so you must feel passionate about the work and be willing to do what it takes to generate the millions in revenue that this business can provide.

FAQ

1. How do I know if I have what it takes to be an entrepreneur?

You need an unflinching belief in yourself and your dreams, and you must have both passion and perseverance.

2. How do I separate myself from the rest of the security firms out there?

Over deliver.

3. How will I know if I've passed my prime as a security consultant?

Steve Jobs, in his famous commencement speech to the graduating class at Stanford, stated that when he woke up every morning he asked himself if he was looking forward to what he was about to do. He said if the answer was no for too many days in a row, he knew it was time for a change.

If your answer is no, then fix your security consulting business, close your security consulting business or sell your security consulting business. If the answer is yes, you're still in your prime.

4. It sounds all well and good, but starting a consulting business costs money. Can I do this on a shoestring?

Absolutely! As an entrepreneur you'll need to embrace the concept of bootstrapping. You won't need US$100,000 to get started. In the following pages, I'll show you how to get your business off the ground for considerably less.

5. What books would you recommend for a first-time entrepreneur?

Here are my top three books for people looking to start any business:

+ *The Art of the Start* by Guy Kawasaki

+ *The E-Myth Revisited* by Michael Gerber

+ *Blue Ocean Strategy* by W. Chan Kim and Renée Mauborgne

Note from the Field

Rio de Janeiro

0820 hours

I'm currently in Brazil for the 2014 FIFA World Cup. Our team has established a command post within a posh Ipanema Beach hotel conference room to monitor our various clients' security activities. SMI is operating in eight cities across Brazil for the games, and we are protecting various media outlets, international corporations and high-net-worth individuals.

In addition to more than a dozen bilingual Brazilian agents, we have a handful of Portuguese-speaking Americans, as well as a few former British Special Forces officers, to manage the operation. We have employed some of the latest technology to monitor all of our clients' movements using cell phones, satellite phones and various GPS trackers. We have incorporated proprietary big-data analysis software to monitor social media and news feeds concerning protests or any other security threats. We maintain constant communication with the U.S. Consulate and the Brazilian law-enforcement community. We're also using specially encrypted communications to ensure our clients' privacy.

Despite these high-tech solutions, there's still no substitute for having great people around you. Our Brazil team has worked together for over eight years, and they take extreme pride in being recognized as the best at their profession. Right now, I can proudly state, SMI's Brazil Security Division is one of the finest (if not the finest) collection of individuals providing security for the World Cup.

2. Getting Started

*The way to get started is to quit talking
and begin doing.*

—Walt Disney

WHETHER YOU'RE A ONE-MAN SHOP, a small boutique firm, or you plan to open your doors with a substantial number of employees, congratulations! You're about to embark on an incredible journey. It could be a positive, even unforgettable experience. Or, like so many others who try the independent business route, your outcome could be negative – and you could lose your shirt.

However it turns out, it will be an adventure. Opening a business is one of the most challenging but liberating experiences a person can undertake. Life is short. You might as well control how you spend your time and enjoy what you're doing. You'll view the world in a new light, and you might have lots of fun in the process. The only guarantee is it won't be easy. But if you have the determination to be a global security consultant, you're in for the ride of your life.

Don't be intimidated. Every great business – and every great businessperson – throughout history had to start the exact same way.

Incorporating Your Business

As soon as you've chosen a professional name – and please try to avoid ridiculous monikers such as Dragon Slayer International Security Group or Night Stalker Tactical Consultants – you'll need to take the legal steps necessary to open your doors to a world of potential clients.

Here are the requirements for starting a global security consulting company in the United States. If you're located elsewhere, you should consult with a good tax attorney to determine the business structure that works best for you.

The first thing you need to do is form a legal entity. Here are two key questions you should ask yourself:

+ Will I be seeking outside investors?
+ How soon before my business will begin making a significant profit?

I've known some lucky individuals who stumbled on a profitable, long-term contract before they even formed their businesses. May you be so fortunate.

Meanwhile, based on how you answer these two questions, you should consider one of these:

+ Limited liability corporation
+ C corporation
+ S corporation

There are advantages and disadvantages to each.

Limited Liability Corporation

An LLC is an inexpensive and easy way to establish a business. Many first-time global security consultants have found it a comfortable avenue into the business world, particularly if their background was limited to the public sector. Owners of the company are defined by the percentages they own. You could be a sole proprietor. You could split ownership 50-50 with your spouse. Or, you could divide the business numerous ways with other individuals who are also equity partners.

An LLC provides the same protection from personal liability as a full C corporation but with much greater simplicity. For example, you don't need to compile and disclose minutes of meetings, accounting practices or shareholder decisions. Instead of filing separate federal income-tax forms, you list the income and expenses from the LLC on Schedule C of your personal return. If you have partners, you can file an IRS Form 1065, which also allows a personal pass-through of income and expenses. In either case, however, always consult your attorney.

LLC owners are taxed in relation to their equity percentages.

Because most startups lose money their first few years, your full or prorated portion of that loss can be used to reduce your taxes on other personal income. You can also carry losses forward or apply them against income from the previous three years.

I've established LLCs for SMI and my other businesses, but an LLC isn't for everyone. If you suddenly find yourself besieged by investors looking to throw cash at your business, you can convert your LLC to a C corp with the help of a lawyer. The costs you incur from such a conversion should be justifiable. If they aren't, then you might not be ready to make the switch.

On the other hand, if you need outside investors to fund your enterprise, you'll probably need to go the full corporate route.

C Corporation

A C corp – the designation refers to its subsection of the U.S. Tax Code – is usually reserved for medium to large-sized businesses because it's a stand-alone legal and tax entity. It requires separate tax returns, but it allows you to claim maximum protection from personal liability. In the United States, C corps are often registered in Delaware because of that state's accommodating legal requirements.

A C corp can issue stock and is owned by its shareholders – hence its utility when you attract outside investors. The problem with a C corp is its complexity: You must maintain a board of directors, adhere carefully to certain reporting requirements, and conform to financial and operating standards. Likewise, C corps present a double-taxation issue, because any dividends paid to shareholders are not deductible from corporate income while they're also considered income on personal returns.

There's an alternative corporate structure. If you're financially independent or solvent enough, you might want to consider an S corporation.

S Corporation

An S corp is essentially a C corp but with special permissions. It is possible to form a C corp and then convert to an S corp if you qualify. An S corp enjoys the same tax pass-through advantages of an LLC, although there are significant restrictions on the type of investors allowed. For example, they cannot be other corporations. Nor can they be venture capitalists or non-residents of the United States. There are also restrictions on the number of shareholders an S corp may accumulate. You're limited to fewer than 100, but even that can vary.

Many private defense contractors – i.e., security personnel who work in the war zones of Iraq and Afghanistan – have formed S corps. In addition to overseas deployment tax advantages, individual defense contractors can also separate themselves from their business entity if an overseas security incident develops (e.g., a shooting investigation).

Using a Lawyer

If you have previous experience in forming a company, you might feel comfortable enough to establish your new entity via an online service such as LegalZoom.com or Incorporate.com. But if you're new to the business world, you'll probably be better served consulting an attorney. Although you could spend us$1,000 or more, discussing your options with a lawyer could save you a hundred times that figure in future legal, tax or financial headaches. A lawyer will also help you decide if you should incorporate in a tax haven state such as Delaware or an international tax haven such as the Isle of Mann, the Cayman Islands or Panama.

In the case of setting up a legal entity, it's usually better – and cheaper – to invest in an attorney *before* you need one. Then, if you ever find yourself caught up in a legal issue – which is bound to happen when you start making real money – you'll have a trusted lawyer only a phone call away. It should be someone to whom you have been referred by others in your field, someone with a reputation of success, integrity and reliability. In other words, protect yourself and your company. Avoid, for example, retaining your buddy from college who has a law degree but works as a consultant in a management firm instead of at a law practice. Or, he practices law but is unfamiliar with global security matters.

The search shouldn't be difficult. Many attorneys now specialize in national security law and have compiled extensive experience working with international defense contractors and on international security cases. Some of them might even have obtained a U.S. Top Secret clearance as part of their need to know. If you're just entering the world of global security consulting, this might be more than you need for a while. But when you begin crisscrossing international borders and dealing with ministers from various governments, you might want to put an experienced lawyer on retainer to watch your back.

You'll also want to hire a lawyer who specializes in international liability to review your client contracts and partnership agreements with foreign entities. It's easy to subcontract a job to a foreign security entity that you only assume maintains full insurance and licensing. As I discovered – early on and sometimes painfully – many of these partnering firms are anything but reputable. Many don't carry proper insurance, and many pay their operatives under the table. If you subcontract a job that takes an unexpected turn for the worse, be prepared to be stuck holding the bag by your client – even if you think you've obtained a binding agreement with your subcontractor. An experienced attorney will anticipate this and head off potential problems.

It's always best to apprise your clients up front, in writing, of your responsibilities – and non-responsibilities. Informing them that you will not accept liability for certain negative outcomes could, in the long run, save you and your business from financial ruin.

Insurance

Never skimp on it. The security industry is riddled with potential liability issues. One misstep and you're out of business.

I recommend consulting with an insurance agent who specializes in the security field. That agent will probably recommend maintaining general liability insurance in excess of US$3 million, with additional coverage for workers' compensation, vehicles, travel, DBA (Defense Base Act insurance for contractors working overseas on behalf of the U.S. government), international medical assistance, and possibly kidnapping and ransom – aka K&R.

Don't accept your insurance policy at face value. Have your lawyer carefully review it and walk through a series of what-ifs with your agent. No scenario should be too outrageous. Consider the following questions:

+ What if one of my team is injured in an accident during a project?
+ What if the client is injured during a project?
+ What if I subcontract an executive-protection job in another country and the subcontractor botches the job?
+ What if one of my subcontractors hits a pedestrian with a rental car during a project?
+ What if during the transport of a client in a vehicle, the vehicle is attacked and one of our team kills one of the attackers?
+ What if we perform an investigation of a person and that person finds out about it and decides to sue our client?
+ What if one of my team is in a plane crash overseas?
+ What if one of my team accidently destroys a piece of our client's valuable equipment?
+ What if a confidential report about a client is accidently released to the public?
+ What if we sell an integrated technology system to a foreign client and the system fails to work?
+ What if the client refuses to pay?
+ What if one of our team members is kidnapped?
+ What if one of our clients is kidnapped?
+ What if I franchise my company and a franchisee botches a project?

The list is endless. The point is you need to protect yourself at all times. Don't try to cut corners just because you're starting up or business is slow. In addition, the more your business grows, the more often you'll need to review your insurance requirements.

It will be a fact of your business life: The global security industry is dangerous and filled with uncertainty. To mitigate that uncertainty, always carry the proper insurance – and even try to maintain extra coverage.

Dun and Bradstreet

After you've formed your legal entity, be sure to register it with Dun and Bradstreet. In the United States, D&B is a public company that provides information on businesses and corporations for use in credit decisions, business-to-business marketing, and supply-chain management. It's important to obtain registration, because it allows clients and other companies to verify your legitimacy. It's also used as a source of information on how well your business is performing. If you don't register with D&B, you'll look like an amateur – something that will cost you clients.

Trademarks and Copyrights

When you've built your business to the point where you can provide off-the-shelf services, such as training courses or consulting packages, ready to deploy at a moment's notice, consider protecting your intellectual property. To accomplish this, I recommend obtaining a trademark for your materials – though you'll have to choose between the two alternative methods available.

Assigning a trademark to your materials with the ^{TM} superscript after the title is the quickest and easiest way to begin the process. It notifies other enterprises that you are either claiming exclusive use of a term or have instigated a formal registration application.

What it *does not do* is guarantee that you can preserve the proprietary nature of your material. That can only be done via the formal registration process, which is best handled via an attorney who specializes in patent-and-trademark matters. If your application is approved, you can affix the coveted ® symbol to your intellectual property. You can learn the basics of the procedure at the U.S. Patent and Trademark Office's website.

Even formal registration can't always prevent someone else from using your unique presentations. These days, anyone can go on the

Internet or take one of your courses then turn around and slightly repackage your hard work into their own brand. It's unfortunate, and it's considerably more prevalent when you work globally. But if you trademark your material, you can at least discourage others from blatantly ripping it off. More important, you can make a strong, credible impression on prospective clients when your products are registered.

The copyright process works in a similar way. Anytime you publish a book or an article for a magazine, your words are automatically copyrighted in the United States when you display the © symbol. The protection also applies to marketing brochures, white papers, PowerPoint presentations and reports, as long as they carry the copyright disclaimer. Again, this will not guarantee you complete protection from plagiarizers, but at least it allows you to make a legitimate claim.

You can formalize your case by registering your material with the U.S. Copyright Office. The cost is modest, particularly given the value of the work you are protecting, and the procedure is simple. You can learn more at the Copyright Office's website.

CARVER Target Analysis and
Vulnerability Assessment Methodology

At SMI, we have a gentleman on our staff named Leo Labaj. Leo retired from the intelligence community after compiling a distinguished career that took him around the globe.

During that time, Leo and his team were tasked to create a methodology to help identify vulnerabilities in potential targets that could be used as both offensive and defensive strategies. To achieve this, he adapted the U.S. Air Force's CARVE methodology, which was developed to identify bombing targets. CARVE stood for:

+ Criticality
+ Accessibility
+ Recognizability
+ Vulnerability
+ Espy

Leo and his colleagues retooled CARVE into CARVER:

+   Criticality

+   Accessibility

+   Recognizability

+   Vulnerability

+   Effect

+   Recoverability

This more elaborate version allows the intelligence and special-operations communities to better assess potential vulnerabilities, either for protection from assault or for covert action such as sabotage using explosives.

Following the attacks of September 11, 2001, the U.S. government required a methodology to conduct rapid vulnerability assessments of the nation's infrastructure. After the formation of the Department of Homeland Security (DHS), CARVER became the methodology of choice.

Leo Labaj now performs monthly training sessions for SMI under the title, CARVER Target Analysis and Vulnerability Assessment™ training course. By designating our course with that symbol, we have not only kept the pretenders at bay, but we have also added legitimacy to the course for government agencies whose employees attend. Had we not trademarked our intellectual property, imitators likely would have surfaced. Not that competition is necessarily a bad thing, but you need to protect your hard work from unauthorized appropriation.

Licensing

Licensing is a quick way to expand your business and revenues without also increasing your workload. In order to do so, however, you'll need a quality product or service to license. In some cases, you can even license just your name – as long as you have developed a stellar reputation and brand-name recognition – think Donald Trump.

At SMI, we've found that licensing our training courses is the easiest way to expand our name, increase our revenues and build a business model that can run on its own. For several of our products, such as our Hostile Travel Course – designed for international businesspeople, government employees or non-profit organization personnel who must travel to high-threat, harsh-living environments around the world – we have developed a strong cadre of independent instructors who license our training materials from us. SMI provides the promotional items, course materials, financial registration and student logistics. We thoroughly vet these independent instructors then allow them to promote the course to their contacts, usually in countries where SMI does not currently operate.

In return for developing new business, the independent instructors receive a commission for each paying student. We use video recordings, personal audits of the instructors and student feedback forms to ensure that the course meets our standards.

By utilizing this system, we can spread the SMI name globally, tap into and cultivate new relations and referrals, and grow profits without dramatically increasing the workload at our home base. Keep in mind, however, that this system is only as good as the instructors, so they need to be the best and absolutely trustworthy. One poor performance from a subcontractor can destroy your reputation. Adhere to that old maxim: Hire slowly; fire quickly.

Opening a Company Bank Account

You'll need a bank that specializes in international transactions. It sounds simple and logical, but these days finding a bank that's compatible with your needs, particularly if those needs extend overseas, can be challenging.

With the international economic downturn, obtaining bank loans has become more and more difficult. Establishing a low-interest line of credit likewise is a challenge. You practically have to sign away your home, life insurance policy, retirement account and first child just to qualify. You'll have to work hard to find a bank that charges reasonable fees.

You'll need international capability because wire transfers to and from other countries will become routine as you serve clients around the globe. You'll also need an ATM card that's compatible with international cash machines; many such cards from smaller banks do not operate outside the United States.

Incidentally, I recommend using separate banks for your business and household finances. Maybe it's just a personal preference, but I don't want my company's bank to monitor my personal account. If a bank can access my business's deposit and withdrawal information, I'd rather they couldn't also see how much (or how little) I might be paying myself or how much I'm maintaining in my private savings account.

Company Credit Cards

It's easier to keep your business expenses straight for tax purposes if you maintain a company check card or credit card – or both. You also should provide separate cards for each of your employees and subcontractors. It's an easy and efficient way to track business expenses, and it will greatly improve your bookkeeping tasks. Obtain credit cards that also provide frequent-flyer miles, so you can accumulate points to use for service upgrades.

Whatever cards you maintain for domestic transactions, be sure to use *both* a VISA and an American Express card for international travel. Many establishments overseas will take only one or the other. Though not as popular in the United States, MasterCard is preferred in Latin America and other regions. And the Ink® business card from Chase offers an attractive array of rewards and benefits for small businesses.

Computers and Communications

You're going to need specific hardware and software. Even if you're not a techie, I strongly recommend investing in a high-end laptop plus a backup storage device, preferably a high-capacity USB flash drive or, better still, an online backup service.

Regarding laptops, I'm a big fan of the Mac. I use a MacBook Air for traveling, along with my iMac desktop at the office. Though it might take some time to learn the slightly different keyboard, the MacBook is incredibly thin and lightweight, and it syncs up easily with other Apple products. The sleek design also looks very professional.

If your budget is limited, I recommend buying the most

powerful laptop you can find and loading it with extra memory. As a consultant, you'll be producing plenty of reports with charts, images and even video, so you'll find that increased data storage and a fast processer are worth the added expense. But I also advise against using this computer for anything other than work. Mixing in your family photos, shopping lists, video and music downloads, household budgets and so forth could leave you vulnerable to identity theft or blackmail if you take that personal information overseas.

Obviously, you'll need a cell phone or smartphone with international calling capability. As a supplement, if your phone or laptop is equipped with Skype or a similar voice-over-Internet protocol (VOIP) application, you can reduce your international calling charges. At SMI, we use VOIP phones in the office and have a fixed international plan with our cellular provider. Negotiating fixed rates is always good. We also have dedicated in-country cell phones because they allow cheaper rates, particularly when our team members travel to places such as Brazil and parts of the Middle East.

Many of the free phone services or apps lack sufficient security from hackers or eavesdroppers, however. So, if you use one, confine your conversations to non-proprietary topics. If your international conversations cover sensitive subjects, buy a disposable cell phone *and* employ an encryption device.

Back at the office, you should maintain a landline with a separate fax number. Yes, the venerable facsimile machine is becoming obsolete, but lots of overseas organizations still use them – we still frequently have to fax documents to South America. So it will speak well of you if you can send and receive faxes. And don't try to scrimp by using a dual office/fax number. It screams "amateur."

Invest in what's called Find Me/Follow Me software, which redirects calls from your landline to your cell phone when you're out of the office.

Office Hardware

Invest in the best possible laser printer, preferably one that can also scan, fax and copy. A quality printer produces professional-looking letters and other communications. And unless you anticipate printing tens of thousands of documents per year, don't rent a printer, either. When you open your business, copier salespeople will come knocking. But wait until you have at least half-a-dozen employees before investing in printing/copying hardware. Be prepared to pay a small fortune for ink or toner, because it's one of today's realities for small business. And use your office printer only for business. For personal documents, buy a consumer-grade version. They're amazingly cheap now – well under us$100 – but the ink's still expensive.

One caution: All modern copier/printers contain memory chips and therefore can retain proprietary or sensitive information. Make sure yours is empty or removed anytime you sell, junk or trade-in.

These days, voicemail services are much more reliable and efficient than answering machines – though more expensive. As you might have observed reading my recommendations so far, I'm all for creating the best impression possible. Speaking of which, it's best to have an office assistant who answers all calls. But failing that, voicemail trumps an answering machine. One example: Voicemail can handle multiple incoming calls simultaneously. You never want a potential client's call to be met with a busy signal.

You'll need other standard office accoutrements such as filing cabinets with file folders, a year At-a-Glance® wall calendar, a Day-Minder planner – or generic equivalents – and a whiteboard. A small office safe is also a good idea; just be sure it can be bolted down securely to something.

Business Cards and Letterheads

Failing a glowing personal recommendation from a satisfied client, your next best opportunity to begin a new business relationship is by creating a strong first impression. The way you dress, the way you speak, how you conduct yourself, all convey competence – or the lack thereof. So it is with your business card.

Don't scrimp. Spend enough to create a card of high quality and distinctiveness, and work with the designer until you're satisfied with the result. Don't create it yourself from some free website and print it out on your home computer. Nothing says "avoid this person" more quickly than a chintzy business card.

Think of your card as an extension of yourself and your business. Examine it and ask yourself if you were a potential client would you want to do business with its owner? Think classy, tasteful and understated; forgo the temptation to add certification letters to your name. Just because you paid a fee and took some test, that doesn't mean you need to display the fact. If you're an M.D. or Ph.D., fine, but that should be the extent of it.

I don't even recommend including your former positions in the military or law enforcement, on Capitol Hill or the executive branch, or with intelligence agencies. In this day and age, everyone checks on everyone else via Google. If you've achieved your intended stature, your prospective clients will find out in two ways: Internet searches and word of mouth. Anything else suggests overreaching, and that's the kiss of death in this business.

Incidentally, there's an art to receiving business cards that can make or break your relationship with a prospective client. In certain parts of the world, it's even ritualistic. You take the card with both hands and immediately raise it toward your face so you can read it easily – and make sure you read all of it immediately. Then place the card in either the breast pocket of your shirt or the top pocket of your suit jacket. Never put it in your pants pocket and especially in your wallet. In some cultures, that's a sign of disrespect. Besides, it's good manners to show interest in someone you've just met.

Your company's letterhead should also be impressive. Don't print out your logo on a sheet of copy paper and consider it your company stationary. Spend a few hundred dollars for an offset-press version. Otherwise you only convey amateurism. The same goes for envelopes.

Invest in Your Website

Unless you are *extremely* tech savvy and can do it yourself, hire a professional website design firm. It will pay for itself in the long run. You might disagree with this advice. You might argue that there are plenty of free templates available on the Internet from which you can build your site.

True, but unfortunately many of those cool-looking designs

are being used by other companies, and they're easily recognizable. They're also usually written in a lower-quality HTML code, meaning they're not being given a higher priority by the major search engines such as Google, Bing or Yahoo. In other words, good luck hitting the top of the first search page for your services.

Yes, it's easy to drop US$10,000 on website design, plus the other special features a web-design or search-engine-optimization (SEO) company will try to sell you. For example, I spent about US$25,000 on the SMI website. It includes several professionally shot videos (which Google has preferred ever since they purchased YouTube), as well as downloadable white papers, a shopping-cart feature to register for our training courses or buy our products, and links to other useful sites. We're also constantly updating our content, posting news feeds, Twitter tweets and blog posts.

The more interesting and visually arresting content you can post on your website, and the more often you update your content, the more traffic your site will draw. Period.

Think about it. What's the first thing you do when you learn about a potential client – or anyone new, for that matter? You get online and examine their website. In today's global business environment, a website is often what creates a first impression – often well before you meet someone. So, you've got to make that impression count. And creating a first-class website is critical to your company's future.

Essential Software

Given the special needs of this business, I recommend that you include the following software in your budget:

+ **Contact database/prospective client organizer.** I recommend SalesForce or PipelineDeals. Both are virtual platforms that will help you keep track of your clients, prospects, proposals and overall business dealings. If your business requires you to maintain numerous contacts, as well as manage several deals at once, these sales tools are more useful than a stand-alone contact database or calendar reminders. As a global security consultant, you'll find yourself leaning on these programs to keep your day-to-day operations in line. They'll help you sort out which client requires a follow-up phone call on a certain day or how you should estimate your third-quarter sales based on proposals submitted.

+ **Accounting software.** QuickBooks or its equivalent is essential for any business to manage its finances. FreshBooks is a bit easier for smaller startups and for those who aren't so computer savvy. Even if you prefer to keep your financial records the old fashioned way, in a paper ledger, you should use one of these services to generate profit-and-loss statements, balance sheets and cash-flow statements.

+ **Virtual Shared Drive or cloud storage.** As your business grows, you will eventually need to share your information with others: employees, subcontractors, clients and others. In our office, we have tried several different services, but we have found Box. com to be a simple program to which everyone can quickly adapt. More advanced options exist out there, but because many of our consultants are older, they prefer a more user-friendly interface.

+ **Mailing-list generator.** You want to be able to send your clients professional-looking updates without wasting hours crafting individual emails. In order to target an email list effectively, I recommend programs such as ConstantContact or MailChimp. We use MailChimp to send our monthly SMI newsletter to all of our clients and potential clients, and we can immediately distribute security advisory notices to specific clients operating in a certain country or region. For as little as US$20 per month, you can stay top-of-mind with your clients.

Essential Forms

Several standard consulting documents can assist you in day-to-day legal transactions. They include:

+ **Proposal Template.** I have included a sample in Chapter 8, but there's a catch: Boilerplate proposals are obvious and easily spotted by a savvy client. Be sure to create a customized proposal that demonstrates exactly how you will be addressing the client's needs. And if you're cutting and pasting from a previous proposal, proofread the whole new document before submitting it. Otherwise leftover names, references and facts could be overlooked and cause embarrassment or even loss of a client.

+ **Nondisclosure and Non-Circumvent Agreements.** If you're entertaining a partnership and require a nondisclosure agreement, include non-circumvent language as well. This can be a separate document or combined with an NDA. As your business grows, you will find more and more "potential partners" showing up on your doorstep. Nine times out of ten, they're looking for you to throw some business their way or introduce them to your clients. Be wary of these types; they do exist. Such individuals have burned me.

+ **Independent Contractor Agreement.** Sooner or later you're going to need a subcontractor. At SMI, we use an independent contractor agreement to handle such situations, and we carefully prepare each one to suit the individual or company. Without a solid ICA in place, which stipulates such terms as billing rates, hours and expenses, you could be robbed blind by a dishonest IC.

+ **Separation Agreement.** Many small businesses overlook this important document. It essentially prevents an employee or IC who is leaving your firm from taking your intellectual property and clients. A strong ICA is important before you hire someone, and an SA will protect you when you close out someone's services.

+ **Invoice Template.** At SMI, we prefer to use a customized invoice template generated from our subscription to Freshbooks. If you prefer to create your own invoices, instead of using Freshbooks or Quickbooks™, make sure you can quickly retrieve them for bookkeeping and tax purposes. Unless you anticipate sending out only a few invoices per year, you should avoid creating homemade documents using Microsoft® Office.

+ **News Release Template.** Depending on your circumstances, you might not need to deal with the media. But if you want to get the word to the public quickly, you should create one of these documents, which includes your company logo and contact information, as well as a headline, dateline and text format. It will allow you to distribute newsworthy information quickly. See Chapter 5 for other approaches to marketing.

A Note about Contracts

After your client has approved your proposal, the question is who writes the contract. If you've reached a stage where you can produce the document, fine; your client will review it or present it to legal counsel. But if your client provides you with a contract, be careful. Even if you've just won a lucrative consulting job, do not – repeat, do not – sign it without your lawyer's review and approval. Why? Because it might contain provisions holding you liable for future disasters that befall the client – often in perpetuity – as well as unfavorable payment terms.

Home Office vs. Virtual Office vs. Office Building

Another question that arises for first-time consultants: Should I get an office? My answer: It depends.

If you're starting out as a one-person shop, you probably don't need a formal office. Wait until you begin generating income *and* are ready to expand. Next to employees, an office will be your biggest expense – sometimes costing more than your home mortgage. But if you think you'd be better served working outside of your den, basement or attic, try a virtual office.

When I started SMI, I spent the first two months working from my one-bedroom apartment in Rosslyn, Virginia, directly across the Potomac River from the Lincoln Memorial. Then I began using a virtual office along the K Street corridor in Northwest Washington. It gave me a powerful-sounding address, and the service offered three professional receptionists who took my calls and transferred them to my cell phone. If I needed to meet a client, I could do so there by renting one of their conference rooms by the hour. Plus, that particular operation included an accidental side benefit: Newt Gingrich, former Speaker of the U.S. House of Representatives, maintained an office next door. Regardless of my prospective clients' politics, all were impressed by my big-name neighbor.

When I determined that SMI was solvent enough, I bit the bullet and leased first-class office space in Northern Virginia – but not before I negotiated the hell out of the deal. I acquired a thousand-square-foot suite in a prestigious building near Tysons Corner with plenty of parking. It contains two small offices, my larger office and a nice reception area – which I consider essential. I always want our current and prospective clients to be seated in a separate room that prominently displays our logo on the wall and features a flat-screen TV and a stylish leather sofa. The receptionist greets our guests with a friendly smile and an espresso machine at the ready.

At first, I decided against getting a bigger suite with a conference room, because my office was large enough to accommodate a sofa and several chairs (à la Mad Men) for meetings. But now, as I am writing this book, we are in the process of expanding to a new office with a glass-enclosed conference room in the same building. Business has been picking up, and we've become too cramped for comfort.

The key point is, don't expand your office space until you absolutely, positively need to. Always play the What if? game. In other words, what if you lose your biggest client tomorrow? Could you still afford to pay the rent? If not, wait until you've achieved a comfortable enough revenue stream to take on a bigger expense. Having a big office with no clients will depress you and possibly destroy you financially.

Security Organizations and Affiliations

I opened SMI in 2010 and joined every security networking organization I could. Now, nearly five years later, not one of them has resulted in new business. I have learned to regard these groups not as allies but competitors. Moreover, some security organizations have received knuckle-dragger reputations, so an association with them could hurt your reputation. I now prefer to keep my distance and operate SMI under a different business model.

Instead of being a traditional firm that promotes solely the physical-protection aspects of security for a fixed fee, we focus on how we can save clients money through various assessment and implementation strategies. We consider our SMI consultants to be as comfortable speaking with senior executives in the boardroom as they would with tribal leaders in the Hindu Kush.

At SMI, our clients are not found on security tradeshow floors. Instead, we interact with them at philanthropic events, international business forums or industry seminars. It's better to be identified by your clients as a respected peer rather than a security company discovered in a random search of some directory.

On the other hand, if you've recruited clients via security organizations and affiliations, then good for you. I won't argue with anyone's success. I'm simply saying that these groups haven't worked in my experience. Unless it's the Council of Foreign Relations, I'm no longer interested in joining security-related clubs.

Company Car

I was raised to regard leasing a car as a bad investment. I still think it's true for a personal vehicle, but I've found that leasing one for my business is a worthwhile tax write-off.

Keep in mind, though, that if you lease a vehicle for your business, you must use it only for business. The IRS doesn't take kindly to individuals who fudge on their vehicle write-offs. What you can do, if possible, to save money is be stingy with the mileage you and your employees rack up. Then, when the lease expires, you can avoid the stiff extra-mileage charge. Also, if you choose to buy the vehicle, either for your business or for personal use, you'll likely get a better deal than if you start fresh on the used car lot.

Another good reason to lease is it eliminates the prospect of your employees using your personal vehicle. And it's easier to break out the liability insurance. But, I have to admit, the main reason I began leasing was it looked more professional to arrive at a meeting in a classy European sedan than a used SUV – my private vehicle at the time. When meeting with clients, your vehicle can say as much about you as your clothes.

Employees

You've established your business, you've rented your virtual office or invested in a commercial site, and you've hung out your shingle for the world to see. The next question is: Do I need employees? The simple answer is: No.

If you haven't achieved an ironclad contract, an agreement paying your company a substantial amount of cash every month for an extended term, then you don't need employees. Only when the money really starts rolling in should you consider, carefully, what type of individual to add to the payroll.

This might surprise you, but in my experience the best person to bring on board first is a personal assistant/bookkeeper. It's surprisingly tough to find a good one, but when you do, that person will be worth his or her weight in gold. That said, you might not need to begin with someone working full time. It might be better to start off at part time – maybe 4 days a week/5 hours a day or 5 days a week/4 hours a day – than take on the extra expenses and legal requirements associated with a 40-hour staffer: health insurance, workers' compensation, vacation, sick leave, OSHA requirements, overtime. The list goes on and on.

Try to find someone who has retired as an administrative assistant for a senior executive in either the highest levels of the government or a Fortune 500 company. These individuals usually already carry their own health insurance and are looking to supplement their retirement checks. You could be pleasantly surprised to find out how quickly they'll be able to make your business operate more smoothly.

A caution: Do your homework – in other words, obtain and check references. If you don't and end up with an incompetent assistant, you could find your workload actually increasing, and it will irk you to sign that check each payday. You don't want to put yourself in the position of seeing your profits going out the door to an unhelpful employee – and these days, it can be tricky to fire someone without risking a discrimination action. As I stated earlier, hire slowly.

Miscellaneous

A few more items to help you get your global security consulting business off the ground, items that will save you time and money in the long run:

+ **Use a travel agent.** If you're going to be an international man (or woman) of mystery, you'll be spending a lot of time on airplanes and in hotels. Why waste hours searching online travel sites or being placed on hold by airline reservation agents? Find a good travel agency and have them do the work for you. The typical booking fee is only around $30 per transaction. Just be sure to use someone who understands your needs.

+ **Courier services.** At SMI, we're registered with FedEx, DHL and UPS, so whenever we need to ship a package, it's easy. We call one of the companies – depending on the destination, urgency, and type of package or envelope – and they send a driver to the office to pick it up. Then they charge our shipments monthly to the company credit card. It saves a ton of time not having to drive to drop-off locations. A local courier service to deliver documents around a busy city is also useful.

+ **Printing/copying.** Establishing an account with a good print shop is must. After much trial and error, we found a great one to handle our printing and copying needs. These include our stationary, business cards, holiday cards, proposals, final reports, marketing pieces and so forth, as well as the occasional report or multipage document that needs to be copied in bulk or professionally bound.

One caution: In certain instances, you might need to print intellectual property, or you might be thinking of having your printer handle confidential client information. Before you proceed, make sure you have a legally binding NDA in place. For sensitive client reports, we print everything in-house – no matter how onerous.

+ **Postage meter.** Another time-saving measure: Rent a postage meter for your office. I can't tell you how many times I rummaged through my desk looking for stamps before I finally broke down and ordered one. Now I kick myself for waiting so long. It's turned out to be an excellent investment. You might even want to consider using an online service such as Stamps. com.

+ **Virtual assistant.** When I first considered a virtual assistant, I envisioned a call center in India where conmen would be maxing out my credit card as soon as I authorized them to perform the first task for me. But after reading Tim Ferriss's book *The Four Hour Work Week*, I revisited the concept and found if I precisely outlined my work requirements and time allotted for each project, I'd have reasonable success. In fact, I *have* used a company in India for the past several years. My favorite assistant, Renju, is intelligent and reliable. For as little as US$8 per hour, Renju does a great job tackling some of the mundane jobs I hate, such as updating my client mailing lists and researching news articles in foreign languages.

If you're considering a virtual assistant, start slowly, and use PayPal for your financial transactions. Just remember virtual assistants work best as part-time help for mundane tasks. Don't incorporate them into your daily business routine.

Conclusion

If you have completed all of the items I've described above, you should be well on your way to laying a strong foundation for your global security consultancy. But infrastructure doesn't guarantee a successful business. To turn a profit and create a thriving company, you'll need clients. This is much harder than decorating your office or designing your company letterhead. To make money in global security consulting, you must master three skills:

+ Cultivating outstanding client relationships
+ Producing superior intellectual property
+ Displaying exceptional management

We'll cover them in the upcoming chapters.

FAQ

6. What executive courses would you recommend if I don't have business experience?

If you lack business training, or haven't previously run a business, I'd recommend taking crash courses in finance, sales and marketing, and negotiation. If you've never had to manage people, I strongly recommend a management course. A talented team will be your company's greatest resource – learn to treat them properly.

7. Don't I need an office right away to look legitimate?

No. As I mentioned, open an office only when you really need one. Meanwhile, sublease from a friend or associate, or use a virtual office if you feel the need for a brick and mortar presence.

8. Should I wait until I get a client before buying business or liability insurance?

No. Purchase basic liability insurance as soon as you incorporate your business. You'll need to protect yourself starting Day One.

9. This sounds like a big initial investment. What's it going to cost?

If you work out of your home to start, as I did, you can accomplish most everything for just a few thousand dollars. Too many consultants break their bank way too early. Be conservative with your money at the beginning.

10. Should I assemble a board of directors?

Unless you're starting a C corp that's charging out of the gate with a multimillion-dollar contract, you don't need a board to manage your company's affairs. If you have some trusted individuals who can provide you with solid business advice, you might consider a board of advisers. But even they aren't necessary until your business starts generating substantial revenue.

Note from the Field
Monrovia, Liberia
1930 hours

I really enjoy Africa. Despite the hardships the continent continues to face, you can still find beauty among the chaos. Liberia, for example, has never reached its full potential. That's a shame. Though the United States never colonized Liberia, the American influence is obvious. Even Monrovia, the capital, was named for the fifth American president. And the desire for a better life is widely apparent.

My hotel room is decent by African standards, which means it would be given about a star and a half by U.S. travel publications. I can't help imagining how difficult it is for the average citizen here to thrive. The immense poverty out on the street is overwhelming. Most people live on just a few dollars a day. Unemployment is astronomical and corruption is SOP.

As a security consultant, I've visited much harsher places in the sub-Sahara, such as the Congo, Zimbabwe, Rwanda, Guinea and Ivory Coast. But I always return to the notion that the success of a nation can be judged by how many people want to get in and how many want to get out. There are always a lot more people trying to leave Africa than are entering Africa. The possible exception is the Chinese, who are looking to exploit the continent's vast natural resources. But then, they're not looking to stay, either.

In Liberia's case, many nationals have been fortunate enough to leave and obtain citizenship from other countries, such as the United States. But many of these individuals also return to exploit their newly earned passports – so much for national loyalty.

I once heard a college professor who was an expert on African studies proclaim in a lecture that it could be another hundred years before any African country reaches par with the West.

Not every trip is the Four Seasons or dinner at a Michelin Guide star-rated restaurant. It's a cold, hard truth that when you travel as a global security consultant, you'll inevitably have to take the bad with the good. I do. But trips like this one allow me to appreciate the blessings I enjoy in life.

3. Maintaining Financial Control

Rule Number 1: Never lose money.
Rule Number 2: Never forget Rule Number 1.

—Warren Buffett

I ADMIT IT; I'M NOTORIOUSLY BAD AT FINANCES. Back during my MBA program, I had to trade NFL game tickets (I was also working in sales, so I had plenty of access to client gifts) to a classmate so he would help me with my accounting homework. It didn't hurt that he was already a CPA at Arthur Andersen – and I held no Enron stock – but it did presage my future struggles with balance sheets.

Recognizing this weakness, at the start of my business I hired a full-time bookkeeper and regularly spent money to have my taxes prepared by a CPA with solid credentials. I continue to work at overcoming my deficiency, but I credit myself with the wisdom to leave the work I can't perform well to the professionals.

In simple terms: Always maintain impeccable financial records.

My bookkeeper constantly updates me on the health of my company. My office manager also keeps copies of the books, both in hardcopy and electronically. That means we have every expense, invoice, payment and receipt in triplicate at our fingertips. Whenever I need a financial item in front of me, I can retrieve it quickly.

I also check our balance sheet every morning and our profit-and-loss sheet at the end of each week. I review our cash flow practically nonstop, and I carefully scrutinize every expense. It isn't sexy, but it's vital for the company's survival.

Business is all about numbers. I call owning a global security consultancy a lemonade stand with a lot more zeros. You always need more coming in than going out.

Simple? Obvious? Sure, but here's a fact never to forget: The U.S. Bureau of Labor Statistics cites the number-one reason that small businesses fail is poor financial management.

I certainly never forget it. The main reason businesses are forced to shut down has less to do with a lousy product, poor sales or a lack of leadership than it does with an inability to control the money on hand.

Even if you hate math, at the end of the day it's all about the numbers. They never lie, they're devoid of emotions and they're relentless.

Perhaps I'm harping on this, but if you're intimidated by financial jargon such as "depreciation," "amortization," "escrow" or "insolvency," you must overcome your fears. Better yet, suspend reading this book for the moment and head straight to your local library or Amazon and get a copy of *Accounting for Dummies* or a similar reference. Read it then ask someone you know who keeps financial records on Quick-Books to walk you through the bookkeeping process.

Make no mistake; if you want to succeed, you'll have to learn to do the numbers. They'll help you pay the mortgage and, more important, allow you to sleep better at night.

Know the Numbers for Each Project

As I'm writing this passage, I'm in New England and it's 5 a.m. I always find it easiest to write first thing in the morning; it's usually the only free time I have during the day.

My SMI colleagues and I are here performing a three-day critical infrastructure vulnerability assessment for a client in the utility sector with whom we have worked for over a decade. We won the project on a firm-fixed-price proposal, meaning the client is paying us a flat fee with no hidden reimbursable expenses such as travel, local transportation or per diem. Therefore, it's in SMI's best interest to keep overhead low.

I will cover extensively the pros and cons of this bidding strategy in Chapter 8. But I traditionally offer FFP proposals on domestic jobs only; there is too much risk involved attempting them for international projects.

It's the final day of the job, and as usual the bill just slid under the door of my modest but very clean and respectable hotel room. The room charges are not bad, because our client negotiated a special rate for us. In addition, instead of having to fly roundtrip from Reagan Washington National, we rented an SUV and drove up together – six hours each way – thus saving roughly US$2,500 in airfare.

When you consider how long it takes to pass through airport security screenings, plus the fact that we would have needed a vehicle on arrival, we probably lost only two hours in travel time each way while saving a bundle. The drive also gave the team a chance to strategize together about the project, so in essence we gained valuable time.

This is an important point about consulting: Try to maximize your work time with colleagues, particularly subcontractors.

Subcontractors

If I hire a subject-matter expert to assist me on a project, and I am paying him or her US$1500 per day, you'd better believe I will create an assignment to be completed while flying business class. Instead of drinking wine and watching movies, that sub – aka independent contractor or IC – will be reviewing documents and working on his or her presentation for the client.

Many security subs have recently retired from government service – military, law enforcement or intelligence – meaning they might feel they've earned the right to make $2,500 per day merely because of their previous positions. Many also think they need only stand in front of a client to earn their paycheck.

No question, there are many fine, extremely competent former government people. But I've also found that some of them don't function well in the private sector and often underdeliver in terms of providing effective consulting or valuable analysis.

It might be difficult to tell a former ambassador, "Please write a 30-page report on your assessment and get that back to me by the end of the week." For this reason, I hire subs only when absolutely necessary and use people who can justify their rates. I also maintain a file on each of my subs, including an updated résumé and contact information, date of birth, social security number, and copies of all pay and expense checks, plus additional notes on their strengths, weaknesses and feedback from clients. The pay/expense records help the bookkeeper expedite IRS Form 1099 reports and allow me to file my tax return quicker. The notes – even brief ones – help me keep a running account of how well each sub has been performing.

SMD

I once worked as a subcontractor to train a group of Fortune 500 executives who were about to travel to a war zone. The client had paid nearly US$40,000 to receive instruction from me and a highly decorated former intelligence official.

Because of the audience – and the amount of money on the line – I prepared and rehearsed my training modules for weeks in advance. I opened the morning session by laying out the threats the executives likely would be facing. I acted essentially as the warm-up act for the Big Gun instructor, so I tried to be entertaining as well as informative.

I spoke for three hours, including breaks, and I used a lot of recent statistics, visual aids, relevant stories and even some humor. The students seemed engaged, and the first part of the day got off to a fine start. Now it was time to introduce the expert with the impressive résumé.

After a lengthy litany of his awards, titles and achievements, the senior official took the podium. I will never forget his opening remarks.

"So, what do you guys want to talk about?"

Everyone but the accountant who had struck the man's sizable paycheck thought he was joking. Unfortunately, he wasn't. He fumbled through an excruciating PowerPoint presentation he had obviously never seen – someone else must have created it for him. He would read each slide to himself for about 30 seconds, which felt like 30 minutes, before commenting on what he had just read. In some instances, he would read the slide, mumble "Hmmm," and then move on to the next one, as though he wasn't even sure what the slide meant. It was a complete disaster.

Apparently, my fellow instructor didn't think he needed to prepare for his audience. He assumed his sheer presence and occasional war stories would suffice.

After the presentation, the client decided to end the training. His representative called me later that day in my hotel room. He told me, "Luke, I'm going to inform your boss that you did a great job and that you should be compensated for your performance. In fact, I asked all the students to fill out evaluation forms on the training, and everyone gave you glowing reviews. But we're going to ask for a full refund from your employer due to the total lack of preparedness and professionalism demonstrated by your colleague."

It was a bitter experience, but the lesson wasn't lost. From then on, I never assumed because someone had impressive credentials they could perform to a client's satisfaction. You should do the same. Vet your subs before they represent you; otherwise they could seriously damage your reputation.

Unless I've seen a sub perform, I make him or her deliver the upcoming presentation to my staff beforehand.

SMD – Subs Must Deliver

Getting a Handle on Your Expenses

We have a tradition at SMI. We always enjoy a nice steak dinner the night before kicking off any consulting project. We also maintain a strict rule limiting employee drinking to no more than two glasses; the only thing worse than showing up late to a client's location on the first day is showing up looking like you attended a bachelor party the night before.

Speaking of meals, we dine conservatively on our trips and never pass the expenses on to the client. On this particular trip – to New England as I mentioned above – it looks like we've done a good job of keeping expenses down. As a wise man once said, expenses are like fingernails; you must constantly be trimming them.

Trimming is probably too mild a word. If you're going to succeed in this business, you have to become tyrannical about cutting *unnecessary* costs, particularly early on.

Let me be clear about this: An unnecessary cost refers to an item or service that would be nice to have but not essential at that particular moment. An example would be ordering matching polo shirts with your company logo for all your team members when they deploy on a project.

Another: offering promotional swag such as customized pens or calendars to clients.

Yet another — and one of the biggest money wasters of all: sponsoring booths at industry tradeshows. I know; when I started SMI, I was one of the biggest offenders.

Looking back on the formation of my company, which basically means re-examining the books (a good thing to do periodically in any case), I shake my head in disgust at some of the expenses I incurred. I've probably peed away tens of thousands of dollars on marketing schemes that paid zero return on investment. These included magazine ads, Internet banner ads, newsletters, glossy company overview books and website videos, to name a few.

When I was contemplating these actions, I thought it was wise to spare no expense to look like the most substantial security consulting firm possible. I had read a quote from Tom Watson, the founder of IBM, which boasted, "I realized that for IBM to become a great company it would have to act like a great company long before it ever became one."

In my mind, SMI was going to act like a big company right out of the gate. It turned out to be a huge financial mistake. To this day, I wish I had all that money back. Sometimes there is nothing wrong with baby steps.

Maximize Your Profits

Stating the obvious, if you want to make money in global security consulting, you need to learn how to maximize your profits.

It isn't about how much money your client pays you. It's about how much of that money you put in your pocket after you've paid all your expenses. Subcontractors, travel and lodging, and professional printing services all have a tendency to add up rather quickly.

Consider this example: You're based in New York City and

agree to perform a two-week security assessment in Indonesia for US$50,000, which requires you to bring along a sub as a subject-matter expert.

What to do? First, account for every possible expense that could be incurred. This should include, at a minimum:

+ Multiple business-class, round-trip airfares (along with fees for unexpected date changes)
+ Your sub's prep time, phone consultations and report writing
+ Country visa/entry fees
+ Immunizations and prescriptions
+ Hotels
+ Ground transportation
+ Meals and other direct costs such as dry cleaning, printing, excess baggage fees, ATM/transaction fees, currency exchanges and so forth

And don't forget one of the biggest expenses of all: taxes. You might actually be taxed *four* times on this deal. Your client could conceivably be taxed by the Indonesian government – with that tax deducted from your payment. You could be taxed again in the wire transaction from the client's Indonesian bank to your bank. And of course you will be taxed by the State of New York *and* the Internal Revenue Service. Consequently, you could see your $50,000 quickly dwindle down to $5,000 profit.

Not to mention the impact if your spouse/partner wants to tag along on the trip. In that case, you could even lose money on the deal.

How, then, do you ensure that as much of the money you earn remains money you can keep? It isn't as difficult as it sounds, but it does require discipline. Basically, you need to determine how much revenue your company needs to generate in order to satisfy your personal standard of living.

The first step is to set a goal for how much net income you plan to make next year. I know I stated in Chapter 1 that setting arbitrary income goals can be counterproductive, but this is a financial exercise. The number is entirely up to you. It could be US$100,000,

$500,000, $1,000,000 or more – in which case I like you're style.

Next, calculate the minimum profit margin you're willing to accept on your average consulting project. Normally, I like to make at least 40 percent on any job and never less than 20 percent. Splitting the difference approximately, or 33 percent, is a realistic goal, though some consultants will shoot higher, as much as 80 percent. If you can hit that mark, you'll be in a class by yourself.

Unfortunately, most security consultants set their margins too low when starting off. They'll build in an uplift of 10 percent to 15 percent on their services, only to find out the hard way that unexpected costs have eaten deeply into profits.

Don't fall into this trap. Be conservative with your consulting estimates, and protect your bottom line.

Have your Client Cover Your Expenses Up Front

When you work internationally, it's always best for your client to cover all of your travel expenses. This includes airfare, hotel, taxis and other direct costs (ODCs). It's even better to have them pay for these expenses up front, preferably via transfer from their bank account.

If you purchase business-class tickets and 5-star hotel rooms with your company credit card, you risk not being reimbursed for an extended period of time. It could leave you holding the bag through a monthly billing cycle with its accrued interest charges. You might say, "Yes, but I like getting all those extra bonus miles on my card. What's the big deal if it takes them more than 30 days to reimburse me? I get to keep all those extra points." True, but when you start generating more business, and if you have to take two or three international trips per month, you'll suddenly find yourself faced with a US$30,000 credit-card bill and a client who decides to take 90 days or even 120 days to pay. That's a lot of credit you're extending and service charges you're covering – out of your margin.

For that reason, I insist on getting my travel expenses up front. If a client in Dubai wants me to fly over to review a security plan, I respond that my labor rate will be a fixed US$50,000, which includes five days on the ground at their facility, plus my time back home to review documents and write up my final report (which could take an additional 2-4 weeks), *plus* the above-listed expenses in advance.

Incidentally, I never volunteer that I'll be staying at a 4-star or 5-star hotel, preferably a Hyatt property. If they're the type of organization worth doing business with, they'll expect it. If not, you'll know early on.

Notice that I didn't mention meals. In most cases, unless it's a U.S. government client that's accustomed to paying per diem, I don't charge for meals. Yes, it's an additional expense, perhaps hundreds of dollars. But I find it unprofessional to present a meal tab to a client for whom I'm providing high-level consulting. Moreover, whose business is it that I ordered a steak and a side of pommes frites at a restaurant? Certainly not the client's accountant or their finance department. Also, what if I want to order an expensive wine with my dinner? I would never hand that receipt in to the client, either. And I know I wouldn't rehire a consultant who did such a thing.

When you travel for a client, you're there to perform a service. Do your job, do it well, and go home. Don't be a tourist or a freeloader.

Coordinating Travel

When it comes to globetrotting for a client, I always like to work with their internal travel department, or better yet their designated travel agency, to choose preferred flights. If I rely on management to make the decision and arrangements directly, it can lead to inconvenient flight times and layovers, airlines not in my frequent-flyer network, or a poor choice of seats (the dreaded middle). So, I work with the specialists.

As soon as the client and I have agreed on a start date for the project, I ask whom I should coordinate with regarding travel. I always prefer this person to be an assistant and not my direct point of contact, or POC. There's a practical reason for this. I never want to get off on the wrong foot with my client by wasting valuable time discussing my flight itinerary.

If the client doesn't maintain a travel department or supervisor, then I offer to make my own travel arrangements and submit them for approval, after which I'll ask the client to purchase the tickets, reserve a rental vehicle and book a hotel for me. Or, if they prefer, they can wire me the travel expenses, and I book everything myself. That means the client forwards a 50-percent deposit for my labor costs along with my travel voucher.

As I mentioned earlier, I use travel agencies, either one I'm familiar with or one the client recommends. Travel agents can make sure you're credited with frequent-flyer points and help you secure a desired seat. They also can answer questions about your destination city that you might be hesitant to ask your client.

Minimize Debt

I could write an entire chapter on how to minimize your company's debt – or better yet, how to avoid debt entirely. Suffice it to say, though, that at some point you'll need to go into the red for a while. Whether it's a bank loan for startup capital, a loan from a friend or family member to cover the month's payroll, or a credit-card charge instead of a payment for a vendor's invoice, accruing debt is sometimes necessary.

Some financial advisers will even argue that carrying debt is good; for example, for helping you to build a credit rating for your business. It sounds fine in theory – as long as you can meet your monthly obligations. But if the unforeseen happens, you can find yourself in a hole from which it's difficult to emerge.

One of the quickest ways to sink your global security consulting business is to take on too much debt. I took on a ton of it early in the formation of SMI. I wanted the best of everything, and I thought my high-priced marketing would pay off tenfold in terms of new business. So I borrowed to finance my marketing efforts. It didn't work. As a result, I spent a lot of time digging back out to solvency. It was a valuable lesson I learned the hard way.

Credit cards can be a big temptation, particularly those so-called introductory offers, which dangle a low-interest or zero-interest trial period as an inducement. Avoid them, and pay off your company credit cards every month.

Having cash reserves on your balance sheet is a sign of success, not aversion to risk.

Even if your ambition is driving you to attempt to grow your company at lightning speed, establish a limit on how much debt you will assume at any one time. This will prevent you from biting off more than you can chew, and it will keep your company sound for years to come.

I posted a quote from Ernest Hemingway's *The Old Man and the Sea* near my desk. It reads:

I try not to borrow. First you borrow. Then you beg.

Dealing with the Taxman

The U.S. Department of the Treasury's Internal Revenue Service requires businesses to file estimated tax returns quarterly based on projections for the current year and usually based on revenues and taxes due from the previous year. Often, however, those prior-year numbers aren't reliable. A fat year can be followed by a lean one. It's important to keep your estimates within a reasonable range to prevent owing a large chunk of money to the IRS, thereby risking not being able to pay and being hit with interest and penalty charges for underpayment.

I've been able to stay ahead of the taxman (knock on wood) by using a simple rule of thumb: I budget 20 percent of my net profits for estimated tax payments. As long as I drop that 20-percent payment in the mail every three months, when April 15 rolls around I usually don't owe any more than I've been paying quarterly. Some years I've even gotten a refund, but that usually means my business performance was below par.

There are certain exemptions that a global consultancy can claim to help ease the amount of revenue taxed. Some of the more common ones are a company car lease, charitable donations, depreciating office equipment and certain client expenses. It is best to speak with your accountant to determine what you can claim as business write-offs.

One caution: Don't get overly creative with your deductions. Too many questionable write-offs can trigger an audit. As my mother once told me, "Always pay your taxes. You can never beat the taxman. Deal with it."

U.S. Government Contracts

For those of you who deal with government agencies, you might have to limit the amount of profit you make. Many federal contracts allow a vendor to make only 5 percent to 10 percent. For multimillion-dollar or multibillion-dollar military contracts, vendors might be allowed to earn only 2 percent. Although that might sound harsh, keep in mind that a fat government contract can dramatically increase your assets and number of employees, thus increasing your equity and your stock price. Suddenly, a 2-percent profit – which itself is still in the millions – becomes gravy to large defense contractors whose stock prices rise 5 percent on winning a bid.

For those of you ready to take on Lockheed Martin, Raytheon or Boeing out of your home office, the next step is to calculate how much gross revenue you need to generate in order to hit your desired net profit, using your average profit margin. This might not be Harvard Business School, but the reality is if you don't set a financial target you'll only be flying blind.

So, if you want to personally make a salary of US$500,000, pre-tax, next year, and your average profit margin is 33 percent, you'll need to gross about $1.6 million. Notice I said "pre-tax." If you do bring in $500,000 the next year, and if you live in the United States, you could end up paying 40 percent or more to your state and the IRS, thereby reducing your take-home to $300,000. For lack of a better phrase, that sucks.

To legally avoid giving away so much of your hard-earned income to the taxman, you'll need a strategy to reinvest profits back into your company, thus drawing a smaller salary for yourself. Although you're still bringing in the same US$500,000 in pre-tax revenue, there are smart and safe ways to decrease your tax bracket without having to suffer the wrath of a government audit. This can be done through taking legal business deductions and establishing a tax-deferred retirement account such as a 401(k) or an Individual Retirement Account (IRA). I contribute to a Simplified Employee Pension Individual Retirement Account (SEP IRA), which greatly reduces my taxes – though the taxes are due when I begin withdrawing the money later in life.

Because this is not a financial book, the only tax advice I'll offer is this: Invest money in a good CPA with a solid reputation and who has experience with international consulting firms. Do not use your Uncle Bob or think that you can do it yourself with tax-preparation software. It's better to spend good money up front than to suffer the potentially expensive headaches in the future.

Some people are under the misconception that if you work in a unique international consulting field, there are ways to hide money offshore. This, for the most part, is fallacy. You can establish a corporate presence in another country that offers a lower tax rate, but eventually any money you repatriate back to the United States will be taxed again, doubling the burden. Don't be naïve enough to think you're going to pull one over on the IRS. The best way to keep what you make in a thriving global security consulting firm is to have an organized bookkeeper, an experienced CPA and an efficient business model.

Invoicing Your Clients

The only thing better than sending a client your invoice is receiving payment for that invoice. Yet some security consultants actually fear invoicing their clients; others go about it the wrong way.

Sending your client a bill should be a point of pride, if you performed your consulting services well. If you feel nervous about billing a client, it could mean you didn't feel confident that you delivered on your promises, or you don't think your services are worth the cost.

Send your client an invoice as soon as you have delivered your work product. Even if they want to discuss your deliverables in more depth, at least the invoice is in front of them and in the pipeline. Usually, the invoice is forwarded to someone in the client's finance department. So, while you're editing your final security assessment report, an accountant has put the wheels in motion to get your firm paid.

In addition, if you followed the advice I gave earlier, you should have already received at least 50 percent of your money up front. If clients are delinquent paying their bills, it directly affects your cash flow and could jeopardize your company's existence.

Always be a nice guy, but don't allow your clients to confuse your kindness with weakness. You don't have to call in Knuckles Kowalski to collect on your deadbeat clients, but do let them know – in a straightforward business tone – that you will not tolerate late payment.

I sometimes nudge a late-paying client with the following email, which includes an attached copy of the original invoice:

Dear Mr. Smith:

I have not received payment yet for our last project together. I sent you an invoice on January 10th and you are currently past due by 7 days. If this is just an oversight, please send payment immediately. I need to reconcile my books on this contract. Please disregard if you have already sent payment.

Thank you for your attention.

Sincerely,

Luke Bencie

If the response is delayed, I next will call the client. Of course, sometimes it's acceptable to cut the client a break. Consider it good karma or a prudent decision for future business to be patient with a client going through some hard times. We've all been there. Just don't make it a habit. Otherwise, you could end up as the one unable to pay the bills.

Final Thoughts on Finance

I enjoy watching the television show Shark Tank. If you're unfamiliar with it, the premise is that entrepreneurs in need of investment capital are each given a few minutes to pitch five successful business people. If these celebrity millionaires like the entrepreneur's idea, they will negotiate like sharks to provide seed money, in return for equity in the entrepreneur's company. Regardless of how interesting the product is, the sharks always seem to ask the same series of questions:

+ What are your sales to date?

+ What is your monthly cash flow?

+ What are your profit and losses to date?

+ What are your operating costs?

+ Who are your current clients?

More often than not, the answers determine whether or not a shark invests in the company. Be sure you know the answers about your global security consultancy at all times. Then ask yourself: Would a shark want to invest in my business?

The toughest shark on Shark Tank is known as Mr. Wonderful, aka software millionaire Kevin O'Leary. In one particular episode, O'Leary told a former U.S. Marine, who had mortgaged his home and his child's college fund to finance his unsuccessful invention:

Money is like an army. I want to send my troops out to do battle and bring back prisoners (i.e., more money). You, sir, are sending your troops out to be slaughtered.

Although an unfortunate statement, it made me contemplate every investment I have made with my money since.

How are you directing your fiscal army? Are the troops bringing back prisoners, or are you sending them out to their doom?

FAQ

11. Should I get an investor to help me start my business?

Investors are a wonderful thing – if you're willing to share equity and possibly sacrifice control of your business. Consider this: When Sergy Brin and Larry Page were starting Google, they maxed out their credit cards to cover costs rather than go to investors. That saved them from giving up 20 percent to 50 percent of their profits. Do you think they don't celebrate that decision every morning when they wake up?

12. How do I know if my business is healthy?

Your business is healthy if you have positive cash flow, your customers are satisfied, and the business can run smoothly without you for three months.

13. I don't know if I'm going to make US$50,000 or $500,000 next year. How do I anticipate my annual sales?

Ask yourself how much net income you want to earn and then determine your gross sales in order to reach that number. If you go above that target, the rest, as they say, is gravy.

14. Should I share my business's financial information with my employees?

Unless your employees have equity in the company or earn a bonus for reaching specific numbers, I would generally say no. It can only lead to problems when you start making real money.

15. What's the single best piece of advice you can give me to get started?

I'll give you two: Without risk there is no reward. Watch your spending.

Note from the Field
Vienna, Virginia
0600 hours

I'm back home. It's a cold and rainy Saturday morning.
I always like to wake up early on the weekends and do some
writing at the dining room table. When my wife comes
down to join me for coffee around 8:30, I usually shut the
computer down for the rest of the day – unless we have
a specific project going that requires constant attention.
Regardless of the industry in which you're engaged, it's
important to unplug completely from work at least one day
a week. When I first started up my consultancy, I was working 12 hours to 14 hours a day, seven days a week. This isn't
uncommon for a startup entrepreneur. But at a certain point
you need to seek a balance. Remember, you start a business
to give yourself more freedom, not to neglect everything
else in your life. Be smart with your time and learn to relax
a little.

4. Leadership, Management and Processes

> *Mediocre people don't like high achievers,*
> *and high achievers don't like mediocre people.*
>
> —Nick Saban, head football coach,
> University of Alabama

THERE'S NO DOUBT IN MY MIND THAT LEADERSHIP IS ESSENTIAL for creating and running a successful global security consultancy. I also firmly believe it's something you must learn and earn and not something you're born with. But that's good news, because it means you can achieve it no matter your background. First, however, you have to find ways to acquire it. The best way, in my experience, is to learn it from your elders and superiors and then incorporate that quality into your own life.

If you spend any time at all observing leadership in others, you'll soon find that it's about deeds, not words. It's about earning the right to take charge. Throughout history, those who emerged as great leaders invariably were individuals who persevered when times were toughest. Think Alexander the Great against the Persians, Henry V at Agincourt, George Washington at Valley Forge and Winston Churchill in the Battle of Britain. These men faced what seemed like hopeless odds. Yet all were able to rally their people to victory.

In more mundane and everyday cases, leadership means being able to deliver when your back is against the wall – like a quarterback whose team is behind, marching his offense down the field to victory during the final minutes of a game. That's what separates leaders from wannabes.

Leadership in the global security consulting business is no different. Running a consultancy means competing for business against other companies. To survive means becoming a shark – but not in the predatory sense. Rather, it means if you stand still, you sink.

Anyone can run a business when times are fat and clients are beating a path to their door. But it takes leadership when the company has just lost a multimillion-dollar contract, when a competitor has stolen your intellectual property, when a con man has threatened you with a bogus lawsuit, or when the bank is demanding repayment on a loan that is no longer in your bank account. Sound daunting? It should, because that's what life in this business can throw at you. The good news is if you can demonstrate leadership, your company can overcome almost anything – but leadership starts and ends with you, so make sure it's something you can handle. How? Begin by asking yourself a few basic questions:

Am I introspective? Do you take the time to think about your actions realistically and consider how they might affect your business and the people around you? You need to be honest with yourself, and more often, you need to be your own toughest critic – but also your strongest supporter.

How well or poorly do I take criticism? Maintaining a thick skin is an absolute must in this business. As hard as you might try, you can't please everyone all the time. When somebody criticizes you, which no doubt will begin as soon as you obtain some success, you need to recognize the circumstances of that criticism and not allow it to upset you.

How well do I handle stress? This is a big one. In the global security industry, stressful situations are endemic. Scenarios ranging from a client's secret formula being stolen, a client's employees being kidnapped overseas, or an explosion tearing through a client's facilities are all plausible, meaning you should expect phone calls to wake you up at all hours of the night, as I've discovered personally. The truth is that you've chosen a profession that's highly untraditional, and therefore you should be prepared to deal with people who are in highly emotional states – if not in immediate danger.

Who are my best role models for effective leadership? You never outgrow the need for guidance and support. Think back to the people who have shaped you, and consider how they might have achieved leadership.

I've been fortunate to have learned valuable lessons from several incredible individuals. For example, when I was a young man, I played college football in NCAA Division I, for Florida in the Southeastern Conference and at Michigan State in the Big 10. At those schools, I had the privilege of being guided by three of the finest coaches in America: Steve Spurrier at Florida, and George Perles and Nick Saban at Michigan State. Even my old high school coach, John Sprague, was once named NFL High School Coach of the Year. Needless to say, I enjoyed a front-row seat to absorb the philosophies these men had developed for leadership and success.

These four individuals are leaders who have won numerous conference titles, national championships and other prestigious awards. All have secured a place in American football history. When people ask me what were the biggest lessons I learned from each of them, here is how I respond:

+ **John Sprague.** My high school coach taught me to ignore the critics. He said that most of the time they don't even have the guts to attempt what you're doing.

+ **Steve Spurrier.** He used to say there's no reason to do things a certain way just because they've always been done that way. I spent only a year under his tutelage, but the most valuable lesson I learned from Coach Spurrier was the phrase: *Nothing in the books says we can't do it this way.* It means, basically, reset the dynamics of the playing field to your advantage, and don't be afraid to shake things up from time to time. You'll often find that people will begin to imitate you.

+ **George Perles.** Aside from learning a slew of colorful cuss words from Coach Perles, most of them directed at me every time I made a bone-headed play – which happened quite frequently – I learned toughness, both physical and mental. The verbal abuse, which I considered more of a form tough love than malicious intent, shaped me into a more focused individual. I'm grateful for how he, and the other MSU coaches, pushed me every day.

+ **Nick Saban.** One of the premier football coaches in the country, Saban taught our team that we constantly must strive to get better and actively seek perfection – but recognize that it's never obtainable. Wasting time doing anything that doesn't make you a better person, football player, businessman, father, husband, whatever, is disrespectful to yourself and everyone around you. He also taught me never, in his words, to indulge myself in the "Poor Me's." He meant I should never feel sorry for myself.

Even now, years later, I take all of those lessons with me in every endeavor I pursue, and I've come to learn that leadership, more than anything, is a state of mind – and it works in the boardroom just as well as on the gridiron.

For example, anytime I'm negotiating with someone in a formal business setting, I remind myself that the person sitting across from me probably has never experienced competing head-to-head against a future NFL first-round draft pick in front of 100,000 fans in a stadium and 20 million more on TV. Also, this person probably has never been to Iraq or Afghanistan or endured the extreme stress of being shot at, something Winston Churchill once characterized as the most exhilarating feeling in life – as long as the shot is "without result."

Keeping such thoughts in the back of my mind usually allows me to maintain a comfortable control of myself during business dealings. I'll discuss international negotiation in Chapter 11.

Be Prepared

As I moved from the academic and collegiate sports environments to the world of intelligence, my observations of leadership continued. I got a chance to learn from some of the legends of the Central Intelligence Agency, such as the late Arthur "Mick" Donahue, Wilfred J.A. "Wil" Charette, and many others whom I can never publicly name.

Of particular importance, I learned that in the intelligence world, there is zero room for error. If you screw up during an intelligence operation, it could easily lead to an international incident and a black eye for your country. Therefore, you'd better be damn sure that you prepare, prepare and then prepare some more. You should also recognize that Mr. Murphy, of Murphy's Law fame, is always lurking right around the corner, ready to ruin your day.

While traveling the world, to places such as Iraq, Afghanistan and Southeast Asia, I had a front-row seat to some of America's unsung spymasters, as well as several well-known military officers. These men and women were extraordinary leaders. Many of them were still quite young. In fact, every time I hear someone say that today's young people will make terrible future leaders, I have to defend the men and women I met in the war zones. I was proud to have witnessed some of my country's finest young people and will be even more proud when they become our future politicians, diplomats and business captains.

Then there was my most valuable leadership role model of all: my own father. Dad was a high school basketball coach and is arguably the most organized person I've ever met. At 6 feet, 7 inches, he's a proud, quiet man. A former basketball player at Michigan State, he played in the Final Four the year Wilt Chamberlain's Kansas team won the national championship. He was a stickler for consistency, teamwork and a hard work ethic.

Dad taught me that you have to strive to do things right every day. You have to stay disciplined. You have to focus on the fundamentals and never become complacent. Most important, he taught me there would always be competition for anything of value. He was a fan of the legendary basketball player Larry Bird and liked to borrow one of his most famous quotes. Someone, he said, was somewhere practicing at that very moment with the sole intention of defeating me, my team or my company in the future. This always was, and continues to be, my main source of inspiration to succeed.

'Just Don't Let Fear Take over You'

You have to operate your business, your relationships and your life in general with a sense of purpose and even urgency. You can't let fear of failure or fear of the unknown stop you. Dad would tell me before my games, "It is good to be a little nervous because it means you care ... just don't let fear take over you." If you don't have that fire in your belly, if you're too scared or if you don't relish that nervous anticipation that comes from competition, you might want to reconsider starting a business.

Leadership isn't about being loud or aggressive – the Alpha Male in the room. Leadership is about inspiring others to follow your vision based on example. As John Wayne used to say: *Courage is being scared to death but saddling up, anyway.*

In the world of global security consulting, your character defines you as a leader. You must lead from the front and never ask your people to do something that you could not, or would not, do yourself. Whether you're a one-man shop or head of a multinational firm with thousands of employees, you're still the one who sets the tone of your company. This includes the way you dress, the type of language you use, your attention to detail and how you interact with customers.

For example, at SMI, I expect our associates to dress and conduct themselves in a professional manner at all times. The men must wear business suits every day but Friday, and jeans are never permitted. Women are also required to wear respectable attire and skirts that cover down to the knee. Because security often means serious business, even life-or-death business, our employees should always look like they understand the gravity of their duties. As a result, you'll never catch me in a Michigan State T-shirt behind my desk (at home, certainly). That isn't to say I'm a stiff. I just want our clients to understand that we're serious people who can be trusted with their security. T-shirts and sandals are fine for an Internet startup company, but not the people tasked with protecting men, women and children.

SMI Employee Expectations

Character is like a tree and reputation like its shadow.
The shadow is what we think of it; the tree is the real thing.

—Abraham Lincoln

How you are perceived at SMI is a direct result of how you conduct yourself and how you perform your work. The following are the traits we expect from SMI employees, based on legendary UCLA basketball coach John Wooden's Pyramid of Success:

Notice that Character is at the base of the pyramid while Talent is at the top. That's because I regard strong moral and ethical character as the foundation of who we are as a company. In order for SMI to achieve our vision, we will always strive to hire those individuals who possess both character and extraordinary talent.

At SMI, we define each employee trait as follows:

+ Character – being respectful and doing what is right, even when nobody is around to see it
+ Consistency – giving a solid, dependable performance every day
+ Cooperation – being interested in finding the best way, not in having one's own way
+ Focus – being observant, detail-oriented and eager to improve
+ Initiative – being proactive and enthusiastic about work
+ Talent – delivering the best whenever the best is needed

SMI Employee Requirements

Never lie; never cheat; never steal.
Don't whine; don't complain; don't make excuses.

—John Wooden

Following are requirements for everyone working at SMI – many of which I adapted from Coach Wooden:

+ Be on time and dressed in business professional attire.
  Maintain good hygiene.
+ Be ready to work with a sense of purpose and enthusiasm.
+ Conduct yourself with class and respect.
+ Strive to improve yourself and your work product each day.
  We don't "half-ass" it here. Take pride in your work.
+ No cliques, no complaining, no criticizing, no jealousy, no
  egotism, no envy, no alibis. This is not a government job.
  Earn the respect of all your colleagues.
+ Keep your area and common areas organized and neat.
+ Be poised, confident, well informed and in control when
  talking with clients and colleagues.
+ Follow up! Always follow up with clients, with colleagues, with
  prospects and with vendors. Do not allow little things to "fall
  through the cracks."
+ Be efficient in your work. We are not interested in your activity
  as much as your productivity. Don't waste a client's time.
+ Work as a team. Support each other and remember we are all
  working toward achieving the same goals.
+ Never talk about a client with anyone outside of the office.
  We are paid to maintain our clients' privacy and solve their
  most difficult/embarrassing security problems.
  Absolute discretion is a must.
+ Do not send out any work product, such as a proposal, market-
  ing piece, report or invoice until management has approved it.
+ Whether you like it or not, as a leader you will always be judged
  by both your clients and your colleagues. Therefore, it is

important to demonstrate consistency on a daily basis.
You need to be a rock. You need to be solid and dependable.
You cannot let your personal problems – or the problems of
others – let the office slip into chaos. Please don't misinterpret
this. It does not mean being a tyrant. Tyrants never bring out
the best in their team. You can still be friendly and should strive
to create an office environment in which people enjoy coming
to work each day. The most important traits of your character
should be that you are honest and fair. Remember, people can
question your decision-making, but they should never question
your character. We all want to be liked, but earning the respect
of your colleagues is much more important – though we all
would hope for both.

Managing People

For some, managing other people can be a dull and thankless activity. This is unfortunate. When I hear stories of a company's management team berating subordinates, or worse, a manager hiding away
in his or her office cowering from employees, I know that business
is in trouble. To me, a good manager gives people meaning in their
work. Whether you are a receptionist, intern or vice president, every
job is important to the overall success of the organization and thus
must be emphasized as such.

In study after study regardless of culture, it has been demonstrated that money is not the greatest employee motivator. Rather, recognition in front of one's peers has actually been proven to
be a more powerful incentive than financial rewards. Yet for some
unknown reason, most managers have trouble acknowledging their
staff's achievements. In order to keep your team motivated, allow
them the opportunity to express their opinions. If not, lethargy will
set in and their work will become sloppy. You'll then find yourself
spending more time on disciplining employees than supporting and
mentoring them.

People inherently have a need to create. This is why Google
allows their employees up to 20 percent of their workweek to
brainstorm new ideas. Although a global security consulting firm is

not exactly in the same category as the world's leading search-engine provider, you still must ask for suggestions from your people from time to time. Encourage ownership of a project by challenging employees to take personal responsibility for its development, and you might be surprised by the sudden passion people display.

It's important to enforce boundaries – or even red lines – for your employees when allowing them to be creative. For example, clearly define your expectations of project concepts ahead of time to avoid confusion. Delays or unexpected budget items, due to miscommunication or misunderstanding of the project scope and deliverables, are possible. But if you've created a solid operational plan, your employees will have enough flexibility to minimize concerns that they'll be performing incorrectly. As a leader, it's your obligation to ensure your team is on the right path. But when something is done wrong, own that mistake.

If you need to delegate responsibility, you also need to think carefully about what you're going to delegate and to whom. One way to work things through is to meet with the person or people to whom you want to assign responsibility and specify what your expectations are.

I've found it usually helps to discuss the 5 W's (Who, What, Where, When and Why) plus How. Present your expectations in these terms then establish a timeline for your person or team to provide updates, which can become critical vehicles for you to contribute feedback. It's also critical, once you establish your expectations, to respect the individual or individuals involved by getting out of their way. Just add that if anyone has questions as the project unfolds, they can discuss them with you at any time.

Sometimes, the best managers are the ones that figuratively throw their employees into the deep end of the pool but remain vigilant and standing by to help.

Another point about managing people: Jim Collins, in his hugely successful book *Good to Great: Why Some Companies Make the Leap… and Others Don't*, suggests that the key to managing a successful company is to "put the right people in the right seats on the bus, and then point the bus in right direction."

I'd suggest one exception to this principle. Even if you have some non-traditional, undisciplined characters on your bus, allow them to sit wherever they want, provided they keep delivering results and don't affect the productivity or morale of the other passengers. I've personally witnessed a bunch of these eccentric personalities make companies a lot of money. Sometimes, it's better to give these people enough space to operate effectively – again, as long as they don't interfere with anyone else's work – than to constrain or even fire them.

It might sound trite, but it's true: a manager is like a quarterback. He or she will always get more credit than deserved if the project is successful but more blame than deserved if the project fails. When you set out to lead, you sign up for both. Regardless of the outcome, good managers must remain even-keeled and appreciative of those they lead.

Managing Time

I consider wasting time a sin. Why? Because life's far too short to burn daylight on trivial matters such as playing video games, sitting in traffic, indiscriminately surfing the web or watching mind-numbing sitcoms. I don't want to sound grumpy, but let me be perfectly clear about something: Time is the greatest resource on the planet. It's also the most democratic resource. No matter where you live, what language you speak, what deity you worship or what constitutes your lot in life, you still get 24 hours every day. It and the air we breathe are about the only things we all have in common.

What separates us is how we choose to spend those hours.

If you run a global security consultancy, a successful version of which will operate across various time zones, you'll quickly discover that 24 hours are only part of what you'll need daily. If you want to maximize your ability to accomplish the tasks necessary to manage your company, consider the following time-management tips:

+ Write out your next day's tasks the night before, and leave them on your desk. This will help ensure that you get off on the right foot each morning, especially if the previous day's work kept you up late the night before.

+ Check email no more than three or four times a day. Email was supposed to make our lives easier and more efficient. I often think it's had the opposite effect, bombarding us with more communications than we can handle. Responding to emails can eat up much of your day, so discipline yourself about how often you open your inbox. Maybe start, as usual, when you first sit down at your desk in the morning. Then, do it an hour before lunch and again an hour after lunch. Last, wait until just before you're ready to leave for the day. The rules should apply whether you're sitting at a desktop or laptop, or you're using a smartphone. Also, try to avoid the temptation to check emails before bed. For one thing, if it isn't an emergency, it can wait until morning – and if it is something dire, that person would have called instead of emailed. For another, it's important to disengage from your business during rest. You don't want to try to fall asleep when a work-related issue has your thoughts churning.

+ Carve out specific times for routine tasks and stick to them. You'll accomplish more by performing a daily routine than by trying to work impromptu style and staying in the office a couple of extra hours each night. Budget your daily time for specific tasks, and focus on those tasks only. Unless the Sultan of Brunei is calling to hire you to secure his kingdom, tell your staff to take a message. If you don't have a staff, let the voicemail handle calls and return them when the task in front of you is done. (Did I hear you gasp as you read that last sentence?)

+ Limit meetings and be sure they have specific agendas. Many managers hold meetings just to have something to do. Don't run your business that way. If you must have a meeting, be sure there's an agenda and impose a time limit. And if you end up needing another meeting as a result of the one you just had, then you failed to accomplish your agenda. At SMI, we have one **30**-minute meeting on Monday morning, and it usually sustains us through the week. We outline what the objectives of the meeting will be as soon as we begin, and we conclude by recounting which individuals will be directly responsible for following through on the decisions that have just been made. Period. Bureaucratic nonsense, such as assigning a party-planning committee, isn't permitted. If we need to say something else to the group, it's often better done by email or a simple conversation in someone's office – though I discourage instant messaging instead of talking face-to-face.

+ If you can complete a task in under four minutes, do it right at that moment.

+ If you get an email from a client or colleague that can be answered in two minutes, do it. Otherwise, why bother checking email at that particular time?

+ If you can send a fax or scan a document quickly, do it. Don't let it pile up on your to-do list. Knocking out the little things immediately will help free up your day.

+ If an employee walks into your office, stand up at your desk to talk to him or her. Have you ever had a colleague who continues to walk into your office every **20** minutes just to ask a question or chat? If you get in the habit of standing up every time he or she enters the room, it will convey the message that the person should not sit down, and it demonstrates that you have been pulled away from what you are doing and have given this person your full attention – so it'd better be important. Do this a few times, and your people will only approach you with legitimate concerns. You'll still seem approachable, which is imperative, but everyone will understand your time is valuable.

+ Skip the business lunches in favor of breakfast meetings. Lunches are time killers and rarely yield the big deal so many people hope they will yield. I call it RLS or random-lunch syndrome. If you meet someone for breakfast instead, you'll save money, the talk will go faster, and the meeting won't cut so much out of your day. Also, because breakfast is less formal, it usually elicits more personal conversations. Try it.

+ Try to schedule meetings at your office instead of traveling to someone else's office. If I have to meet a client or new potential business partner, I much prefer they come to my office. It means

I don't have to waste time driving to their office – and trying to find parking. Also, if I think the meeting's going nowhere, I can make an excuse to get them to leave. I've learned that some people just want to meet with you to feel important. They promise big things, but more often than not they just want to see what kind of work you can throw their way. There have been plenty of times where I left a meeting at someone else's office only to think it was a waste of time, realizing there was more important work I could have done. Of course, if you don't have your own office yet, this approach won't work for you. But keep it in mind for the future.

+ Instead of taking clients to dinner, invite them to your house. Hosting clients in your home saves you time and money; it creates a more personal atmosphere, which offers you the opportunity to build closer relationships with them. Taking clients out for expensive dinners might seem impressive, but you could also get them wondering if you're doing so by inflating costs on your contracts. As I've noted already, human relationships will be the essence of your long-term business. So, don't be so quick to treat for dinner at an upscale restaurant.

+ Schedule at least an hour of personal time for yourself during the work week. No two ways about it, as hard as you labor, you'll also need down time. Otherwise – count on it – you'll crack up. I know it isn't easy. Every hour seems so valuable, especially when you're just getting started. But trust me; you need to decompress. Once a week I drive to my bank to conduct international wire transfers. There's a nice bookstore a few doors down. I turn off my phone and allow myself to wander the aisles. After a good twenty minutes in the bookstore, I move to the wine outlet right next door. Even if I don't buy anything, I've spent some time where I feel relaxed. When I throw in a cover-to-cover read of a favorite magazine, with the door to my office closed and my shoes off, I'm fully recharged for the remainder of the week.

The SMI Playbook

The best way to direct your people is through well-defined processes and procedures. As of this writing, Alabama head football coach Nick Saban has won four college national championships. He accomplished this tremendous feat by constantly refining what he calls The Process. It's a step-by-step itinerary on how to maximize every minute of every day. It's meant to bring out the best in every player, coach and water boy while minimizing everyone's time and effort.

The Process requires discipline and sacrifice to follow; thus it is never taken for granted by the Alabama team. Not surprising, many other football programs have tried to emulate Saban's system, as do many well-known corporations. Yet, most of them have not come close to achieving the same success. The reason is leadership. Alabama's players and coaches have all bought into the philosophy, mainly because of Saban's passion and personal dedication – something you can't fake. Your people must believe in the mission.

At SMI, we also have our own version of The Process. It's been an evolving set of procedures developed over several years. Some companies might call it an operations manual; we call it our SMI Playbook.

Michael E. Gerber, author of the successful *E-Myth* series, is one of the biggest proponents of the value of processes and operations manuals. He repeatedly cites the McDonald's manual as the poster child for the concept in all his books. Although I've enjoyed the *E-Myth* books, it's always bothered me that the author never provided a concrete example. Therefore, in order to demonstrate that I practice what I preach, following is a segment from our own SMI Playbook on carrying out a direct-mail campaign. The two-page excerpt contains instructions for sending out a Brazil Travel Advisory Notification.

You will most likely be expected to create Brazil Travel Alerts or Newsletters using MailChimp. To do so, follow this action plan:

Benchmarks	Accountable Position	Timing
1. Receive credible threat information from an SMI credible source, SMI-BSD office, media outlet, etc.	Research Department	As Needed
2. Forward information to SMI Managing Director to determine if it should be sent out as a travel advisory. If Managing Director is on travel or does not respond within 30 minutes, follow up with an SMI Senior Associate for approval.	Research Department	ASAP
3. Should SMI Managing Director or Senior Associate approve the information for release, access the Mail Chimp website at www.mailchimp.com	(All subsequent steps)	
4. Enter the login name: XXXX@smiconsultancy.com Enter the password: XXXPasswordXXX		
5. Upon logging in, you will be directed to the MailChimp Dashboard. Click on the red "Create Campaign" button on the left. Choose "Regular Ol' Campaign" from the drop down menu.		
6. Select the "Brazil Travel Warning!" list and choose "Send to Entire List"		
7. Under the Setup tab, name the campaign something you will recognize such as "Brazil Alert-___ Threat" and make the message subject "Brazil Security Alert". Leave the "from" name and reply emails as they are.		

Benchmarks	Accountable Position	Timing

8. When you click "Next", you are directed to the Design tab. Choose "My Templates" at the bottom and select the "SMI-Brazil Travel Warning!" template.

9. Click into the document and edit your content while maintaining the layout of the template. Save your content and click "Next".

10. Under the Plain Text tab, make sure that your plain text content matches the content of the HTML document. When it does, click "Next".

11. Review your choices on the Confirmation page. **Before sending the document to the entire list, send a test email to yourself and officemates.** This can be done under the "Preview and Test" button by selecting "Send a Test Email." Fill in the email addresses to which you want to send a test by separating each with commas and click "Send Test."

12. After your document has been reviewed and checked for mistakes (which often takes multiple attempts), click "Send Now" at the bottom of the Confirmation page to send the travel advisory to the entire list.

Result Statement

To successfully send out a Brazil Travel Advisory notice to SMI-BSD clients within 30 minutes of receiving credible threat information.

Language also plays a key role at SMI. The vocabulary we insist on using among ourselves and our clients is of paramount importance to our identity as a security consultancy. As I've repeatedly mentioned, we avoid the stigma that comes with the word "security," and it's always our intention to shatter the knuckle-dragger stereotype associated with it. Toward that end, within the SMI Playbook, I include the following text, which originated with McKinsey & Company founder Marvin Bower in 1953. It describes the approach we take toward our internal and external communications:

We are what we speak – it defines us – it is our image. We don't have customers, we have clients. We don't serve within an industry, we are a profession. We are not a company, we are not a business. We are a firm. We don't have employees; we have firm members and colleagues who have individual dignity. We don't have business plans; we have aspirations. We don't have rules; we have values. We are (security) management consultants only. We are not managers, promoters or constructors.

Measuring Success

At SMI, we quantify everything in order to track our progress. As I've stated before, the numbers don't lie. Therefore, it's imperative we maintain precise records of all our activities. Only by measuring our progress, or lack thereof, can we determine how best to streamline our process and achieve greater results.

For example, the following chart is a breakdown of results from the 76 total proposals SMI sent to or discussed with clients in 2013:

PROPOSALS

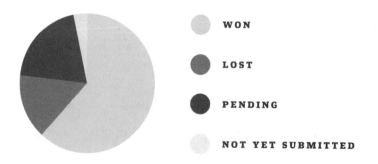

Notice we achieved a majority of successful closings in 2013. Although this number is considered strong in the consulting world – many firms typically close only 10 percent to 20 percent of their prospective client leads – at SMI we are always striving to improve on that number.

Only by measuring every aspect of your global consulting firm can you truly get a handle on your business. Your bottom line is always the first thing investors will want to see, and you also need to understand constantly how you're doing. Only by tracking your daily activities and comparing them over time will you know where to make the necessary push to improve.

Here's another list of items that we track at SMI:

+ Company Expenses

+ Brazil Division Expenses

+ Middle East/North Africa (MENA) Expenses

+ Sales Closing Ratios

+ Prospecting Calls

+ Marketing Piece Expenses/Response

+ Individual Project Times/Expenses

+ Time Spent with Clients/BD Expenses

+ Travel Expenses

+ Training Course Development Time/Expenses

+ New Product Line Development Time/Expenses

+ Use of Independent Contractors/Outside Vendors

+ Employee Billable Hours/Overhead Time

We make it a point to track as much of our business that we can. For example, in order to gauge our sales success, we use the web-based software PipelineDeals. This program allows us to see quickly what prospects are in our sales funnel, how much new business we've brought in, how much repeat business we've closed, how much referral business we've received and how much time we've devoted to each. It also helps us determine our return on investment and success rate for the proposals we submit. I give a more detailed explanation of the sales process in Chapter 7.

Until the cash register was invented and made affordable, many businesses had trouble determining whether they were making or losing money on a day-to-day basis. You're lucky in this day and age to have access to some incredible tools; you should be able to know continually how your business is performing.

Conclusion

Leadership isn't easy. If it were, most businesses would succeed instead of fail. To own and operate a global security consulting firm, you've got to be stubbornly determined with extra-thick skin. You must walk through your front office door each morning inspiring confidence in others, all while maintaining a complete belief in yourself. You must establish a vision for the business, empower your team with the resources to carry out and achieve that vision, and you must maintain the focus of the business when times are tough.

Above all, always lead from the *front*.

The concept of leadership is very personal to me. For that reason, I hope you don't mind my frequent personal anecdotes. When you start your own global security consultancy, remember that the road to success will be filled with potholes and that your leadership skills will be tested daily. Through painful experience, I've found that leadership isn't something acquired by reading a few books. You have to earn it over time and through your own tribulations. But perseverance pays. One of my favorite quotes on this topic is from John Wooden, who said: "Don't measure yourself by what you have accomplished, but by what you should have accomplished with your ability."

FAQ

16. What is the best leadership quality?

Integrity. At SMI, integrity is not a bonus characteristic of our people – it's considered a basic requirement.

17. I was a senior manager in the government for several decades. Does this mean I will make a good businessperson or lousy businessperson?

It depends. Everyone's different. Your lessons from your government service could be totally applicable to your new job, or they might turn out to be useless. Don't let a lack of business experience intimidate you. Start slow, don't bite off more than you can chew, know your financials and continue to develop your business acumen, and you should be fine.

18. Now that I have employees, what is my primary obligation?

Your biggest obligation as a boss is to be fair to your people. This doesn't mean you're running a welfare system. Outline everyone's responsibilities and then stick to them.

19. How do I know if the people I hired are right?

The majority of people you hire will probably not be perfect for the job. Even if the person is a star on paper – or arrives with great references – you'll never know at the start if they'll be a good fit. It's important to establish expectations and benchmarks right away and provide continuous feedback to each new hire for at least the first 90 days. It's more expensive, in the long run, to hire the wrong person than waiting to hire the right person.

20. What do I do if my employees are not buying into my vision?

There are probably only two reasons for this: lack of leadership or people who just don't care. You need to carefully and honestly assess which one it might be. More often than not, lack of leadership is the cause. You might want to have a frank discussion with your team to get their input. But don't forget you're their leader, not their master. Honest feedback from your team is vital to keeping your company's overall direction in line.

Note from the Field
Singapore
1146 hours

Writing relaxes me. That's why I'm always knocking out chapters on the go. It often strikes me how surreal it is that I should be in a position to offer business advice when not so long ago I was running this company out of my apartment. Now, I'm sitting at the desk of my room in the Four Seasons Hotel Singapore, looking at the astonishing lights of the city outside my window. The amount of money in this city-state is staggering, bordering on the absurd. Ferraris, Lamborghinis and Bentleys line the driveway below. Singapore is truly growing into its nickname as the Switzerland of Asia. In business you get a lot of obvious-sounding advice, such as "Follow the money." Sounds good, but how do you know where the money is? Well, I've found it. It's in Singapore. One of the basic tenets of security consulting is where there's money there's a need for security. It's really that simple. Keep your eyes open – and your frequent-flier number memorized.

5. Marketing

Profit in business comes from repeat customers,
customers that boast about your project or service,
and that bring friends with them.

—W. Edwards Deming

A LOT OF MARKETING BOOKS AND COURSES out there try to
deliver a formula fit for every industry, a one-size-fits-all approach
that makes marketing appear so easy even a monkey could do it.
Well, in one sense they're right. Often, marketing means going simple, and there are lessons available that apply across all sectors. But
that logic only goes so far. As a new consultant, you don't have the
resources to dump money into every popular trend, and you certainly don't want to attract the same clientele as, say, a GAP commercial.
In this chapter, I'll address these issues.

Successful marketing is truly an art, not a science. At SMI, we've
been blessed to have an outstanding marketing team. Our webmas-
ter Michael Asker is an IT genius. Michael not only has designed for
SMI one of the finest websites in the security industry, but he also
continues to find creative ways to drive traffic to it. Our marketing
director Jacqueline Asker is the brains behind our brand imaging.
With decades of experience working at some of the top advertising
agencies in Europe, Jacqueline has put a face on SMI. Then there's
my secret weapon, Josh Tallis, who coordinates our day-to-day marketing campaigns and allows us to maintain top-of-mind awareness
with customers. In fact, because Josh is such a talented writer, I've
asked him to contribute his marketing expertise to the bulk of this
chapter.

Everything I'm presenting here is applicable to a range of
budgets. That includes streamlining costs to make marketing a reality even for firms still in their nascent stages. It used to be that

marketing and advertising were luxuries that new businesses could never utilize effectively. Today, with creative use of online media, plus a few tricks I've picked up along the way, that's no longer the case. Moreover, I wrote this chapter specifically for security consultants. It's a quick-tips guide to marketing to get your business growing faster than you ever thought possible. These same suggestions took SMI to international proportions faster than you could earn a college degree. They can do the same for you. And, learning from my mistakes, you might even be able to do it faster.

I've divided the chapter into three sections:

+ Social Marketing

+ Stand Up and Say Something

+ Nobody Wants a Toaster

Each will take you from online media to public speaking to corporate advertising, but the core message will be the same: You're in charge of giving your consulting company a voice and personality. That means thinking deeply about what you say and how you say it. Marketing is how most people will encounter your company, and in security first impressions are usually all you'll get.

Social Marketing

I continue to emphasize the need for personal relationships. Whether it's choosing subcontractors you trust or landing deals with clients, consulting is an intimate profession. It's all about shaking hands and building friendships. In every aspect of your marketing strategy, always keep that in the forefront of your thinking. Ask yourself, "Is this the personality I want my company to have?" Or, "How will this campaign help me strengthen old relationships and forge new ones?" At SMI, one of the best ways to reach clients is to interact with them directly through social media.

I know this might sound strange, especially for the older hands who prefer the clacking of a typewriter to the hollow clicking of a keyboard. After all, aren't Twitter and Facebook for youngsters? Partly, but to a dramatic degree these sites have also attracted millions of professional users and organizations. Just as important, they're free. Likewise, portals such as LinkedIn, WordPress, Blogger, YouTube, ConstantContact, MailChimp, iTunes and even Pinterest, Instagram and Flickr can be tremendous assets in building your brand.

In Chapter 6, I'll discuss my **Ten Commandments for Success**, but here, in a nutshell, are two of them:

Commandment 4: Cash flow is king.

Commandment 9: Document and measure everything.

Both relate to the websites listed above, because they'll allow you to network free of charge, and with their incredibly sophisticated tracking software they can give you complimentary reports on your progress.

Facebook, for example, generates statistics on how many people mention your page weekly, how many people see your posts, and how quickly your page is growing. Twitter offers similar options. WordPress and Blogger document how many hits your blog receives, calculated as both unique views and total views. MailChimp and ConstantContact offer in-depth analyses of who opens your emails, in what countries they're located, how many people clicked on links contained in your emails, and even which links are the most popular.

Here's a quick rundown of how you can use the sites I've mentioned to your advantage:

Facebook. Not only is it an extremely popular Internet destination, on which users can create profiles and Friend – a proprietary term – one another, but also with more than a billion active users it's become the biggest public website in the world. Furthermore, Facebook is growing so rapidly that its user base will be larger than the population of China in a few years.

Facebook is used primarily by individuals, but many so-called public figures – politicians, entertainers and journalists, for examples – use it as well. And so do many businesses, creating their own profiles, called Pages, which members can Like – another proprietary term, which made its inventor a billionaire. When someone Likes your Facebook page, from then on they can see updates as soon as you add anything new. That simple interaction can quickly expand a small network of 15 or so Likes into a network of followers numbering in the hundreds or thousands.

Facebook also offers progressive advertising technology, with options that will accommodate even micro budgets. Using it, you can specify who sees the ads based on the information they share, such as where they work – e.g., aerospace industries, State Department, etc. – and their age and where they live.

The mission of your Facebook account should be simple: generate interest. Seventy-percent of your posts should be informative, unique or fun, with as much personality as possible to encourage followers to check in frequently. The remaining 30 percent should be soft sells or information specific to your courses and products. Social media entrepreneur Gary Vaynerchuk calls this "jab, jab, jab, right hook," based on his book of the same name. Facebook offers the ability to appeal to clients visually and project a sense of stature. Pictures from interviews, professional logos, YouTube videos, merchandise, blogs and page banners all can be used to reinforce that perception. Meanwhile, your ultimate objective is to attract traffic to your website. Pictures and content should frequently carry links to encourage interest in the products or services you offer.

Even if you choose not to make social media a major part of your consulting brand, be sure to claim a Facebook profile in your company's name. You need to control your brand identity. If you succeed in this business, you don't want to face having to buy your namesake back from someone else who holds it on a social media site. In our new and media-rich world, this is called cybersquatting. Though it's technically against the law pursuant to the Anticyber-squatting Consumer Protection Act (ACPA) of 1999, it falls into a legal gray area and can cost a lot of money to resolve if lawyers get involved. So it's best to beat squatters to the punch.

Here's an example of what I mean: I have a buddy who owns a cosmetics business. Recently, he began using social media at his daughter's insistence. As they went to set up an account on Facebook, they discovered that his business name had already been taken. It turned out one of his overseas vendors had been interacting with clients online as if he owned the brand. My friend managed to resolve the situation without incurring a major financial burden – but the lesson should not be lost.

Twitter. This is a much simpler version of Facebook. You create a brief profile then Follow other accounts and try to get other Twitter users to Follow you. Each account has a name, such as Luke Bencie, SMI Consultancy, or Among Enemies (my previous book) and a handle using this format: @Luke_Bencie or @SMI_Consultancy or @Among_Enemies. As soon as you're similarly equipped, you can publish, or Tweet, an unlimited number of brief messages of up to 140 characters. Each message is preceded by what's called a hashtag (#) followed by a word or phrase indicating its theme.

Here's an example:

@SMI_Consultancy I've got a new book coming out all about global #consulting, I'm thinking of calling it #GlobalSecurityConsulting.

The hashtags allow me to connect with users who are interested in consulting and to build awareness about my upcoming project. Notice how simple the message is – this particular one runs well under 140 characters – and there are no spaces in the hashtag phrases. You use capital letters to distinguish between words.

Your mission for Twitter should be guided by the two types of followers you want to target: clients and journalists. The aim of developing a sizeable social media presence is to generate publicity and, eventually, business. Of the two, publicity should be your primary Twitter goal. Use the site as a free resource for sending out news releases, following the trend of many larger businesses. To do it effectively, craft your Twitter content to be insightful and original.

When you post, try to adhere to that 70/30 ratio, with 70 percent of posts being informative, such as links to a blog or Facebook, PR announcements, tips, fun facts and so forth, and 30 percent soft sells, such as new services, links to your website, direct appeals and links to text from email campaigns. Twitter content should also sound personal whenever appropriate. People like to interact with people, not faceless brands.

My advice for Twitter is the same as for Facebook: Whether or not you think you need it, claim an account name as soon as you create your business.

Blogger and WordPress. According to the Internet analysis site Alexa, these sites are the 11th and 24th most visited in the world, respectively and as of this writing. They offer extremely simple templates that enable users to create semi-personalized blogs – short for web logs – on any topic they like.

For a global security consultant, however, don't rely on these services as substitutes for investing in a real website – as I discussed in Chapter 2. You might wonder why you should bother establishing a blog. The answer lies in the most visited website in the world, Google. Nowadays, almost all online interactions begin with a Google search. Therefore, if you want to maximize your company's online visibility, you'll need to have your name attached to as many popular platforms as possible.

By blogging, and frequently, you can kill two birds with one stone. First, you'll be creating content that you can post on your other social media platforms, thereby keeping your followers engaged and drawn to your website, where they can view other content about your courses or products. Second, you'll increase the likelihood that someone looking for a security consultant will encounter your firm's name.

LinkedIn. You could call LinkedIn the professional version of Facebook. Here, you also create a profile, but in this case it's specifically so you can build and maintain a network of colleagues and associates. Chances are you already have a LinkedIn account, but if you don't, create one now. Being a consultant means promoting yourself and maintaining as many trusted relationships as you can. LinkedIn is a perfect way to do so digitally, with the added benefit of the marketing potential inherent in a community focused on the same area of business.

Managed carefully – and by that I mean respecting the site's etiquette – LinkedIn is ideal for the soft sell, for keeping your name in the mix, and occasionally for even interjecting a blog post or two to generate interest among prospective employees and clients. LinkedIn's tone is more formal, but the principles remain the same:

Interacting with more people is an easy and free way to expand your reputation and visibility among peers.

At SMI, we frequently use LinkedIn to speak directly to the security or corporate communities. It is, in the end, a substantial demographic that has already self-identified as interested in what you have to say – so don't stay quiet.

YouTube. If you visit our homepage, you'll notice videos we've also posted on YouTube. They were professionally produced, and we use them as a vivid introduction to our company – and, as you'll see, yours truly.

You should consider making the same investment. Beyond just looking good and letting vendors know you're a well-funded and serious firm, producing a sharp-looking introductory video and then posting it on YouTube can get your company noticed. Granted, it costs some money – and under no circumstances should you scrimp in this particular area, because a poor-quality video is a sure way to drive potential clients away – but in your early years this type of online media is a great way to stand out.

It also pays dividends. Not only do we have a YouTube channel, which draws viewers to topics we want to promote, but back at our website, we can also use these videos to keep people visiting longer and even attract greater attention in email campaigns.

This is the one social media area where investing – in terms of money and creatively – is necessary. The options noted previously in this section are free or cheap. Video in many cases is not, though you can see that some of our YouTube posts consist of recordings of speeches and conference sessions. In those instances, the video is basic, but its value is communicated by the prestige of the events.

MailChimp and ConstantContact. Technically, these aren't social media sites, but they do fall into the category of marketing. Both offer free or low-cost subscription services that allow you to create professional email templates for your business. You can build subscriber lists, send digital mailing campaigns and track your success all on comprehensive and simple platforms.

At SMI, we use both services religiously. For example, we send out monthly newsletters to communicate to our clients and prospects to display our recent achievements. We also maintain subject-specific email lists. such as sending clients or prospects associated with the Brazil Security Division special alerts on Latin American security that might not interest our domestic critical-infrastructure clients.

The objective of our email campaigns is to remain relevant without becoming bothersome. We've found that if we reach out too frequently, we notice higher levels of unsubscribing. On the other hand, reaching out too infrequently risks not building enough brand awareness, and your audience might even become more unlikely to read your material when it does arrive.

In the consulting field, MailChimp reports an average open rate of 37 percent and an average click rate of 3.4 percent for large email campaigns. Use these as benchmarks. But remember, getting to that level could take years, and your open rates will take dramatic dives if you add new subscribers in bulk, so be sure to pay attention to content rather than trends. Automatically generated reports will help you home in on popular subject lines and lists, so you can easily make adjustments.

How do you build an email list? For one thing, start accumulating business cards and compile your first lists from them. Then create simple templates to interact quickly with them.

Be sure to populate your emails with links to your social media accounts. It might sound like oversaturation, but if you do so in an unobtrusive fashion, you'll begin to build a network that allows you to engage with clients in several ways.

In short, social media are, hands down, the most popular places people now visit when logging onto the Internet. You risk nothing by being there and everything by not.

Working the Web

For all your social media accounts, keep your posts interesting and keep them consistent. Create mission statements that foster continuity in your marketing voice no matter who's in charge of managing it, and include goals that keep you actively engaged online.

For example, here's a brief statement the SMI marketing team prepared for our blog:

MISSION: Our mission for the blog should be twofold. First, it should generate interesting content that encourages people to read it. This is not the place for hard selling. Content that attracts readers encourages them to actively return to the Social Media sources on which the blog is published (Facebook and Twitter), which will increase the likelihood that business or PR-related content will make it to these viewers. Second, the blog should drive traffic to our websites. It should contain links imbedded in relevant content, images and words/phrases related to SMI services to help encourage an organic interest in our business.

OBJECTIVE: Our objective should be the publication of one blog post a week. For the end of this year we should be striving to achieve 60 views a month reaching a total of 530 views by year's end. The blog should be a familiar staple of any weekly Social Media activity.

If I've inspired you to create a presence for yourself and your firm on social media, I also want to advise you to use moderation. Supposedly hot new sites emerge all the time, but that doesn't mean you need to join every platform available. In fact, if you do it could diminish the quality of the content you post on all of them.

The best way to avoid overexposure, and possibly unwise platform choices, is to track the social media sites your clients frequent. See what's in demand, and pay attention to long-term Internet trends. If there's one site that seems to garner disproportionate amount of attention among your audience, that should be your target.

Use social media for social marketing.

Paradoxically, sometimes it means generating content that has no direct marketing value but establishes you as an innovator among your industry's community. To be taken seriously as a consultant means being part of the conversation, and the social media have made it easy.

Now that I've laid out what is essentially my own company's social media strategy, I have a confession to make: I actually hate social media. I realize that sounds hypocritical, but hear me out. I also hate accounting. But accounting is a vital part of my business and must be done. I just don't want to do it myself. Likewise, social media has become a vital part of my company's marketing strategy. But I don't want to be the guy who's posting blog comments all day. I have better uses for my time. So, just as I've hired a skilled accountant, I've also hired a tech-savvy person to bring SMI's message to the appropriate social media and keep it there.

I've sought out the best possible social media and website people and carefully explained my vision to them. Then I turned them loose to do what they do best. I've never heard of anyone making millions from a deal initiated on LinkedIn or by the number of Likes they received on Facebook. Now as in the old days, business isn't done that way. Besides, I want prospective clients to judge me through personal interaction, not clever Tweets. The purpose of social media is to build your brand, to establish name recognition and to keep your company in mind – period.

That said, you've got to keep putting your brand out there. We do so much social marketing that when someone Googles "Security Management International," "Luke Bencie" or "Among Enemies," they find search results that continue for many pages. They also find images and YouTube videos. Consider that 80 percent of new business relationships begin with a prospective client typing a search subject into a web browser. We constantly keep that figure in mind. Likewise, you must be sure your company shows up prominently in a search. In today's competitive business world, which bombards us with electronic communications, only those companies that can establish and maintain their web presence will succeed.

Stand Up and Say Something

If you've worked for a company or government agency, odds are you've attended a few conventions and tradeshows. If so, I'd bet you had some pretty good times. After all, you got a holiday from the kids, a night or two in a hotel, free booze and the chance to meet some interesting people. Heck, if you were lucky, you even learned a thing or two or met a valuable future contact.

For the same reasons you once loved business gatherings as an expenses-paid employee, however, as a cash-strapped business owner you now should be wary of them. The truth is, tradeshows can waste your time, money and energy. But if you take my advice, you might be able to avoid some of the pitfalls involved while still showing clients and competitors you're a serious presence in global security consulting.

Let's talk more about the downside. Tradeshows are usually packed with vendors, the biggest of which tend to garner attention equal to their dominance of the total market. It's difficult to make a splash when someone bigger or more famous is making waves and drawing crowds on the other side of the room. Chances are, they've also provided the keynote speaker and taken the top sponsorship spots. That means the whole event is essentially a well-orchestrated marketing statement by one or a handful of companies, no matter who else participates.

What about the other sponsors who were thanked at the kickoff breakfast? You know, the ones identified only by the small logos printed at the bottom of page 3 of the event program. I often felt motivated and energized after hearing some particularly effective conference speakers; I can still visualize them and hear their words in my memory. But I'll be damned if I can recall any of the minor sponsors. Think about your own experiences. Aren't they similar? You remember some interesting lectures you attended, but you can't recall who sponsored them. Make that Lesson 1 on tradeshows: If you're not a top sponsor, the expense isn't worth it.

That said – and as I've stated repeatedly – becoming a top-tier security consultant means engaging in the global conversation; not showing up at all will leave you at a terrible competitive disadvantage. What can you do? Several things:

Bite the bullet and be a top sponsor. This buys you the most ideal locations on the exhibit floor, a position of prominence in the printed material, frequent mentions from the stage and one or more primetime speaking slots.

Naturally, this costs money – lots of it – so you'll have to wait until your business starts producing substantial revenues. But you can reduce your exposure somewhat by negotiating a lower sponsorship price. You'd be surprised how often conference organizers will accept counter offers. You still might have to stretch your budget, but by being a skillful negotiator you can ease some of the strain while greatly increasing your visibility.

Write a book. Capitalize on your body of experience and perception of the world at large by doing something that will allow you to avoid paying for tradeshows at all. If you're not a writer, hire someone who is. Better yet, find a publisher with a skilled editor who will work with you to realize your vision. Not only will a good book become your best calling card, as well as a source of credibility and potential revenue, but it will also keep you in the minds of event organizers looking to schedule speakers.

Flash forward a bit. You've written that book, and it's quickly become a buzz topic, landing you your first speaking gig. Now you find yourself on a podium in front of your peers and potential clients. I hope at that moment you'll remember the advice I'm giving you here, Don't tell your audience everything you know; tell them only what they *need* to know.

The tradeshows you'll be attending are also populated by your competition. Many of those individuals and companies are respectable, admirable even. But some will have no reluctance to take – steal – your intellectual property (IP) and use it for their own benefit. Avoid the impulse to show off to your colleagues. Think twice before uttering something sensitive about your topic, such as a new program or initiative your company has in development.

Again, having a book helps. If you've published something, it means you're comfortable with the contents being available to anyone. If you stick to talking about your book, you can promote your work and avoid leaking IP to the competition.

If you land a speaking gig, try for lunchtime. Midday speeches at conferences are perfect venues. That's when people are content to sit and listen while they eat – and they're no longer ignoring the speaker because of growing hunger. On the other hand, you can easily lose a lunch crowd if you bore them. You can tell when this happens, because you'll notice more and more of the audience chatting happily with their neighbors instead of paying attention to you.

What to do? Be light, witty and just a *tad* controversial. Too little, and you'll find the background noise swamping you; too much and you'll start a food fight. If you're a confident and practiced speaker, lunchtime is your time. If not, gain some experience at smaller functions before you try the big league.

Record your speeches. One great way I've found to promote myself and my firm is to post videos of my appearances on YouTube. To use a biblical phrase, go and do likewise. Anytime you speak at an event, that's news for your company. Ask the host organization to record your speech. If they can't, ask for a free ticket to have a friend or professional record it for you. Then, when you're done, you've gained a nice bit of marketing material to email to your client list, put up on your website and post on your YouTube channel. That way, a speech seen in person by dozens or a hundred people can be viewed later by thousands via digital media.

Meet clients outside of the venue. If you're trying to attract a potential client, the odds of connecting with that client among hundreds or thousands of attendees are slim at best. So, why pay us$1,000 for the privilege of being unsuccessful? Instead, call or send an email to your prospect and ask to meet in the lobby of your hotel for drinks. By doing so, you've drastically cut the cost of your meeting while still demonstrating you're part of the global security consulting community.

An alternative: Ask a trusted existing client who's attending the conference to have dinner with you and invite the prospect to join them. I know, I advised earlier against spending money on restaurant meetings. But this is an exception. It's a way of getting someone's attention by having them accompany a satisfied customer.

In the end, however, most consultants don't walk away from tradeshows with contracts. What they can do – and what SMI has done repeatedly – is to solidify working relationships with other firms. But for the most part conventions and the like should be viewed with caution. Use your cash-flow situation to determine how you approach them.

Don't forget the world beyond security consulting. It's a big world out there, and much of it involves companies and organizations that have little or nothing to do with your business – but that doesn't mean you can't derive benefit from them.

I'm talking about professional organizations, alumni associations, universities, the FBI's Infragard group, the Rotary club, even country clubs and unions. They all represent venues where you can pitch directly to clients. They're where you can be the keynote speaker and the center of attention. Often these organizations sponsor functions that are free of charge and offer you the potential to make connections normally unavailable to the small fish in the big pond.

When I wanted, for example, to pitch SMI's Counter-Espionage for Business Travelers course, I spoke to executives at my local FBI-sponsored Infragard chapter. When I wanted to pitch our CARVER Threat and Vulnerability Assessment Methodology, I had my critical infrastructure guys speak to engineers and corporate-safety officers at The Infrastructure Security Partnership (TISP). And when I wanted to pitch SMI's Shopping Mall Assessment and Response Training (SMART) Course, I asked my strategic partners at All is One International to speak at the International Council of Shopping Centers (ISCS) conference.

In all three cases, the events were free to me and my guys, and all expenses were covered. After my Infragard appearance, I walked away with a pocket full of business cards and great leads. After TISP, I developed both a world-class partnership with a renowned engineering firm and, eventually, some of the most sought-after courses in explosives mitigation. And after ISCS, I won some relatively minor but still worthwhile contracts. In every instance, the successes started small, but with virtually no initial investment the returns were tremendous. Multiple referrals later, it's hard to calculate just how lucrative those engagements were.

Never underestimate the power of thinking creatively. Wrestling contracts from consulting giants is incredibly difficult. Building your own network with the full attention of private audiences is always the better option. That means seriously engaging with education-based marketing as well, something I touched on without naming directly in the social marketing section.

If you follow my company (@SMI_Consultancy) or my previous book (@Among_Enemies) on Twitter, and if you receive our emails or visit the Resources page on my website, you'll notice a large amount of material that begins with, "Did you know…?" or "FYI…" That's because every time we make an effort to educate the public, we become more of a reference point for potential clients. And if you hate doing direct sales, education-based marketing is a great alternative way to introduce yourself to new clients without having to lunge into a pitch.

For example, if I want to interest security directors in my Counter-Espionage course, I could try the standard sales model, phoning them with the pitch, "Have I got a product for you!" But let's be real; that approach doesn't produce much of a success rate.

Instead, I could send this:

> Did you know that every year $300 billion in intellectual property is stolen from American businesses like yours, mostly when employees are in transit? If not, SMI is offering a free white paper: The Top 5 Espionage Threats to Business Travelers. If you are interested in learning more about IP theft or brand protection, please feel free to reach out to me.

Using this approach, you can whet someone's appetite and show them you are an educator, not simply a businessperson. It's also a great way to be invited to speak at university symposia or business conferences, as I have numerous times. And it will lead to more prospective clients and your establishment as a brand-name consultant. Your angle is you're there to help, not sell. In reality, you can and are doing both.

A final point about speaking engagements: As I'll explain in the next chapter, the first commandment of consulting is Know Yourself; the tenth is Never Stop Improving.

You can't be an effective leader of a global security consulting firm without commanding attention on the podium. Your clients will look to you for reassurance and guidance, and potential clients expect the same qualities in the contractors they hire. If you're not a good public speaker, you can be, with practice and lessons. If you're serious about making it big in business, you can't fake that skill. It might not be pretty, but it's true; stand up and say something, or sit down and shut up.

Nobody Wants a Toaster

Let's assume you've done your homework and refined your sales pitch to a high luster. You can speak confidently, you've been attending professional functions on a budget, and you're plastering the Internet with your brand. If so, great! But there's one more marketing tool you must tap into: advertising.

Advertising, as I mentioned earlier in this chapter, despite the expense involved provides no guarantee that you're going to win new business. In fact, ads often seem to be an exercise in vanity rather than a valued sales tool.

I remember walking through the Washington, D.C., Metro system once and seeing the ad spaces in entire stations bought out by the same government-services firm. None of the ads said anything of significance, and a few didn't even feature the company's name prominently. Perhaps the characters on the cable TV series Mad Men would have something to say about subtle marketing techniques and brand identification and exposure, but in the end that company spent a great deal of money to reach mostly ordinary commuters. If you're big enough to do that, fine. But for everyone else, these next paragraphs are for you.

I want you to focus on four specific concepts: corporate material, gifts, print ads and online ads. I've listed them in descending order of importance, and if you handle them wisely you can make back your investment, and then some.

Corporate material. Some marketing activities should remain optional for startups in their first years because of the high cost, but corporate material is essential.

I've gone on at length about making presentations to your clients and prospects, getting them to trust you, and making your pitch concise and professional. But the ultimate closer after any meeting involves heading straight to your vehicle and immediately producing a handwritten thank-you note.

I'm not talking about signing the thing, slipping it into an envelope and traipsing back to the office you just visited to present it to the receptionist. That says "amateur" and "over-eager."

No, I'm saying write out the note while the meeting is still fresh in your mind. Try to remember a detail that's complimentary to your host, such as his or her professionalism, the helpfulness of the staff or even the pleasant atmosphere of the office, building or grounds. Then drop it in the mail when you return to the office.

I can't overemphasize the importance of a prompt and polite thank-you. It will go a long way to making you appear bigger than you might be. And chances are that piece of paper will remain on the person's desk for a while, so it becomes a small advertisement. That should be the substance of your communications – polite and professional. Regarding the form – meaning your logos, fonts, colors, phrases and proportions – that's something to be standardized on any piece of paper you put out. At SMI, our colors are red, white and black, and our font is Georgia. Everything matches that: our business cards, PowerPoint presentations, tri-folds, envelopes, letterheads, folders – and our thank-you notes. It's not only business material, it's also advertising.

Nowadays, doing it all doesn't really cost very much. For example, I found a guy who printed our note cards on high quality stock for us$60 for a hundred pieces. On occasions such as the one I mentioned above, each card can be worth its weight in gold. Consider them an imperative expense for your new venture, and budget accordingly. The same for business cards, tri-folds and folders. All are great investments that should be seen as more-than-necessary business items.

Consider these two scenarios. In the first, you hand your prospective client a business card you had printed at Staples and your presentation enveloped in a plain white folder. At best, the prospect will think you're cheap; at worst they'll pay no attention to what you've handed them.

In the second instance, you present the prospect a glossy folder embossed with your company logo and containing a pocket into which you've slipped your glossed business card. Inside the folder is your bound presentation, also matching in design and style. The prospect is bound to take note of your brand's identity. That will help him or her recall your name later, and it reinforces the image that you're an established name. Such material should always complement your sales. As your consulting business expands globally, you might also want to consider a double-sided business card that presents the front-side text in other languages. For example, I also carry SMI cards that display my contact info in English on one side, while on the back it's printed in Arabic, Portuguese or Chinese.

Incidentally, tri-folds constitute a versatile piece of corporate literature; they can be used anywhere. Attending a conference and need to hand out reference material? Tri-folds fit in suit pockets or purses and provide a good mix of information and visual stimulation. Meeting a client? Again, tri-folds are easy to carry and don't seems as intrusive as larger-format material.

Feel free to think creatively. Tri-folds fit in standard business envelopes, meaning you can mail a letter to a prospect and include your brochure without paying more than a stamp's worth for them to see it. Just as with the note cards, there's enough competition among local print shops that you can easily find someone to print a hundred pieces for less than US$1 each.

Gifts. They go hand-in-hand with corporate material. I don't mean spending thousands for briefcases or even club ties. But when it comes to gifts, go classy or don't go at all. Pens can be a great business giveaway, and people always seem to be short of them. In my office, we use pens that we custom-ordered. They look good, but more important they perform well – much better than the stuff you get in bulk at the office-supply store. They're black with our name and logo on the side of an elegant twist top, and I often carry a few on me, though I never force them on anyone. Instead, I wait for the inevitable circumstance when a client asks if I have a pen they can borrow. I give them one and tell them to keep it. Then it becomes a small advertisement.

In the same vein, notepads with your company's logo are relatively cheap to produce and make convenient giveaways.

Whatever you do, try to avoid giving out standard fare only. Pens and pads are fine, but something different would be even better.

Over the years, I've experimented with several alternative giveaways. Ceramic mugs are popular, but I found that metal camping mugs with a logo or short phrase can catch the eye even more. They're also lightweight and unbreakable, making them easier for people to carry away from conventions, meetings, courses or other gatherings.

In recent years, challenge coins also make a unique and popular option. They're easy to carry in your briefcase or purse, and when you hand them to potential clients they're usually appreciated. You can also sell them, as I do for my first book *Among Enemies*.

Gifts are good, but they're not essential. If you don't have room in the budget for them, wait until you do. Advertising has a hierarchy. Some expenditures, such as the signs plastering Metro stations in D.C. are more for status or vanity than for closing deals.

Print ads. Advertising as a consultant can be tricky. It's probably the least cost-effective way to invest your marketing budget. You're not trying to attract everyday consumers; you need to reach C-Level executives, government procurement workers and security directors. Starting out, your ad material will be localized and mostly hand-delivered to clients. If you try to broaden your advertising pool, your audience is what you should be paying for, not the ad space.

When I began advertising SMI, I cut a great deal with a popular security and counterterrorism magazine. In return for a better rate on a set number of full- and half-page ads, I agreed to supply one or two articles for the magazine's quarterly circulation. As a result, I ensured that my ads were reaching the desired audience, *and* I got to establish myself, my associates and my company as an industry leader in the field by appearing in the publication.

My strategy worked because I thought about how to maximize my investment – how to get the biggest bang for my buck. At this writing, my associates and I have contributed over a dozen articles to the journal. They've all been great giveaways at meetings. We've also sent reprints to clients and prospects – along with a handwritten note wishing them well.

So, my ads have gotten my company noticed within the right community, while we've used our articles as calling cards. We've also thrown them into our company folder along with tri-folds and presentations at our pitch meeting.

If you do the same, you'll likewise look like a player in this industry. As my credibility has grown as an author, I'm being approached more and more to write articles for other security, business and travel magazines. I happily accept, with the stipulation that the publisher provides me with at least 50 copies to mail out at a later date. Because most magazines usually appear in online editions as well, I post those links on the NEWS page of our website. It all increases our visibility.

Consider also a proactive alternative: Approach security and business media websites and offer to write an article for free. Blogs and online publications are always hungry for content on a daily basis. You could even allow their writers to appropriate an essay that you've written – as long as they mention your company or quote you as an expert. To learn more about this admittedly self-serving technique, I encourage you to read *Trust Me, I'm Lying: Confessions of a Media Manipulator* by Ryan Holiday.

Online ads. I'm not a huge fan of paying for Internet advertising. For one thing, it can be incredibly expensive, depending on the site. For another, it's difficult to know who you're reaching. Nevertheless, like social media, online ads are now an essential part of marketing. But keep some things in mind. For example, shy away from big security sites with expensive ad space. As with tradeshows, you're sure to be overshadowed by huge banners from the likes of Raytheon or Lockheed Martin.

Instead, find the sites your prospects are likely to frequent, such as professional organization pages. Or, target them with sophisticated search functions on Facebook. In either case, the rules from print marketing apply. You're paying for the audience, so no matter how good the price is, never shell out cash for something aimed at the wrong demographic.

In addition – and I shouldn't even have to say it at this point –

never pay full price. It's your prerogative to ask for a deal. More often than not, you'll get one. As always, keep your material simple, and link to your home website. That is where you're king on the Internet and where there are no competitors vying for attention.

If you haven't turned a profit, yet – which is the norm for businesses in their first two or three years – this is a luxury item, pure and simple. Concentrate your efforts on the social media sites, and save any revenues coming in for landing clients, not building a name.

One last tip. Use your email signature as an advertising tool. You probably send thousands of messages each year from your business account. Many will be forwarded to other people whom you've never met before. Why not add a little something extra for the reader to notice, such as a link to your site or to your book, or even an article or interview you've recently done? A quick endorsement or award from a well-known person or entity is also helpful. Here's how I sign off:

Luke Bencie
President/Managing Director
Author of *Among Enemies:
Counter-Espionage for the
Business Traveler*

**SECURITY
MANAGEMENT
INTERNATIONAL,** LLC
Intelligent Security Solutions

Security Management International, LLC
7600 Leesburg Pike
East Building, Suite 340
Falls Church, VA 22043 USA
Office 703.962.1545
Cell 703.627.5248
Fax 703.997.8827
lbencie@smiconsultancy.com
www.smiconsultancy.com
www.among-enemies.com

You should consider Among Enemies *a must-read if you travel overseas.*
—William J. Esposito, Former FBI Deputy Director

Caution: Don't overdo it. It's easy to get carried away with your email signature. Instead of impressing a potential client, you could annoy them with too much promo. Also, use your signature only once during a back-and-forth email exchange. It can be aggravating when someone inserts his or her signature in every email reply, forcing the reader to scroll through the mess of contact info, company logos and favorite quotes.

Closing Thoughts

Keep in mind that selling and marketing are not the same thing. You can sell without advertising, and you can advertise without selling. While the two complement each other well, selling is definitely more important in your startup years. Again, we'll discuss selling further in Chapter 7.

Successful marketing requires building a recognizable brand identity. Remember, there's a great deal of marketing you can do that costs very little or nothing at all.

FAQ

21. Where should I advertise if I am just starting out?

Start by investing in a good website. Eighty percent of all business begins by someone doing a Google search. You need to maintain a respectable online presence.

22. How much of my budget should go toward advertising?

Initially, you want to spend very little for ads. Sure, produce first-class business cards and stationary, as well as other marketing collateral that you can mail out. But as far as advertising goes, I wouldn't recommend spending more than 5 percent to 10 percent of your revenues in the early months of your business.

23. I'm a one-man business. How in the world do I build a name for myself overnight?

You don't. Rome wasn't built in a day. Make a list of your ideal clients and then contact each of them. If you're fortunate enough to land one, provide unmatched customer service and allow them to help establish your reputation.

24. Should I skip the tradeshow and security conference circuit entirely?

I've never found security tradeshows to be of value, particularly sponsoring a booth. As an alternative, become a speaker at the conference — have *them* cover your travel costs — and you'll probably end up with lots of leads, appear more credible and save a ton of money.

25. It seems as though there is so much advertising already out there. How do I distinguish myself from all the noise?

You're correct; there is a lot of noise. The way to break through it is by building a community of followers who are interested in what you have to say. That requires you to give away interesting content, regularly and usually for free. Start by creating your own webinars or podcasts on pertinent security matters. These usually cost nothing to create, and if you're credible and interesting, people will begin following you online.

Note from the Field
Above New York City
1445 hours

Manhattan, even from 30,000 feet, is still an impressive sight.
As I write this, I'm returning from Vienna to Washington, flying
Austrian Airlines. I'm sitting in Seat 1A, so I feel as though I'm
tucked away in my own private space. There's nothing quite
like looking down on the greatest city in the world, especially
with Frank Sinatra's "New York, New York" wafting through the
headphones, while I'm enjoying a glass of Chilean Carménère.

I find the fiery red uniforms worn by the flight attendants
unflattering, particularly with those matching red leotards and
shoes, and the sky-blue scarves around their necks don't soften
the impact. But they're all attractive middle-age women, and
though their Austrian accents project a somewhat disciplinarian
tone, they're attentive and highly professional.

The night before my flight, I had enjoyed a traditional Vien-
nese dinner with a client to discuss security recommendations

for a government in the Middle East. Those recommendations could mean the difference between safety and danger for the top echelons of that government.

Sometimes, when I think back over the years to when I start-ed working in this field, I have to pinch myself. Here I am, a former kid from the Midwest, now a globe-trotting security professional helping governments fight terrorism and criminal activity. But if I can do it, so can you. You just have to be willing to take the hits. I've discovered that when it comes to starting a business, most people allow their fears to outweigh their dreams. Instead of laboring away at a job, take the plunge at least once in your life and build a career that makes you raring to go to work every day.

6. Ten Commandments for Success

The most basic form of human stupidity is
forgetting what we are trying to accomplish.

—Friedrich Nietzsche

BEFORE YOU CASH OUT YOUR LIFE SAVINGS and open up the next great global consultancy to rival the likes of Kroll, Pinkerton and the other big-name security firms of the world, it's essential to make the following list an instinctive part of your business life. I call them the Global Security Consultant's Ten Commandments for Success. These rules to live by constitute what many of us swear by, rules developed over decades of trial and error. You can avoid the pitfalls of the past by taking them seriously.

They say that in order to succeed, smart people find successful role models and emulate them. Even smarter people study the mistakes made by successful role models to try to avoid repeating them. But not-so-smart people ignore both and choose to learn for themselves the hard way.

Whatever your method of absorbing knowledge, I hope you eventually reach the conclusion that the following points are essential to building a sustainable global security consultancy.

Legendary Green Bay Packers football coach Vince Lombardi made famous the phrase: *Winning is a habit; unfortunately, so is losing.* Commit these Ten Commandments to memory, and you'll position yourself to be a winner in your chosen new field.

Commandment 1: Know yourself.
This simple statement, updated from the Greek philosopher Plato, represents the cornerstone for any businessperson. As an entrepreneur,

you must be brave to strike out on your own. But you also must be honest with yourself and recognize clearly what you can and cannot do, particularly in terms of performing international consulting work.

Too many security consultants immediately say "yes" to any job or partnership that comes their way without considering the consequences of their actions if they can't deliver the goods. In the realm of global security consulting, the jobs often involve physical protection of people and assets. This isn't something to be taken lightly. Unlike party planners who, if they screw up the invitations, risk a loss of business and bad online reviews, when security consultants make a mistake it could get someone killed. Even the consequences of giving bad advice could be severe, if not life threatening, to the client.

With all due respect to Plato, I still prefer the advice from Clint Eastwood ... remember? *A man's got to know his limitations.*

If your expertise is in intellectual property investigations in Latin America, and you receive a call from a prospective client who asks for antipiracy assistance off the coast of Somalia, you'd better be damn sure you have a trusted and expert subcontractor at the ready before taking the job. Otherwise, you've just put your client, your team and your reputation in harm's way.

If you don't want to turn away business, line up your resources ahead of time and devise an operational plan that can be quickly implemented when the need arises. As my good friend, Pablo Gonzalez, a former director of emergency preparedness for the City of Miami, used to say, "If you're exchanging business cards during an emergency, you're already too late."

To know yourself means being honest with yourself. Many consultants choose to fake it until they make it. That might work for a time with those who don't know you well enough, but the worst person you can try to fool is the person in the mirror. And whether you choose to listen to Plato or Eastwood, knowing what you can and cannot do provides the intellectual scaffolding for building your consultancy.

Commandment 2: Charge what you're worth.

Many people think the difference between charging a client US$5,000 and US$50,000 for a security consulting project should be based on the consultant's experience or the quality of the deliverables. The cold, hard truth of the matter is, you decide what you're worth, not the client. If there are phrases that best summarize a losing mentality when it comes to security consulting, it would be these three:

"I could never ask for that much money from a client."

"A little bit of something is better than a whole lot of nothing."

"How could I justify charging that as an hourly rate?"

These aren't the utterances of a successful businessperson in any field, let alone a security consultant. If words like those have crossed your mind, you need to lose that attitude. Instead, start thinking in terms of the value (i.e., the convenience and ultimate cost savings) you're providing. The service that you perform for, say, US$50,000 could cost your client millions if left unattended or delegated to unskilled hands.

Let me give you an example. SMI specializes in educating international executives on how to best protect their intellectual property and business intelligence (IP/BI) from hostile foreign intelligence services and business competitors while traveling overseas. It's a good specialty to have. Over US$300 billion in IP/BI is stolen from American business travelers each year, and on average every Fortune 500 company is targeted at least twice a year.

In other words, the odds of travelers being victimized are fairly high. In fact, it's estimated that each targeted attack costs a Fortune 500 company between US$50,000 and $500,000 – not to mention the possibility of public embarrassment and resulting erosion of shareholder confidence. When SMI consultants train executives on how to ensure their corporate materials are not exploited, we don't charge a basic daily rate of $1,000 per instructor. Why? Because we don't charge a company a few thousand dollars when we're helping them to save millions. Instead, we let the client know what we're doing for them and, in most cases, they recognize the value. If they don't, we try to educate them further. If they still balk at our price, we wish them well.

You will gain more respect and create greater value for your services by sticking to your guns about price. It would be easy to say "yes, we will train your people for US$2,500." But if you do, you have devalued your own intellectual property.

Alan Weiss, known as the Rock Star of Consulting who wrote the bestseller *Million Dollar Consulting*, coined the phrase "value-based fees" – which he also turned into a book of the same name. Weiss states the following about the concept:

Establishing value with the client is key. If the focus is on fees and not on value, the client has taken control of the discussion, and the client's focus will never be on maximizing your fees.

This reminds me of a great line from the movie *Rocky Balboa*, the final installment in the *Rocky* series. In the scene, Rocky (Sylvester Stallone) explains to his son, who feels overshadowed by his father's reputation, "If you know what you're worth, go out and get what you're worth!"

As a global security consultant, if you truly feel you have the knowledge and expertise to better your client's situation, then always charge what you're worth and avoid falling into the trap of leaving money on the table by charging hourly or daily fees.

Commandment 3: Get your money up front.
This might sound like a negative concept, but it's of vital importance. When you do business overseas, you need to get paid up front, or at the very least get your expenses up front. In the global market, Net 30 is not always considered a payment term; it is merely a polite suggestion. In dealing with global clients, I stipulate that my travel and lodging expenses must be paid up front, and I receive at least 20 percent of my fee, wired to my bank, before beginning the job. If the funds are not in my account by the day of travel, I don't board the airplane. Period. I also inform my clients of this at least twice, once before signing the agreement and once immediately afterwards.

As Ronald Reagan was fond of saying about the Soviets: *Trust, but verify.* You might have a good feeling about doing business with your newly signed client from the Middle East or Africa, but how successful do you think you're going to be in collecting your fee if he stiffs you on the invoice? Do you think you can hire a lawyer and sue? Unless your consulting fee is over US$200,000, your legal fees alone will eat up the eventual award – particularly in the international market.

You say you have a signed contract? Good luck. Every country has different laws pertaining to business agreements. Sure, a good attorney should review your documents prior to signing any international deal and advise you of worst-case scenarios, but a better way to avoid getting shafted by your client is to collect up front. An attorney who specializes in international contracts will cost you, but that precaution could save you thousands or millions later.

Commandment 4: Cash flow is king.

Every global security consultant dreams of landing the one big job they can use to retire. It could be protecting a royal family member of a wealthy Gulf nation, providing all of the security for a major sporting event such as the World Cup or Olympics, or being put on retainer by a Fortune 100 company for investigations or training.

Go ahead and pursue bagging the elephant, but never forget the monthly revenue – or those piddling jobs, as they're known – you'll need to sustain the day-to-day operations of the business. Let's face it, those little two-day investigations or week-long vulnerability assessments add up, at least enough to cover the cost of your office space, staff, phone bills and gourmet coffee machine capsules. I hate to repeat an already overused expression, but cash flow is king; it's the lifeblood of any business.

Other consulting books might tell you to jettison your bottom 5 percent to 10 percent of clients each year. In some instances, I agree. Many smaller clients can provide you with the biggest headaches and consume more of your time than the larger revenue-generating clients. Plus, in business schools, as well as *The New York Times* best-selling business books, you're usually taught to think big.

Yes, thinking big is useful – I always like to keep at least three dream clients in my sales pipeline at all times – but I've also had some lean years where those little headache-makers paid my rent.

In my own practice, I've made it a point to track all of my clients' spending habits over the years. What I've noticed is sometimes those little clients become big clients; not always, but on a few occasions. What's more likely to happen, at least in my experience, is that those little guys refer me to other, bigger clients. In fact, when I add up the revenue from my smaller clients each year, it turns out I actually generate more income from the referral business they provide than the revenue I collect from them individually. This might change from year to year, but never underestimate the power of your clients – even the small ones.

Think big, but always think cash flow first.

Commandment 5: Understand the territory.
It has always amazed me the number of people who travel to a foreign country without studying their destinations prior to departing – and no, a Wikipedia search doesn't cut it.

I remember one instance when I was staying at a hotel camp along the White Nile River in South Sudan. The reason I chose the compound over a traditional hotel was because the camp was behind barbed wire fencing with guards brandishing AK-47s. Usually, I try to mix with the locals on my trips, but in this case I'd received a country report from my staff before my departure, and it warned that violent crime was so bad in the city of Juba that a compound was the safest option.

On that same trip, which took place in the middle of the rainy season, where flooding was rampant and the mud was 6 inches deep, the subject-matter experts from Fortune 500 consulting firms were foolishly wearing penny loafers, dress slacks and button-down shirts with their company logos. Others even attempted wearing suits. These clueless and unprepared travelers were continuously falling victim to heat stroke, malaria, food poisoning, slip-and-fall accidents, allergies, infections and dehydration from horrific diarrhea.

My colleague on the trip, a retired Special Forces combat veteran and an expert in jungle warfare, would just shake his head in amusement and disgust. We wondered how multibillion-dollar consulting firms could send their employees to the Third World so unprepared.

The point is you should always know the country, culture and climate well before your trip. You should also speak with others who have been abroad recently and can educate you on what to expect and what you'll need to bring. One of the best ways to look like a seasoned global security professional, and not a naïve tourist, is to invest in the book *Kiss, Bow, or Shake Hands*. This regularly updated reference guide will provide all types of useful tips you can use for business or social settings. For example, it explains why you don't touch food at a dinner table in the Middle East with your left hand – it has to do with bathroom traditions – or why you don't give the "Okay" sign (thumb and index finger touching) in Brazil. Also, if you're going to work with international clients on a regular basis you should give serious consideration to taking a cultural awareness and diplomatic protocol course. At SMI, all new consultants must undergo a mandatory one-week program on how to behave in foreign environments so as not to offend our clients.

In addition to clothing considerations and medication and vaccination requirements, it's imperative to understand the local laws and customs thoroughly. For this, consult the country's embassy website and the U.S. Department of State website – in particular the Overseas Security Advisory Council section.

At SMI, we even provide in-depth reports for business travelers who want the inside scoop. There's no excuse, for example, for not knowing the visa requirements of your destination county, such as:

+ Do you need a business visa or tourist visa to enter that country?

+ What would the penalty be if you were caught conducting business while in the country on a tourist visa?

+ Can you obtain a visa at the airport and can you extend your visa if need be?

+ Does the country require a letter of invitation (sponsorship) from a local business or government agency?

+ Can you acquire a longer-term visa if you expect to make multiple trips to that country?

Even more important than entry requirements, for many first-time consultants the fastest ways to lose money while consulting overseas is through international taxes and bank transaction fees. Knowing the banking regulations and tax laws of the country in which you're doing business can make the difference between a healthy margin and enduring a quarter in the red. Let me repeat: Know the banking regulations and tax laws of the country in which you're doing business.

Case Study: São Paulo Office

As part of our operations at Security Management International, we maintain an office in São Paulo, Brazil. We call it our Brazil Security Division, or BSD. The office coordinates all of our consulting services within Brazil, from executive protection to armored transport, investigations and infrastructure assessments. When we first started operations down there, we decided to open a virtual office so we could establish a physical address and a bilingual (Portuguese/English) receptionist who could answer the phone and redirect client calls either to our country manager or back to me in the United States. The small monthly lease and service charge sounded all well and good, until I started receiving tax invoices from the Brazilian government. In addition, when I went to pay my office manager via wire transfer, I was shocked to discover Brazil had imposed an international wiring fee of over 20 percent. Needless to say, it became expensive to maintain our virtual office in São Paulo. Then, when BSD began to take off, local security companies became very jealous. So much so that a particular competitor even confronted us and claimed we were costing them business with our "American ways." The grim reality about consulting globally means you'll inevitably tread on someone else's turf. Before you do, make sure you've learned the local laws, inside and out.

Commandment 6: Ask the right questions.

Being considered a great consultant boils down to two things: 1) you understand your clients' problems better than they do, and 2) you deliver your clients the results and answers that make their lives better. If you can lay claim to both, you are succeeding as a consultant, no matter in what city or country you work. Unfortunately, it sounds easier than it is.

To accomplish the first part – understanding their problems – you need to be able to ask smart questions. I judge intelligent people not by the statements they make but by the questions they ask. A good question can quickly identify the sharpest person in the room. Learn to ask those questions. Do this by asking your client to start at the beginning. There's nothing worse than a consultant who pretends to know the client's problem too early in the discussion. This is like a doctor who prescribes a medicine or suggests an operation before the patient even gets on the examination table. One of the easiest ways to understand your client is to ask these five questions:

+ What do you think the problem is?

+ Why do you think that is?

+ What have you done so far to address the problem?

+ Why do you think that didn't work?

+ Could it be that something else is actually the problem?

This should get the discussion flowing in rapid fashion and move you and the client to the same page. It will also open up new lines of questioning that will help you determine how best to address the problem. Don't go looking for solutions until you've answered all of them. Nothing looks more unprofessional than going back to your client weeks after a project has started and asking a basic question that should have been addressed at the beginning of the job.

It also helps to do your homework prior to meeting with the client. Conduct as much open-source research about the company as possible, and seek out a trusted colleague who already works within that organization. He or she can help answer questions you might be too embarrassed to ask in front of a C-Level decision-maker.

Likewise, you don't want to look foolish by asking a question that should be obvious to anyone who consults for a living. Don't sink a deal by not being prepared for a meeting – ever. You need to think of yourself as an athlete going into the arena every time you meet with a client or prospective client. You're not there to compete with them, but you should have practiced your game plan well before kickoff. Compile an agenda before you arrive. Explain to your client what you expect to cover during your time together. Ask if they agree with that agenda and if they have anything different or additional that they would like to cover.

As Woody Allen famously said: *80 percent of success is just showing up.* In global consulting, we aim a bit higher. Let's say that 90 percent of success is showing up fully prepared.

Commandment 7: Work only with subcontractors you trust.
This is a big one, particularly if you're going to do business overseas. Just because you know someone in another country doesn't mean you can claim to have a presence in that country.

I've seen this time after time. Security consultants will say something like, "I have a great guy in country who can perform the job." This can be the kiss of death for your business. At SMI, our test to determine whether or not a subcontractor is worthy of performing work in our name is simple. We ask two questions: 1) Has anyone in our company worked shoulder-to-shoulder in the field with this potential subcontractor? 2) If so, what were the results and can we verify them?"

If the answer to either question is "No," then it's game over. If someone at SMI has worked with the potential sub, I as owner of the company will request a CV and references – which we check – and conduct a Skype or in-person interview; I want to see the person we would be presenting to our clients. Then I instruct our research team to conduct an open-source background investigation. If everything is so far, so good, I require the sub to sign nondisclosure and non-circumvent agreements with us.

As I mentioned previously, NDAs are often worthless in other countries. Nevertheless, I use them to convey a message early on that SMI takes client confidentiality and ethics very seriously.

If it's our first time using an international partner on a project, I also like to forward them an operations checklist, a code of conduct for how to behave, and a budget to stay within. If possible, I prefer to send an SMI representative to oversee the project, even if they occupy a junior position, to ensure that the sub's performance meets our high expectations. If not possible – usually for cost reasons – I require the sub to check in with me on a regular basis or email me a daily report that answers specific questions about the project.

Why go to so much trouble? Because I'm ultimately liable for anything that goes wrong. If one of the subs upsets the client, it's hard to defend yourself by saying, "Don't blame me, that guy was just a sub." You should never allow other people to get you fired – or worse, sued.

If you're going global, start slowly. Don't try to build a network in Asia, Africa, Latin America and the Middle East overnight. It astonishes me the number of individuals on LinkedIn groups who are begging complete strangers to be their international partners. I must receive 10 requests a day from individuals in Pakistan, Nigeria, India and various other countries who offer to be SMI's exclusive partner in the region. If I need an overseas partner, I have other ways of finding credible professionals. The Internet, despite being an incredibly useful tool, is not my first choice.

Finding good, on-the-ground partners is essential for expanding your network and building your business. But choose these people wisely. The only way to do this is through solid referrals from those you trust. And always prefer face-to-face meetings.

Keep this in mind as well: Don't allow your subcontractors to become too cozy with your clients, or vice versa. Clients aren't stupid. If they require ongoing consulting support in an overseas location, and they interact with your sub every day instead of you, it won't be long before the client wonders why they're mailing you a check every month and not just hiring the sub directly. To build a successful international business, you must be willing to hop on a plane and fly the flag from time to time in places where you subcontract work. Also consider including stipulations in your agreements that your subs carry your logo or business cards to ensure the brand you are building maintains visibility with the client.

Commandment 8: Always ask for referrals.

The fastest, most assured way to grow your business is through referrals. Yet for some reason most people are hesitant, or flat out afraid, to ask for them. It's mind-boggling when you think about it. You have a client who's pleased with your work as a consultant, so why not ask that person for leads to other individuals and companies that could also benefit from your services? If you do your job as a consultant well, a referral becomes a three-way win. You win because you receive a lead that can turn into a client. The new prospect being referred to you can win by benefiting from your services. And the client offering the lead can win thanks from their colleague for recommending a fine consultant.

The only time you should be afraid to ask for a referral is when your service has not performed to your own standards. If you believe in yourself as a highly competent and highly experienced security consultant, never hesitate to ask for a referral, especially when the client compliments you on your work. Do it the next time your client remarks positively about you. The exchange might go something like this:

CLIENT: We just received your report; it looks outstanding — much more detailed and useful than we were expecting.

YOU: Thank you. I sincerely appreciate it when clients tell me they're pleased with my work. I wonder if I might ask for a favor in return.

CLIENT:: What can I do for you?

YOU: I have built my consulting practice on referrals from satisfied clients. Could you provide the names of one or two other who might be able to benefit from my services?

CLIENT:: I don't see why not; you've done a great job for us.

YOU: Thank you. If you could phone or email them, it would facilitate my introduction.

CLIENT:: It would be my pleasure.

YOU: Thank you very much.

Such simple exchanges can grow your consulting business exponentially. They're sincere, honest and proven to expand your client base over the long run. The next time your client praises you, try it. On the other hand, if you haven't been receiving accolades from clients, maybe you should reexamine your deliverables.

Don't ask for referrals too soon, however, particularly with a new client. Prove yourself first, then strive to strengthen the relationship. You wouldn't want to ask for a referral and then deliver a service that doesn't please the client.

Commandment 9: Document and measure everything.

Even if you operate a one-person shop, you need a system. As a global security consultant, organization is the key to success. This organization can be easily accomplished by documenting everything you do in your business.

Michael Gerber built an empire on his book *The E-Myth Revisited: Why Most Small Business Fail and What to Do About It.* The premise essentially is that every business, regardless of size or industry, needs to establish operating procedures as well as metrics to gauge efficiency and progress. McDonald's is frequently used to demonstrate how even the most mundane tasks can be written down in a step-by-step process to improve company operations.

The purpose of such minutiae? So you can franchise your business and be able to sell it at a later date. It will also help you determine where time, money and resources are being expended and possibly wasted. The concept might sound boring and unnecessary, but I guarantee it will pay off as your business starts to grow. As you start to take on employees or subcontractors, having a detailed operations manual will make plugging people into place that much easier. It will also allow you to set standards for how you would like everyone to perform.

At SMI we document everything. In addition to tracking our monthly revenues and expenses, we also track the number of inquiries we receive, the number of marketing materials we send out and their response rates, the number of proposals we produce, the amount of time spent on writing reports, and so forth. We also constantly update our SMI Playbook by allowing employees the freedom to find more efficient ways to perform their jobs.

Again, even if you're just a small consultancy right now, don't get lazy on documentation or metrics. This is much more effective than trying to follow a business plan that you wrote years ago and are just now dusting off the shelf. Your operations manual should be a living document that grows as the company grows. Believe me, you'll be glad you created one when you're ready to sell your business to a larger firm for millions.

Commandment 10: Never stop improving.
I'm talking about strengths and weaknesses. Sometimes, it's better not to improve on your weaknesses but play to your strengths. You can always find someone else to supplement your shortcomings. Even so, self-improvement and ongoing education should remain a key element of your core beliefs. Never stop learning.

The easiest way to improve your competency quickly as a global security consultant is to become a voracious reader of all things related to international affairs. This includes books (historical and biographies), magazines (*The Economist, Foreign Policy, Foreign Affairs,* etc.) and newspapers. I start every morning by perusing the A sections of the following newspapers:

+ *The International Herald Tribune*
+ *The Washington Post*
+ *The New York Times*
+ *The Wall Street Journal*
+ *The Financial Times*

This is a habit I picked up interning for a well-respected congressman on Capitol Hill. Each morning before the congressman arrived at his office, he expected those first sections to be sorted and laid on his desk (along with a cup of strong black coffee). We interns kept the Sports and Entertainment sections; the congressman considered them a waste of his time. For the first 30 minutes of each day, he drank his coffee and scanned the headlines. He also read all the editorials to get a feel for where the topics of national debate were headed. That way, he was always up-to-date on global current events and was never caught off guard. While knowing himself was likely the reason he was elected the first time, never stop improving was probably what got him the next nine terms.

Working as a global security consultant means you'll be expected to know about the security issues affecting the world at any given time. More important for you, you'll need to know what can and cannot be done. But first you should be aware of what needs to be done. Do it by investing time and money in further education. Earmark funds in your annual budget for:

+ Magazine/newspaper subscriptions

+ Continuing education or security certification classes

+ Membership in reputable security organizations, such as ASIS International, OSAC or the Council of Foreign Relations

+ Personal improvement classes (public speaking, negotiation, accounting, etc.)

+ Business coaching

+ Extracurricular activities (golf, wine tasting, volunteering)

When was the last time you tried learning another language? As a global security consultant, being multilingual enhances your skill set and opens you to a world of new opportunities, both professionally and personally.

When it comes to continuing education and self-improvement, remember what Voltaire said:

The more I read, the more I acquire, the more I realize that I know nothing.

The Missing Five

In the Mel Brooks comedy *History of the World: Part I*, there's a scene in which God gives His commandments to Moses (Brooks). Moses leaves the mountaintop and, standing before the Israelites, suffers an accident:

Moses: I give you these Fifteen… (He drops a tablet) these Ten Commandments!

I n that vein, I'd like to offer five more rules to help you shape your business. Let's call them The Missing Five.

If business were as easy as following 10 simple steps, we could all be rich. Moreover, why do 80 percent of all businesses fail in their first year? The secret lies in the rules most people don't like to talk about, rules usually absent from business-school curricula or motivational speaking tours. They're rules that would most likely be declared not by Moses but by Michael Douglas's character Gordon Gekko in the movie *Wall Street* – or maybe Rodney Dangerfield's loveable, self-made millionaire Thornton Melon in the movie *Back to School*.

Commandment 11: Learn to be a salesman.

Few people really like selling. Some professionals claim to love it or are motivated by rejection, but we all know that's BS. I've been in sales for over 20 years, ever since my first job straight out of college. And although I've made a good living from commissions and incentivized sales contests, where the awards included all-expenses-paid vacations to exotic locations, there are some mornings – and some people – I just don't want to pitch.

For the rest of you out there who also hate to sell, I have some good news: The Internet has made your life much easier. You can now be a nameless/faceless entity – or a hyper-glorified avatar of yourself – and avoid human interaction altogether. You can even make a decent living, hocking items on eBay or from your personal website.

The bad news is the real world still exists, and nothing happens in business until something is bought and sold, and you shake (non-virtual) hands. So, if you want to have your own security consulting business, at some point you're going to have to persuade someone to trust you and your services. The more people that buy your brand and the greater the trust you can win, the more money you'll make.

What's the most important component of successful sales? Isn't it self-evident? You must believe in what you're selling. If you don't, you'll diminish the product.

Steve Jobs was a salesman. His pitch was that Apple products – the Mac, the iPod, the iPad, iTunes – would change the world for the better. But he wasn't selling electronic gadgets. Rather, he was selling the idea of a more convenient and enjoyable world. In the process he built one of the highest-valued companies in history and changed forever the cultures of music, personal computing and telecommunications.

Regardless of your product, you must overcome your distaste for selling. Some people feel that way because of fear of rejection. For others, it's a matter of public speaking or shyness. Even the best salespeople feel apprehensive at times. But they also know that if someone has slammed the proverbial door in their faces, it wasn't personal; it was just business.

One big step toward overcoming sales shyness is to establish a reasonable definition of success. In a nutshell, you can't close every deal.

Consider Ty Cobb, probably the greatest hitter that Major League Baseball has ever produced. His lifetime batting average – a record that has stood for nearly 90 years – was .366. That means out of every 100 times Cobb went to bat, he failed to get a hit nearly 64 times. Likewise, the legendary and beloved Babe Ruth, who hit 714 home runs during his career, also struck out 1,330 times. So, two of baseball's biggest stars failed at the plate significantly more than they succeeded.

Translating this to the world of global security consulting, if you win three out of every 10 sales calls, you'll end up in a mansion on the beach.

There are plenty of good books and courses available on sales. But I've found that an effective way to overcome an apprehension of selling is by repeatedly role-playing a sales call with a trusted colleague. It's like that old saying your gym teacher used to repeat: The only way to get stronger at doing chin-ups is by doing chin-ups. If you repeatedly role-play different sales presentations, and you field both anticipated and unanticipated objections in private, before you know it you'll have all the confidence you need to call on prospective clients.

Beyond that, the easiest way to be a good salesman is to be passionate about your product. And if you've started your own global security consulting firm, your product is you. If you're not sure whether you can be passionate about your skills and what you can offer prospective clients, you need to go back and read Commandment 1 again.

Commandment 12: Keep in shape.

Yes, this one might sting a few of you out there. But if you're going to lead a successful global security consulting business, you need to be in shape. By in shape, I mean getting rid of that beer gut. You must be able to put up with the physical stress that comes with intense international travel and the dramatic hours running your own business demands.

I fly over 100,000 miles every year. I know what it does to your body. Jet lag, a queasy stomach, poor diet and muscle fatigue are all inseparable parts of the job. High altitudes, poor living conditions, lack of sleep and difficult terrain are likewise givens. Worse, your body becomes more susceptible to injury and sickness after you've arrived at your destination. In some of the harshest Third World environments where our people operate, they must be well-conditioned athletes. An out-of-shape consultant not only looks unprofessional but also fails to inspire confidence. The bald truth of our business is a significant portion of it is pageantry. If you don't look the part, you're at an immediate disadvantage.

I don't mean you need to qualify for the Iron Man in Hawaii. But you should at least look the part in your suit. So, make room in your weekly schedule for exercise. Even when you deploy overseas to work for a client, build in some time – preferably in the morning – to run, lift or swim. Just be sure that you're not cutting into your client's time. Your energy will increase, as will your productivity. In addition, I've never met a client that became upset because his security consultant was hitting the gym at 6 o'clock every morning. If anything, it gave the client something else to brag about when referring the consultant to one of his business colleagues. Maintain your image and your health. Look good in your suit.

Commandment 13: Surround yourself
with smarter and different people.

Enlisting people who are smarter than you might sound like a recipe for disaster. And many bosses seem to live in paranoia that their employees are going to overshadow them. Perhaps it's fear of being found out that as the captain of your company you're not as smart as some of your crew, that the discrepancy might lead to embarrassment, lack of respect or even mutiny.

If that's the way you feel, get over it. At SMI, I'm always on the lookout for people who are not only smarter than I but also vastly different from me. Not that my personality is so awful that the thought of two of me might be too much to bear. But in this profession, groupthink or a one-track mindset is not in your client's best interest.

For example, I feel very confident in my ability to conduct due diligence on an offshore company or speak about corporate espionage to a group of security directors. But I definitely don't know enough to instruct Afghan soldiers on how to perform close-quarter battle during a hostage rescue. For that I employ former SWAT and Navy SEALs, the undisputed experts in CQB and rescue operations. The point is it isn't what you know, it's your ability to find those individuals who can do the job better than anyone else and put them on your team.

I also like to have a few people who hold different opinions and display demeanors that are different from mine and the rest of the staff's. You might say, "If I put someone of a different mindset on our team, it could mess up our strong dynamic." Maybe, but if you want to make sure you're always examining your clients' problems from all angles, you need to throw in at least one outsider to stir things up and offer a unique perspective.

While I was writing this book, I was hired to help promote the Blu-ray video release of the latest Jack Ryan spy movie to a group of entertainment reporters in Hollywood. The reporters got to spend time and perform operational training exercises with former CIA officers, some of whom had been in Moscow, as a tie-in to the Russian setting of the movie. I flew in over a dozen former intelligence officers to demonstrate how to conduct clandestine street surveillance. I also brought in one former FBI agent just to mix things up.

There's always been a respectful rivalry between the CIA and FBI. As it turned out, my FBI guy, William Esposito – a former deputy director of the bureau – quickly became a class favorite because of his natural demeanor, developed over years of conducting surveillance on the streets of New York. The event was a tremendous success, and Bill's input made the exercises that much more fun.

If you remain unconvinced, here's a compromise: Consider bringing outsiders in as subs only for the duration of the project.

I once heard a speaker say, "Never hire someone exactly like you, because it means they're just going to learn what they can from you, steal your intellectual property, and then open their own business and be your direct competition." That person added, "Because that's what you would do."

Commandment 14: Publish a book.

Years ago, when I was a young account executive with a Fortune 500 telecom company, which was my second job out of college (my first was as a stuntman at Universal Studios Florida, but that's another story), I was attending their annual sales conference in Philadelphia. During the weeklong event, motivational speakers would take the stage hour after hour and dispense advice on various topics ranging from "How to Ask for the Sale," "Dressing for Success," "Organizing Your Life" and so on.

Some of the speakers were exceptional, and some were, let's say, less so – not everyone can be Tony Robbins. After one particular gentleman gave a hilarious talk on the negotiation principles he learned while "cutting fabric" – his term – in New York City's competitive Garment District, I decided to compliment him and ask how someone goes about becoming a public speaker. His answer was short but profound. "It's very easy," he replied. "You gotta write a book." Writing a book equals bona fides. Bona fides equals more consulting work, speaking invitations and higher fees.

If you plan to make it as a big-time consultant, writing a

commercially published – not a self-published – book can help put you on the fast track. A book is a fantastic calling card for a consultant. It can give you instant credibility, particularly if it's selling well in stores and receiving positive reviews by national media outlets. A book can bring you exposure that you could never receive otherwise.

Writing a book does not mean slapping 50,000 words down on paper about some random topic, however. I'm talking about doing the real work of writing something that has market value. It means producing a manuscript that will be picked up by a professional publisher, is thoroughly edited and revised to ensure quality, and then marketed and distributed in national bookstores.

To write a successful book, you must first have something to say. Then you need to be able to say it in a way that holds the reader's attention. If you can't or don't wish to do that, I still urge you to publish a book. But you'll have to resort to a ghostwriter or skilled copyeditor for assistance.

The Book-Publishing Process

When I started writing my first book, *Among Enemies: Counter-Espionage for the Business Traveler,* I had no idea what I was doing. The longest thing I had written up to that point was a 60-page master's thesis in college. Only after I consulted a professional author/consultant did I learn everything that would have to be involved. First, I needed to write a book proposal, which included a 20-page summary along with the complete first chapter and another random chapter. Next, I had to shop the proposal around to find an agent who would agree to represent me. I received numerous rejections, and they all seemed to follow the same suspicious line – that for unspecified reasons it didn't "meet their 'needs' at this time." Eventually, a close friend referred me directly to Mountain Lake Press, which agreed to publish the book. I hired the writer/consultant to produce the manuscript, which Mountain Lake Press revised ... again, and again and again. We also went through an elaborate design process plus a mandatory content review by the CIA's Publication Review Board. The book finally hit the store shelves in the spring of 2013. When it was all said and done, the book took 18 months to complete. It was a difficult and challenging process, but it's given me a calling card on steroids. Now, I use it to market both SMI and myself, and I've won more jobs and have been able to charge higher fees.

Commandment 15: Find a rabbi.

When I worked within the intelligence community, there was a common phrase young officers would often hear early in their careers: Find a rabbi. It meant searching out a mentor who would watch your back and help you climb the bureaucratic ladder within the system. If you were fortunate enough to land the right rabbi, one with a lot of clout and seniority, he or she could pull enough strings to get your career on the fast track. That meant you could get promoted quicker and you could get posted in some of the nicer and more prestigious locations around the world.

In other words, if your rabbi had some juice, you could win a three-year prime assignment. But if your rabbi was weak, you could end up in a backwater. If you didn't have one at all, you might get stuck in the basement at headquarters. In business as in government, the mentor/protégé relationship has always played an important role, and the game doesn't change much when you get older and transition into a new career.

If you recently retired from the military, law enforcement or intelligence community, and your aim is to start a global security consultancy, be prepared to seek out advice from someone who's been there – even if that person is younger. Sometimes it's necessary to suck up your pride and admit you need help. Sometimes, it's even necessary to become a protégé all over again. But fear not, if you find the right rabbi, you can learn from their mistakes, leverage their existing contacts and eventually become your own rabbi someday.

If starting from the bottom has you feeling like a rookie, remember what Leonardo da Vinci once said about the mentor/protégé relationship: *The student should always surpass the master.*

None of these rules will be easy to follow, and they're certainly not all self-evident. But they could help push you into the successful 20 percent of startups that survive beyond their first year in the business.

My Own Rabbi

In my own career, I was fortunate to learn about global security consulting from one of the finest individuals in the business. Jon Monett retired from government service after a distinguished career that took him around the world as a senior manger conducting special projects for the intelligence community. Although his career remains mostly classified, he occasionally acts as an adviser to Hollywood for espionage movies. He even landed a role in the Robert DeNiro and Matt Damon spy vehicle *The Good Shepherd*.

After retirement, Jon opened his own security consulting firm in his basement, but within a year he had to move to professional office space. Over the next two decades he grew the business to employ more than 200 people and won several large government contracts. He eventually sold the company to Raytheon, one of the largest defense contractors, for a substantial amount.

I had the distinct privilege to work for Jon over several years. When it was time for me to strike out on my own, he was one of the few people who supported my decision. At the time, I was earning close to us$200,000 per year and was living a comfortable life. Just about everyone I knew thought I was crazy to cash in my savings as startup capital, but Jon encouraged me never to look back. Through the initial 18 months of the business losing money, Jon would listen to all my ideas, gripes, fears and sales pitches. He was quick to offer his advice and, more important, his contacts. We like to refer to him around SMI as our Consigliere, in homage to Robert Duvall's role as counsel to Don Corleone in *The Godfather*. At last, the tide started to change, and SMI began making money. I doubt success would have come so quickly – and in this business 18 months is quick – if I hadn't had Jon in my corner.

FAQ

26. I've developed a great product, but now everyone is copying it. What should I do?

That's to be expected if your product is good. Look at Apple. Every idea they have seems to be copied by the competition a year later. Always keep reinventing yourself and upgrading your products, and you'll continue to leave the competition in your rearview mirror.

27. How much should I outsource?

Provided you have trusted vendors, as much as you can. Heed the old KISS principle: Keep It Simple, Stupid.

28. Are you sure writing a book will help my business?

No question. But before you try to write a book, be sure you have something of value to say and that the book is professionally published. Don't be tempted by the ease of self-publishing platforms. Some books produced that way have taken off, but most scream that dreaded word "amateur." Practice your writing skills by publishing some articles and blogs first. Ernest Hemingway used to write 500 words religiously every morning just to keep his skills sharp.

29. The security consulting business involves increased risk of liability from physical danger, so am I better off growing my business and selling instead of risking an incident down the road?

Every business has risk. Restaurants risk lawsuits with every plate of food they serve. If you feel, however, that it's only a matter of time before a problem jeopardizes your safety, then you should sell it as soon as possible. How well you sleep at night can be an unerring tool for making business decisions.

30. What's the best business advice you ever received?

Easy: Just do it. You'll learn more about business, and about yourself, by starting something than you ever will from continual planning and preparation. At the end of the day, you either make money or not. Life is short. If you believe in yourself, bet on yourself.

Note from the Field
Dubai

0820 hours

Sitting with my wife on the balcony of our hotel room overlooking Jumeirah Beach, it's been absolutely incredible to see the transformation the United Arab Emirates has undergone over the past two decades. Once a dusty little city, Dubai has grown into a global metropolis, containing some of the finest restaurants and shopping, and some of the most unusual attractions found anywhere on Earth. Equally surprising has been how the royal family has avoided the mistakes of Saudi Arabia and allowed the UAE to be an open economy that caters to foreign investments. It goes to show that capitalism can work hand-in-hand with monarchies and religious/cultural traditions.

We haven't eaten breakfast yet, and the temperature is already approaching 100 degrees Fahrenheit. I have an afternoon meeting with a gentleman who wants to discuss the idea of SMI providing security in Yemen. I doubt anything will come of it, but it's always interesting to talk with others about security in different parts of the globe.

Meanwhile, I think I'll cool off in the pool.

PART II

Growing Your Business

7. Selling – and Closing

> *If people like you, they'll listen to you, but if they*
> *trust you, they'll do business with you.*
>   —Hilary Hinton "Zig" Zigla

THEY SAY THE THREE MOST IMPORTANT WORDS in entrepreneurship are "sell, sell, sell." And if you've ever tried to sell anything professionally, you've probably heard the acronym ABC: Always be closing. This classic line was spoken by actor Alec Baldwin, playing a highly successful salesman delivering an aggressive motivational pep talk in the movie version of David Mamet's Pulitzer Prize-winning play, *Glengarry Glen Ross*. ABC became a call to action, and a personal challenge, to the manhood (or womanhood) of salespeople everywhere. It stipulated the only thing that matters in life is to "get [the clients] to sign on the line that is dotted."

That might be stating things a bit obsessively for our purposes, but we can't ignore the fact that selling is an essential and inescapable part of global security consulting. When I was a young account executive fresh out of college, I joined a Fortune 500 company that adhered to this aggressive, take-no-prisoners approach. It was exhausting for me. I did close deals, but the process took its toll. Even though I made good money, the stress of prospecting, sales quotas, keeping clients satisfied and renewing contracts always lingered in my head. Nevertheless, I stuck with it.

Not long thereafter, I transitioned into big-ticket items such as advanced military systems, serving as an international business-development executive for a large defense contractor. The title sounded more important, but the duties remained the same: sell, sell, sell.

Now, some 20 years later, I'm still selling. But this time I'm selling for my own company, not someone else's. It's a much more rewarding experience. It not only feels different, the objectives are also different. How? Instead of concentrating on closing deals, I'm focused on developing new and potentially long-term client relationships. The hard-sell tactics I previously employed – such as time scarcity (These prices are good for today only!) or bundling (Buy two; get the third one free!) seem like remnants from a bygone era. Likewise, I no longer play the numbers game, calculating that if I make X number of cold calls, I'll acquire Y number of sales appointments, which will generate Z number of closes.

If you want to eat, you have to sell. That's a simple fact of business life. But in today's highly competitive, information-accessible, globally interconnected environment, you need a fresh approach to rise above the crowd. This chapter provides just such a strategy.

The New ABC

Popular author Daniel Pink in his terrific book *To Sell is Human: The Surprising Truth About Moving Others* has rebranded the ABC mantra to stand for Attunement, Buoyancy and Clarity. Pink defines each of them as follows:

+ **Attunement:** Get out of your own head and learn to see things from your customer's perspective.

+ **Buoyancy:** In sales, you face a lot of rejection (not a pond's worth but an ocean's worth). Try to get over it and move on.

+ **Clarity:** To persuade someone to buy your service or product, identify the problem they are trying to solve and then explain how you can help.

To sell effectively, Pink says the modern salesperson must "shift from the skill of problem solving to the skill of problem finding – that's what innovators do. They find problems that other people didn't realize were problems."

As a global security consultant, that's your job as well – solving the security problems of your clients. But before you can solve those problems, you first need to uncover them. Then you must persuade your client that the problems exist. And most important, you must get the client to hire you. If you can accomplish all three, and if you can perform the necessary tasks with excellence, then no competition in the world will stand in your way.

If you worked in law enforcement or the military or the intelligence community, you might not have been asked to sell before – and maybe you don't want to start now. As much as I can empathize with your dilemma, the cold, hard fact is in the private sector you must get other people to pay you for your product or service. Otherwise, your venture won't last long.

That's all selling is – no stigma, no greasy backroom deals. It's a natural and utterly common transaction, and virtually nothing happens in the real world until something is bought or sold. You're being pitched hundreds of times a week, though you probably never think twice about it. Then why feel anxiety about selling your own services?

Be yourself and believe in your product, and you'll quickly lose your fear of selling. You might even find it fun. And if you're under the naïve impression that your phone is going to ring off the hook the day you hang out your shingle and launch your website, you'd better lose it, and fast. There's no other way to succeed than getting out on the streets and telling the world you're open for business, and you're worth every penny someone is willing to spend on you.

The PCAN Model

Following the advice of Daniel Pink, as soon as you've identified your prospective client's problems, you must find an effective way of solving them. Armed with that information, your next step is to get paid for your expertise – in other words, to close the deal. It's where selling becomes more than mantras and spreadsheets, where the rubber meets the road. But if you've identified the problem and developed the solution, you can win the contract.

When I worked for that large defense contractor, they sent me to the Wharton School at the University of Pennsylvania to attend a two-week executive course called Strategic Persuasion. It was outstanding. Taught by G. Richard Shell and Mario Moussa, and based on their book *The Art of Woo: Using Strategic Persuasion to Sell*

Your Ideas, the course allowed me to practice my negotiating and persuasion skills alongside some terrific business professionals from around the world.

Because the class included that international mix of executives, we could interact with and try to persuade people of different cultures each day. We learned to adjust our selling tactics based on the unique individual we were pitching. But despite our national differences, we could succeed if we touched the core human emotions that make persuasion techniques so universal.

Networking aside, the biggest take-away from the course was a simple sales methodology Shell and Moussa called the PCAN Model, which I've used ever since. PCAN stands for:

+ Problem: State the prospective client's problem.

+ Cause: State the cause of the problem.

+ Answer: Describe how you can solve the problem.

+ Net Benefits: Explain the net benefits of using your solution.

The PCAN model might sound simple. It is, but it isn't simplistic, and it works extremely well. No one said sales had to be complicated.

PCAN doesn't mean, however, that you march into a client's office and say, "Now this is your problem ... this is the cause of your problem ... this is the answer to your problem." Spoken without context, it sounds arrogant and patronizing.

Instead, if you use the model as an integral part of a logical discussion with your prospective client, you'll quickly discover how PCAN will help you come across as a reasonable, common-sense thinker. And your prospect will view you as a competent global security professional – as you should be.

For example, whenever I interact with prospective clients, I first allow them to tell me what they think their problem is. Then I try to zero in on that problem with a series of questions such as "Why do you think that is?" or "Why do you think that matters?" I've found that you can often identify a problem just by talking it through during your initial discussions. As far as prescribing a solution, that's where your consulting expertise comes into play. You don't have to lay out your step-by-step blueprint right away. But you should be able to describe what you can do for the client.

All the client cares about is his or her own net benefits. The more quickly you can solve the problem, the more valuable – and expensive – your services become. In the security consulting world, it isn't "time is money" so much as "speed is money."

PCAN is no trick; it's a tool – and as a consultant it's always wise to keep several tools in your kit.

The point is, whether you want to use the word or not, when you're engaged in presenting your case to a potential client, you're selling. So get used to the idea. Start practicing your pitch and learning the methods I'm discussing here. Then someday soon, you'll experience the burst of pride that occurs when your first prospective client agrees to retain your services and becomes your first client – because you've successfully sold yourself and you've just closed the deal.

The Secret to Becoming Rich: Referrals

You're probably familiar with the 80/20 Rule: 20 percent of the people perform 80 percent of the work. When it comes to sales, I've amended it to 90/10, meaning 10 percent of the sales force brings in 90 percent of a company's revenue.

How can you achieve the 10-percent echelon? One word: referrals.

Referrals are what make you rich. Referrals are what can take your one-man security practice out of your spare bedroom and onto the international stage, with offices scattered across the globe.

Most successful businesses can trace the majority of their current clients directly back to their first few. Think about it. You can be in business for 10 years or even 20 years and still have derived the majority of your business from those few early customers who were willing to take a chance on you. It's why you should treat your first clients like gold and stay focused on the importance of your reputation, as I keep stressing.

My advice about referrals is a variation on that earlier acronym: AAR – Always ask for referrals. When the job's done and your client is smiling, that's the time. A little later, when you receive final payment on the contract, make a phone call to say a personal thank-you – and ask again. You should re-engage previous clients with whom you haven't conversed from time to time. I'd recommend reaching out to former clients every few months to see if they need your services again and to ask for new referrals.

It should go without saying, however, that you always complete your contracted services successfully before asking for a referral.

How do you ask? It isn't so difficult. First, always try to ask for a referral in person. A typical request might sound something like this:

> Mr. Client, I'm so pleased you and your team had such a positive experience with my firm. That's the kind of feedback I like to hear. As you know, the security industry is strongly competitive, and as a businessperson you can't trust just anyone. Whoever you retain must operate at the highest level of the profession and with the utmost discretion. Based on your response, I'm confident that my firm meets those standards. Because my business is based almost entirely on referrals, I hope you will recommend me to several of your colleagues whom you think can use my services.

That's all it takes. Most of the time, the client will oblige you. If so, be sure to ask for an additional favor: Ask them to call – or email if necessary – the new prospect to let them know you'll be following up with them. That will pave the way for you to meet with the referrals. If it looks as though they won't need your services, there's no harm in asking for two or three new referrals. If you're professional, there's no downside in doing so.

Referrals are the most proven, effective way of growing your global security consultancy. They're also the most underutilized. So keep my acronym in mind as you strive to win clients: AAR.

Prospecting

I admit it; I'm a get-out-there-and-meet-people type of person. If you've watched any of the videos on my website, I think you'll reach that conclusion on your own. My preferred way of doing business is face-to-face. Yet, I also strongly believe in taking thoughtful, measured steps. You can't just walk into somebody's office and win business, particularly when it involves protecting life and limb, as well as property. You need to know what you're selling, know you can deliver exactly what you're selling, and know where to look for clients. This is called prospecting, and where prospecting is concerned, you should take the same educated approach that you apply to your security methodology. You can't just wing it.

For many businesspeople, prospecting for clients requires attending events and drinking cocktails while telling war stories. Personally, I'm not a big fan of networking events such as defense-industry trade shows or conferences. In fact, I attend only two security events regularly: the Overseas Security Advisory Council (OSAC) conference at the U.S. Department of State, and an international conference in an emerging market, such as Brazil, India or Singapore. That's it.

Many consultants think they need to attend these security expos to keep up with the latest security technology or learn what the competition is doing. I prefer to travel my own path. Yes, I'm gregarious, but I'd rather not share a room with a hundred or more of my competitors. I'd rather be the *only* security consultant in a room full of prospects – such as a conference of investment bankers.

Before you ever set foot out of your office/bedroom/garage, there's one task you should be sure to perform each quarter: Make a list of the 25 new individuals or companies you'd most like to do business with. In my case, I send each of them a handwritten note, enclosed in an envelope with a copy of my book *Among Enemies* and perhaps a recent magazine article I've written. I explain that I'd very much like to sit down with them to discuss how my company can help with their security needs. And I suggest a time I'll be calling to follow up. In many cases, I'll receive a thank-you call or email before then.

Of the 25 prospects, I might secure five or, in a good quarter, 10 face-to-face meetings. If they're located close enough, we'll meet at my office or theirs. If they're located in another city, we'll agree to meet the next time one of us is in the other's vicinity.

You might be thinking this process sounds a bit random. Well, it is. But I don't send these notes out without forethought. I don't want to gallivant around, making unqualified sales presentations to people I barely know. On the contrary, I use this technique to establish initial contacts – planting seeds in prospects' minds.

The result: Along with the new leads, on more than a few occasions a prospective client, someone I've never met in person – someone who has never even utilized my services – has referred another potential client to me. That's no guarantee I'll win work from either company, but I've expanded my name recognition and created the prospect of more future business. And as I'll describe in the next chapter, developing personal relationships with prospects, even if they take a long time to cultivate, is the only good way to build your consultancy.

Send something of value along with the note. And think of this process as a series of first dates. As in romance, take the time to let your prospective clients get to know you before you pop the big question.

NWWAM

Here's a funny-sounding acronym to apply to your quest for business. I first heard it from self-improvement guru Tony Robbins. It opened a whole new world for me in terms of understanding human emotion as well as how to use the power of persuasion. NWWAM stands for the following:

+ **Needs:** What does the prospective client absolutely require?

+ **Wants:** What does the individual or company not necessarily need but would like to have?

+ **Wounds:** What pain is the potential client experiencing that I could relieve?

+ **Authority:** Does the person I'm meeting with have the decision-making power to sign this deal?

+ **Money:** Does this person have the necessary funds to pay for my products or services?

As soon as I learn the prospect's NWWAM, I become much more capable of closing the deal. Of the five criteria, the most important is wounds. You might argue that authority or money should top the list, but believe me, neither is primary. On more than a few occasions, I've sat in a room with a decision-maker who had the authority and available money to hire me but refused to do so. Why? Because just as with information-technology (IT) services, some executives don't understand there are products that won't make them money but should be the most critical items they buy. Without solid IT, their devices miss getting emails, their data get hacked and their desktops crash from viruses. Likewise, without security, their business continuity suffers, their people are put in danger and their competitive advantage is lost to companies in China and elsewhere.

To put it more succinctly, companies, like people, are highly motivated by pain. When a client feels pain, the client wants the pain to stop. And when you can explain to the client how you can accomplish just that, you can close the deal. The more you can do to ease your clients' pain, the greater your chances of winning new clients.

How do you uncover an organization's NWWAM? That's where the next odd acronym comes in.

SCREAMPIGS

I know, I know, it sounds like I'm getting ridiculous. But I assure you, this one's deadly serious.

When I worked in the intelligence community, we used a common technique to extract information subtly from others during seemingly normal conversations. It's called elicitation, and I wrote extensively about it in my previous book, *Among Enemies: Counter-Espionage for the Business Traveler.* Intelligence officers will employ elicitation when talking with people on airliners or at cocktail parties, just about anywhere they need to break the ice with a stranger and learn more about that person. By engaging in active listening and asking open-ended questions, the intelligence officer can slowly draw out information on topics such as the individual's background, what professional projects he or she might currently be pursuing, and how much access that individual has to sensitive information. Essentially, the intelligence officer is gathering NWWAM for use in espionage.

How do you initiate a seemingly innocent conversation? I'm restricted from spilling anything classified, but I can tell you how businesspeople do it, and it isn't dissimilar. Business professionals use an acronym widely known as SCREAMPIGS:

+ Smile

+ Compliment

+ Referral

+ Exhibit

+ Ask

+ Mystery

+ Poll

+ Information

+ Gift

+ Schedule

Here's how the process breaks down:

+ Smile. Always approach someone with a smile on your face. You want disarm him or her by conveying you mean no harm. This is an ancient human gesture, equivalent to the days long ago when you met a stranger approaching on foot or on horseback and the first thing you did was open your fist and raise the palm of your hand, thereby indicating you had no weapon at the ready. It's true that some people regard a smiling stranger approaching them as someone who wants something, but a smile is always better than a frown.

+ Compliment. So, put your best smiling face on and then start looking for a way to pay the person a compliment. It's the best way to break the ice. I see this happen between women all the time. When they meet, inevitably one of them will immediately say something like "I love your shoes." Yes, it could be disingenuous, but it's a way of getting the conversation off on a positive, excuse the pun, foot.

+ **Referral.** This is important, because it helps verify who you are and why you've approached the person. Here's an example of something you might say while extending your hand. "I'm Luke Bencie, Mr. Omar. We have a mutual friend in Odair da Silva from Brazil. He told me you two were friends back in São Paulo and that if I ran into you I should introduce myself." Suddenly, you're no longer a stranger; you're associated with a known acquaintance or a trusted friend. A referral is disarming and establishes a connection.

+ **Exhibit.** To exhibit yourself means giving a brief overview of who you are. It's a further justification of why you've approached someone. Like referral, it's important. If you're going to be asking questions, you don't want them thinking, "Wait, who does he think he is?"

+ **Ask.** This is another age-old technique. Part of Dale Carnegie's landmark book *How to Win Friends and Influence People* – which remains a best seller nearly 80 years after its first publication – the rationale is you can put people quickly at ease by getting them to talk about themselves, and asking is the vehicle. It builds rapport and makes the other person feel in control of the conversation, because you're essentially seeking permission to continue. You can even use qualifiers such as, "You're in new-product development? That's fascinating. May I ask you something? How to you go about creating something new?"

+ **Mystery.** Putting on a smile, citing a referral and asking questions are all effective tools for elicitation, but they'll only get you so far. Keeping a person engaged also means creating interest in you. But that doesn't mean you should start tooting your own horn. Initially, you should prepare some attention-getting but vague self references, such as, "I own SMI, a security consultancy out of Washington, D.C."

+ **Poll.** This is the real meat of SCREAMPIGS. By polling someone you're starting to extract the wounds from their NWWAM. A good poll question would be, "What do you think about...?"

+ **Information.** Only after you begin learning about the person with whom you're talking should you start to provide him or her with substantive information about yourself and your company. This is a non-aggressive, subtle way of introducing your services, because you're not pitching, you're only conversing. Therefore the tone should remain appropriate for casual discussion, not a multi-point sales pitch.

+ Gift. This can be symbolic. A gift in the world of commerce always starts with a business card. You present yours and, if all goes well, the other person gives you one in return. That might be the extent of things at first. But if the meeting progresses, you should take this one step further by following up at a later date. For example, if you mentioned an article or book you wrote, send a copy along with a note and perhaps a marketing brochure. Maybe even refer *them* to a prospective client.

+ Schedule. Last but not least, remind yourself to follow up on the initial contact – continue the momentum. Never walk away from a lead without a plan to reconnect, and soon, down the road. You want to schedule an appointment to meet again. For example, "Mr. Omar, it was great to talk with you. I'll be in town for the next few days, so how about breakfast next Tuesday at the Four Seasons, say 7 a.m.?" And if the appointment is for drinks, make sure you buy the first one. Give to get.

That's it, an awkward acronym but a highly effective tool for engaging virtually anyone, a way to find out if your prospect has the money, influence and need to become a client – their NWWAM. Plus, if you struggle with smalltalk, this could help you. It isn't espionage or cheating; it's just two people talking business and building rapport.

What Selling is About

In order to be a good salesperson, you must know how to ask the right questions, all the while keeping your prospective client's attention and interest. Let's face it; the individuals to whom you're trying to sell are busy people. They don't have time for some security guy to walk into their office and lecture them on why they need his or her services. Before you burst through a person's door extolling your phenomenal capabilities, you've first got to establish rapport. It can be defined as a relationship between two people that involves mutual trust, respect and common ground.

In order to gain rapport with a prospective client, you must lose the mindset that you are *just* a salesperson. As I wrote at the beginning of this chapter, the ABC of always be closing is valid, but in the global security business you need to adopt a frame of mind that you're your client's equal – and if you're as good at the job as you should be, you are.

It might surprise you to discover how many people you'll deal with who will genuinely respect you for being in this business on your own – particularly if you're developing a solid reputation. Therefore, whenever you enter a room to do business, your demeanor should suggest you're one of two senior executives who have carved out time from their busy schedules to discuss a mutually beneficial opportunity. But if you allow the prospective client to intimidate you, it will become immediately and painfully evident. Your credibility will evaporate, and you'll no longer be taken seriously.

Anytime you ask someone to disengage from his or her schedule, make it count. *Never* waste anyone's time, especially your own. Be prepared to conduct a serious and meaningful discussion in the briefest time practicable.

Sometimes, you'll have only a short interval to make your case. This is where familiarity with the PCAN model becomes critical. It means you should have already done your homework on the potential client; you should have determined their problem and its cause. It will enable you to ask pointed questions about the problem they're currently experiencing and how to resolve it.

No matter which of the previous acronyms you found most helpful, you'll notice they all share a key element: They all require you to listen effectively.

For example, you might think you know what a client's wounds are but later discover you were mistaken. If you're lucky – and if you've taken my advice – it won't be too late to correct your error, because you didn't blurt out an assertion. Instead, you listened intently, and when someone revealed what you immediately recognized as their wounds, you still didn't immediately jump up and exclaim "I can fix that!" You continued to listen, you asked smart questions, you listened some more, and only then did you calmly and professionally deliver your assessment – and in the process you closed the deal.

How to Sell in a Prospective Client's Office

Allow me to present an example of how a typical exchange might unfold between you and a prospective client in that person's office. Try to identify where PCAN, NWWAM and SCREAMPIGS are being used.

In this scenario, I'm meeting with Steve, the VP of international development for a manufacturing company. Mike, a recently acquired client of mine, has referred me to Steve, whose company has just acquired the rights to establish a factory in a remote area of West Africa. As a result, the company will have to send several employees to the area, which they rightly consider to be dangerous.

LUKE: Good morning, Steve. It's a pleasure to finally meet you in person. Mike has spoken highly of you, and thanks for freeing up some time out of your busy day.

STEVE: Pleasure to meet you, as well, Luke. Mike also told me you did great things for his team regarding their last international project. So, how can I help you today?

LUKE: Mike referred me because he thought my firm's services could be useful to you. I've been thinking about your situation, and I'd like to cover three specific topics with you this morning. Depending on how much time you have, I want to start by discussing what you believe your particular security needs are, rather than go into detail about everything that SMI can do. Does that sound fair?

STEVE: Sure, that's fine. I have about 30 minutes before I have to leave for another meeting.

LUKE: Great. As you may or may not know, we operate a rather unique global security consultancy that specializes in several particular areas of interest, such as critical infrastructure protection, counter-espionage, due diligence and executive training, to name a few. If you're comfortable with the idea, perhaps you can tell me what your security concerns are going into the project, and I'll tell you from my experience how we might be able to help. That way, we can maximize our time together.

STEVE: Very well. As you know, we recently extended our operations into West Africa, and we need to send a handful of people over there to begin establishing a new manufacturing plant and local office. The first team would probably need to be on the ground for about 9 to 12 months in order to get things up and running. Afterward, we would send in a more permanent team, as well as begin training local workers.

LUKE: Do you know who you're sending yet?

STEVE: That's one of the first things we need to decide. We don't exactly have people lining up to volunteer. Their salaries won't change much, except for some overtime, and whoever goes will have to live in a low-budget hotel the entire time. We also can't risk allowing family members to accompany them.

LUKE: Along with time away from family, what are your employees' other concerns, and what are management's concerns?

STEVE: The employees are afraid they're going to get deathly sick, or worse, be killed by local villagers who are upset that a foreign company is moving onto their land. Management is equally concerned that if something happens to one our employees, we'll lose everything in a liability lawsuit.

LUKE: Why do they think that? Has anyone actually been threatened?

STEVE: No – but it could happen.

LUKE: What would it cost the company if something harmed one of your people?

STEVE: I can't imagine; maybe hundreds of thousands of dollars, probably millions.

LUKE: Would you agree, then, that it would be better to make an investment up front to prevent this from happening?

STEVE: Of course, but I'm not sure it would do any good.

LUKE: Why would you say that? Have you already had these discussions with management?

STEVE: Management hasn't had any formal meetings about the security situation yet. But even if we did provide our employees with some training, and took out a hefty insurance policy on each of them, the negative publicity we would receive as a result of a security incident could destroy our reputation – not to mention investor confidence. That's the reason our CEO has tasked me to resolve this situation.

LUKE: Does that mean you're the final authority over what your company does to protect your people?

STEVE: The CEO will make the ultimate decision, but he ordered me to determine the best alternatives.

LUKE: So that I understand this correctly, you have a terrific business opportunity to make money in West Africa, but you're deeply concerned about the blowback from a hostile security incident, an event that could cost your company millions?

STEVE: Absolutely.

LUKE: And you believe that at the core of this danger is the threat from the local villagers who, you are certain, will retaliate against you for moving onto their lands?

STEVE: Yes, that's it, exactly.

LUKE: But you haven't actually performed any due diligence, had a direct threat against the company, or had an on-the-ground team perform a threat and vulnerability assessment of the area. Is that correct?

STEVE: Yes, we haven't done any of it yet.

LUKE: Steve, I've seen this situation before. Sadly, violence against corporations in the least-developed areas of Africa is not uncommon. You're correct that a harmful incident against your people will result in negative consequences against the company – both financially and publicly. But I'd advise you not to pass judgment yet on what you think the threats really are. I mean you should be cautious not to assume that one particular thing is dangerous and spend all your time, energy and resources on protecting against it. In fact, how do you know that the villagers won't welcome you with open arms, because you're bringing employment opportunities and injecting cash into their local economy?

STEVE: You're right, we don't really know yet.

LUKE: Why don't you begin by assessing what the actual threats are in your operating environment? Until you perform what we call a target analysis and vulnerability assessment, along with an open-source threat assessment, you really won't get the full picture of what you're dealing with, security-wise. That requires a professional team on the ground, working in tandem with locals who know the area. Once that's done, you can transition into proactive measures to ensure the safety of your people, such as finding the proper housing, vetting local staff you can trust, providing physical security such as armored vehicles and armed escorts if necessary, conducting emergency medical training or high-threat environment training for employees, establishing emergency response plans, and possibly even having social scientists engage in liaison meetings with the villagers. That's just off the top of my head.

STEVE: That's a ton of stuff! I had no idea all that needed to be done. What would it cost?

LUKE: It depends. We can do a lot of things to minimize the risks to your people. But to do it right, I'll need to drill down a bit more on specifics. That will take more than 30 minutes, and only then could I give you a ballpark estimate on cost.

STEVE: Tell you what. This is important, so let me cancel my next meeting, so you and I can keep talking.

LUKE: I appreciate that. The more details I can collect from you, the better I can construct a clear picture of how to solve the problem. Could I ask a favor?

STEVE: Sure.

LUKE: If your CEO is going to be the ultimate decision-maker, and because he'd ultimately be the one held liable if something terrible happens to one of his people, could we bring him into our meeting? I recognize it's short notice, but this sound likes a make-or-break proposition for your company. If he isn't available today, you and I can keep talking, and we could schedule a later meeting when he would be able to join us.

STEVE: Good idea. Let me call him and see.

Get the picture? My objective in this first discussion with Steve, which I've condensed a bit for our purposes, was to uncover his NWWAM, particularly his wounds. Again, wounds are the underlying reason people buy anything; you must be able to remove their pain in order to make the sale. Even people who buy fancy cars, watches or clothes are doing so not only because they want to show off but also to relieve their perceived pain that comes with the alternative of possessing cheap products, receiving low-quality service or feeling stigmatized socially.

Never misinterpret a person's wounds to mean a type of character flaw or weakness. Identifying wounds also doesn't mean you're exploiting a person's vulnerabilities. Rather, identifying wounds is an effective way of getting to the core of the problem. It saves time and allows you to service your client more effectively by solving the cause of their greatest pain.

Along with asking Steve the basic questions, Who? What? Where? When? Why and How? I also filled out his Needs, Wants, Wounds, Authority and Money. You might also have noticed we established that my services could save Steve and his company millions in damages. Therefore we were subtly discussing the value of the product he needs.

Now, let's jump ahead to the end of the meeting. The CEO, the real decision-maker, joined our conversation. I resumed asking open-ended questions pertaining to security concerns, as well as the potential budget. Then, before we concluded, I perceived that the sale was already a done deal, and I proceeded to close.

Never forget to ask for the sale. Repeat: *Never* forget to ask for the sale.

LUKE: Gentlemen, this has been a valuable conversation. It truly sounds like any security incident could be devastating to your company. It's also apparent that your development team is significantly behind schedule in terms of fully understanding the on-the-ground realities of the threats facing your people. I would certainly like to help, and I know my firm can help, but I want to be honest with you – and state right up front – that this is not a quick-fix solution. Frankly, there isn't a quick fix to overseas security, and anyone who tells you there is, is lying.

CEO: Fair enough. But what are you getting at?

LUKE: My point is I can begin the due-diligence process as

early as this afternoon. I can call my African contacts to assist with the local situational realities as well as gather information about the villages in question. But the real key to security is going to be deploying an on-the-ground team, sooner rather than later, to conduct a full-scope security assessment. Once we determine what the genuine threats and vulnerabilities are, we can put together a security plan in Africa as well as schedule employee training back here.

CEO: That makes sense, but what is all this going to cost us?

LUKE: A lot less than the cost you would incur if one of your people is harmed and you haven't taken the proper steps against it.

CEO: Agreed. So, what's that number?

LUKE: I'll give you some different options, with some ballpark figures, that will land maybe US$10,000 to $20,000 on either side of the actual figure. Keep in mind that our pricing is based on the value of the job itself and not on hourly fees. Also, you will be responsible for reimbursing all of our expenses at actual cost. Agreed?

CEO: Agreed. Now, how much?

LUKE: To gather intelligence, call in favors from some people already over there and deploy a team to Africa this weekend, you're looking at US$50,000 plus expenses, half of which is required before my guys get on the plane. Their time on the ground will depend on the threat and won't change the cost for you. Any follow-up work such as training, investigations or physical security integration will be discussed on an as-needed basis among the three of us. A handshake now gets things rolling, and I'll send over a proposal/agreement within the next 48 hours. Are we agreed?

CEO: Yes. Make it happen.

Sound far-fetched and fanciful? Believe me, it isn't. These types of discussions take place every day. In fact, I've made the price intentionally low in this example so you don't throw this book down and think I'm pulling your leg.

Now that you've established rapport with the new client and made an initial agreement, the follow-on services will come easily.

The deal has been closed. It's time for the global security team to do what it does best: consult.

Being an International Broker

Some people in this business think the way to make the most money is by selling security products, either hardware or software. They've become convinced that by leveraging their international contacts – the ones they made in their previous careers – they can sell high-end security systems for large profits.

They're right.

Without question, advanced technology and military hardware (such as weapons, computer systems and vehicles) are big-ticket items. Many security consultants have discovered that by transitioning away from the traditional business model and becoming brokers – consultants who leverage their international contacts – they can earn a substantially greater return than if they stick to performing assessments, conducting investigations, or providing physical protection or training.

If you or one of your associates has developed international contacts over the years, you should indeed leverage those contacts to the fullest. They will help you open doors and alert you to opportunities you might never have considered before. More important, you can make millions by acting as an intermediary between multinational corporations and government agencies. Even if you hate selling – which, if you've read the chapter up to this point, should be a fading thought – you must develop the knack for putting the right individuals together when opportunities arise. That means becoming an international broker who facilitates large security deals.

So, I hope you've kept that Rolodex full of international contacts, because you're going to need it. The next step is how to find a company that will pay you to broker a bilateral or multilateral deal. For that, I have good news and bad news. The good news is finding a company willing to hire you to sell their security products overseas is easy. The bad news is the actual selling part can be extremely complicated.

If you want to become a licensed representative for a security company and earn commissions from selling their products, all you need to do is ask. Getting a sales director to hear you out is usually not a big deal. Most sales directors are always keeping an ear to the ground for hot international prospects. It will be your job to persuade that person that you have developed valid connections and can deliver a legitimate deal.

In essence, you'll have to sell a salesperson, so you should be well prepared for your presentation. Here's how:

+ Deliver your credentials and list where you have established connections – but don't disclose those connections. At this point, the person to whom you're pitching has no obligation to you. So, if you list the name of a contact, but you don't get the job, you've just given away an entrée overseas – you've cut yourself out of the deal before it even begins.

+ To avoid such situations, require the company to sign a nondisclosure agreement before meeting with their representative. In addition to covering your backside, it will also demonstrate your competence and legitimacy.

+ If the subject of money arises, immediately respond that you would expect only a commission on sales. This removes any immediate financial obligation for the company, and it boosts your chances for an agreement. It also means the only reason the company should turn you down is if they don't trust you to represent their product ethically – in other words, they've heard your pitch but they don't trust you or your connections. That's why it's imperative to be thoroughly prepared for the meeting and to present yourself properly, as I discussed in Chapter 2. Your persona can make or break a pitch.

+ Be ready to discuss monetary specifics as soon as you reach agreement on all other issues. Finder's fees can vary across industry. In the security field, big-ticket military items can run anywhere from 1 percent to 10 percent, depending on the size of the deal. And, as a rule, the larger the sale, the smaller your commission will be.

For example, if you broker a deal to sell 10 American security systems to a government in the Gulf, you'll usually receive a commission of

2 percent. At that point, your client might also agree to compensate you for expenses incurred before the deal was closed. Good luck trying to get your expenses covered before you prove yourself, but if you complete a multimillion-dollar contract you'll be surprised at how quickly you can renegotiate your terms.

Everything I'm describing here is not only possible but also likely if you're constantly on the watch for new possibilities. Don't underestimate the power of your contacts, and don't shy away from opportunities you didn't initially consider if they suddenly present themselves.

A Warning

Before you begin reconnecting with every international contact you've ever had, or worse, you start making big promises to private companies that you can make it rain, you must first fully understand the law. I'll provide information about the Foreign Corrupt Practices Act (FCPA) in Chapter 9. When you reach that passage, tattoo the information on your brain. Meanwhile, here are two other bodies of regulation you should study in detail: The International Traffic in Arms Regulation (ITAR) and the Export Administration Regulations (EAR). If you plan to do any international business from within the United States, these two export controls will affect your dealings directly. Their aim is to control foreign access to specific types of technology and associated data to prevent the disclosure or transfer of sensitive information to unauthorized persons or governments.

For your own protection, and for the protection of your clients, *do not move forward with a deal involving international security products before reviewing ITAR and EAR regulations with an experienced attorney.* Otherwise, you could find yourself in big trouble.

To Reiterate

Alec Baldwin's character in *Glengarry Glen Ross* also throws down a challenge to his audience. He asserts: *The money is out there; you pick it up, it's yours. You don't; I have no sympathy for you.*

Without being as blunt as Baldwin's character, here's my challenge to you. Over the course of the next month, use the techniques outlined above. Use at least one of them every day. Use them to be more comfortable talking to people, asking penetrating questions, listening proactively. Hone the skills you'll need to make you an effective consultant and salesperson. If you do, I promise you'll build momentum. You'll begin to see results and maybe even grow to like the dreaded "S" word.

FAQ

31. How can I learn if the person I'm meeting has decision-making authority without directly asking?

Actually, there's nothing wrong with asking a prospective client if he or she needs to consult someone else prior to engaging in an agreement with you. But if for some reason you're reluctant to do so, you could ask, "If I were to fully satisfy all of your criteria this morning, would you be willing to shake hands and allow me to begin assisting your organization immediately?" If the person says yes, he or she is the decision-maker. If no, chances are someone else holds that authority.

32. What do I do if the prospective client says they would love to utilize my consulting services, but they don't have the money at this time?

Everyone in the business has heard this line before. Even if the client claims not to have money, there usually are ways to allocate funds from another source within the organization. You just need to demonstrate why this particular allocation is vital. Continue to drill down to the real cause of the problem by asking, "Why do you say that?" You might just uncover the real reason and be able to refute their true objection.

33. What's the best sales advice you can offer to a novice salesperson?

Two things: Ask the right questions, and ask for the sale.

34. If I'm concerned about pricing myself out of a potential job, shouldn't I ask the client what his or her budget is before I offer my price quote?

It's always good to know what a prospective client's budget is ahead of time – but only if it's the real amount and not some made-up figure meant to deter you from charging full price. As a security consultant, you always need to charge what you're worth. Low self-esteem is the number-one reason most security consultants don't charge enough for their services. They think it's more important to break even and hope for follow-on business to boost their bottom lines. Often that business never materializes. I'm a big proponent of the advice "Think about the fourth sale first," but you also need to recognize that you're an expert. You must always believe in your ability and what value you can bring to your clients.

35. How much should I charge for my consulting methodologies?

Your clients don't care about your methodologies. They only care about getting their problem solved – and solved quickly. After discussing the problem with the client, figure out how much it would cost if they didn't hire you. That's your true value. People hire you, not your methodology.

Note from the Field

This time, I'm at 38,000 feet above the North Pole, flying from Washington, D.C., to Tokyo via All Nippon Airways – one of the finest airlines in the sky. The 15-hour flight actually traverses north to south, going over the top of the globe, instead of east to west. An interesting phenomenon of such a route is that, looking out my window, the sun has remained perched on the horizon line for hours. It looks as though the sunset has been frozen in time.

Sitting in an empty business-class section, the unmistakable hospitality from the Japanese flight attendants is astonishing. I'm halfway through the flight, and already I've wiped my face with at least five lavender-scented hot towels and had my glass of South African wine refilled equally as many times. I've also just enjoyed my second meal in the air: hot udon noodles garnished with dried sea lettuce and a shot of Wataya Kounosuke Inden sake. If I keep this up, I'm never going to drop the 10 pounds I promised my wife I would lose on this trip.

My client – in this case, the U.S. government – paid for a fully refundable economy-class ticket, I went into my own pocket to upgrade to business. It's one of the few luxuries I allow myself in my work. If you're going to spend half of your life in the air as a global security consultant, then travel like one. Life is too short, and – at 6 feet 4 inches – I'm too tall for economy class.

8. RFPs, Proposals and Doing Business with (Hostile) Governments

The secret of business is to know something that nobody else knows.

—Aristotle Onassis

LET ME OPEN THIS CHAPTER BY MAKING a statement many of you might consider controversial:

Most government requests for proposals (RFPs) are rigged.

If you're surprised or offended, I'm sorry – sorry that you're so naïve. I know many of you can claim that you or someone you know has won a government contract fair and square. Yes, it's sometimes true, but I repeat: *Most* government RFPs are rigged.

How do I know? Because I've observed the process hundreds if not thousands of times. Does this mean all government contracts are corrupt and their managers are being paid off by winning bidders? No, though corruption is endemic in some Third World countries, particularly in Africa. But in the United States it isn't so much a matter of faulty ethics as prevailing legal requirements.

It's human nature. A law requires an agency to issue an RFP for a particular contract that the project's manager wants to go to a certain individual or company. Sometimes, of course, corruption is involved. But other times, and perhaps more commonly, the manager has concluded early on that someone is ideal for the job. So, the agency will tailor an RFP with a particular individual's qualifications already in mind. That's why if you study RFPs you'll find they often specify bizarre characteristics:

> Bidder must be certified in the CARVER Target Analysis and
> Vulnerability Assessment Methodology, must possess 35 years-plus
> of overseas experience in intelligence operations, must have

completed Navy EOD School, and must have previously worked in the country of Angola. Knowledge of Portuguese is preferred, as is at least 10 years of writing emergency response plans for diplomats in hostile environments.

Don't be surprised if you encounter even stranger language. What's important for our discussion is that you learn to recognize a setup when you see one and therefore avoid wasting your time and effort. Here's another example:

Bidder must have exactly 8 1/2 years of security experience within the Middle East, plus at least 3 years of experience in Southeast Asian woodcarving, 1 year of experience in Peruvian interpretive dance, and a background in Thai Chi breathing techniques – preferably obtained from an accredited university located in Northeast region of the United States.

You might ask, "But what if I fulfill the exact qualifications of an RFP and can bid a price that's cheaper than the expected winner?" That's a great question and one that often leads companies to petition agencies to reconsider their awards. Few such petitions succeed, but many companies realize this and still submit them. Why? They do it to drum up support for future contracts. Call it positioning for top-of-mind awareness.

Imagine a government bureaucrat responsible for writing RFPs worrying that if he doesn't award a contract to the company that petitioned the previous time around, the oversight might trigger an investigation. Many bureaucrats would discount the idea, but others would begin to give the petitioner more serious consideration.

Still, in most cases, the odds remain against companies that are qualified but unfamiliar to the agency that issued the RFP.

Here's a firsthand experience: SMI applied, over several years, to a county government's RFPs for various security and emergency-response training courses. Several of the requests even involved how to deal with an explosive device planted at a local high school sports stadium or shopping mall.

SMI applied for every one of those potential awards. Not only do we conduct such training all the time, but our team also includes individuals who have worked as responders to and investigators of some of the worst terror bombings in the world over the past 20 years. These qualifications, if they didn't give us a lock on those contracts, at least should have given us a distinct advantage over our competitors. In all cases we were shortlisted but not awarded the contract.

I finally conducted an Internet search of the winners; I found that one of two companies always won the awards. Both were small businesses headed by, respectively, a recently retired, small-town fire chief and the former director of emergency management for that county. Neither of them had completed explosives training other than perhaps a six-week course from their local police academy. At first, my discovery didn't bother me. I recognize that in some instances it's better to work with a known local than to bring in people from the outside.

On further consideration, I decided to petition. Their current director of emergency management responded to inform me that the county had a policy of taking the lowest bidder as long as the bidder was qualified. So, the next time the county announced a similar RFP, I decided to lowball. I bid a meager us$16,000 – for a contract I had determined would normally be worth $25,000-$50,000 – to fly a team of six experts to the location and conduct the requested training course. It was, I admit, mostly out of spite. But I also really needed to win the RFP at the time.

A few weeks later, an envelope arrived from the local government's procurement office. I was prepared to smile in victory. Instead, the letter stated that the winner – another local company – had bid $15,500. That cinched it; the award had been fixed. And the experience cemented in my mind the attitude that spending hours responding to government RFPs was not worth the hassle.

Also in hindsight, I was lucky we didn't win. I could not have withstood my wife's wrath if she'd discovered I had been such a poor businessman.

How Government Agencies Steal Your Intellectual Property
Even if an agency doesn't write an RFP with a specific company in mind, its bureaucrats can employ another trick to manipulate the

outcome: They can put out a request for qualification or a request for information. In such cases, the agency is saying, essentially, "We are thinking about doing a project but don't exactly know how to design it, so please send us some free ideas."

Usually, the request will ask for your methodology or best practices in solving a particular problem. In many cases the respondents will submit step-by-step checklists and usable spreadsheets, after which the agency will perform the work with its own people. And why not? After all, they've received free private consulting from various firms with varying experience. It's exactly what happened to us.

Each morning we receive an email that lists all of the active RFPs in the security industry. On one occasion we found an RFP seeking a security consulting firm that could perform threat and vulnerability assessments on 70 public schools. The proposal offered a fixed fee of US$180,000 and a timeline for completion of about six months. Because of our extensive experience in this field, the job seemed a no-brainer, so I tasked our team to begin the proposal-writing process. Not a real moneymaker, but we decided to bid in order to beef up our company résumé on school security assessments.

Proposals are interesting animals. Some people earn good money as proposal experts. Larger companies maintain full-time positions filling this role, usually called directors of proposals. At SMI, I usually ask one of our research staff to begin the outline, working from a previous RFP response. Starting with the basics, such as highlighting the specific responses required, the writer forwards the document to one of our directors with expertise in that particular subject, who in turn fills in the details.

In Chapter 2, I warned against using boilerplate contracts. I repeat that caution here. Most astute businesspeople can easily detect precooked proposals. So, always try to customize yours as much as possible. If you do, you'll have a greater chance of winning.

In our case, after about two weeks, my team put together what we considered the perfect proposal. We had assembled a solid team of individuals with stellar bios who could perform the work with ease. We also laid out our proposed methodology with a concise timeline of deliverables.

A few weeks later, we heard from the agency. They said they were thoroughly impressed and would like to shortlist us for a face-to-face presentation with the agency's decision-making committee, which comprised the director of emergency operations, the fire chief, police chief, superintendent of schools and a former FBI consultant.

Incidentally, I've learned to be cautious about your chances whenever a consultant is involved in the decision-making process.

As requested, two of our team members flew to the county to make the presentation. Their expenses weren't covered by the agency, nor could we recoup those expenses if we won the contract. Their flight, hotel, meals and labor all came out of my pocket. Call it the cost of doing business, but I figured with a 1-in-3 chance of winning, the odds justified the expenditures.

The two people I sent, a retired CIA officer and a retired Navy SEAL with an MBA, gave a strong presentation and answered a drawn-out set of questions from the committee. When they finished, the committee basically told them we were much more impressive than the other two companies in the running, and the job was all but ours. A few days later, the consultant called and claimed he needed to check our references as a formality. Again, he declared that the job was ours. He even asked if we could send over a more detailed timeline of our proposed plan, so he could begin lining up the schools for our arrival.

Then a few weeks passed without a word from the agency. I would call and email them periodically for an update, and they responded that "things progress slowly in government." After two months, we received a letter stating that because of budget constraints – they had listed the project's budget as us$180,000 in the RFP – the committee had decided to have the consultant handle the project.

No question, the agency had duped us. They took our methodology, our formulas, our spreadsheets, our checklists – all of our intellectual property. Trusting souls that we were, we had shown them, step-by-step, how to perform the work, how long to spend at each school, and how to lay out the final report. The whole RFP process had been a ruse. The consultant most likely was brought in by the agency to create an internal threat and vulnerability assessment capability – but he couldn't have developed it on his own. We ended up spending weeks of our time providing the necessary information, spending a lot of money in the process, and thereby delivering everything on a platter. I must admit, it was a deceptive but brilliant plan.

The lesson for you is to exercise caution in presenting any business information or intellectual property in your proposals. Of course, you have to demonstrate a competitive edge, and you want to highlight your unique business processes and methodologies. Just be sure not to give away the secret ingredients. Mark each page of your proposal **PROPRIETARY BUSINESS INFORMATION – NOT FOR PUBLIC DISTRIBUTION**, and copyright the document.

Yes, when dealing with public agencies, you can never prevent plagiarism completely, but you can give yourself some legal leverage if the worst happens. Also, never send a proposal as a Word document. Always use the PDF format. Doing so can't thwart a truly dedicated plagiarist, but you must constantly trumpet the message that your property is valuable and you will fight to protect it.

If you truly have your heart set on pursing government contracts, you should strive to win what is known as an IDIQ, an indefinite delivery/indefinite quantity arrangement. This federal government contracting acronym allows an indefinite quantity of supplies or services during a fixed period of time. If you're fortunate to have a connection within the federal bureaucracy that will designate your product or service as a necessary sole-source acquisition, you could land yourself a nice, fat federal contract quickly. They're usually not common or easy to win, but it's worth investing some time to see if you qualify. You can find more information about IDIQ contracts at the Federal Acquisition Regulation website.

The Two Types of Proposals

There are, basically, two types of proposals. The first is the long and boring one, running from 30 pages to 100 pages about the nature and background of your company and why you're best qualified to win a particular job. Long-form contracts typically take time to write, are bogged down with charts and graphs, packed full of legal jargon and contained in big 3-ring binders. No one really reads them cover to cover, and the odds of winning with these multi-colored monstrosities are low.

I prefer the second type. They run only 2 pages to 5 pages and usually don't contain as many specifics. They state the five W's – Who, What, Where, When, Why – plus the price. Some people also include the How, which basically describes some sort of consulting methodology. But it isn't necessary; if you've established trust with your prospective buyer, you should have gotten past methodologies.

The great thing about short proposals is they can double as contract agreements. If you lay out what you can and will do for the client, and then leave a space at the bottom for them to sign, chances are you can begin work right away. We conduct the majority of our business at SMI using this format. And not surprising, our clients prefer the simplicity.

On the other hand, if you want to use the short-proposal format, you must develop a solid relationship with the client and know exactly what needs to be done. You also need to know exactly what you're going to receive in return. In both case, you need to uncover, beforehand and via questions and answers, the information I laid out in the previous chapter when I discussed PCAN, NWWAM and SCREAMPIGS.

You also need to learn the difference between a client's needs and wants. Usually clients think they know what they want, but it's really up to you, the subject-matter expert, to help them determine what they really need. When you've both agreed on what's needed, then you must satisfy those needs. This is where managing client expectations becomes so important. Before you send your proposal, make sure the client knows what's coming and approves of it. If you've put in sufficient face-to-face time beforehand and built up a strong rapport with the client, and managed their expectations, then sending the proposal – which also serves as the contract – becomes merely a formality.

I'm a big fan of renowned business consultant Alan Weiss. If you haven't read any of Alan's dozens of books, know that he's truly established himself as a role model for the modern-day consultant. I mention this because I've adapted many of his ideas in our proposals, particularly his stressing that you request your fees up front.

Sample of a Short Proposal

Here's a facsimile of a proposal we recently submitted for a medical training course. It can serve as a template for many of the projects you seek to win:

 PROPOSED AGREEMENT BETWEEN SECURITY MANAGEMENT INTERNATIONAL AND ACME WIDGETS, LTD.

[DATE]

Security Management International is pleased to provide the following Agreement for training services to ACME Widgets, Ltd.

Client	ACME Widgets, Ltd.
	Attn: Joe Smith
	1000 Main Street, Suite 100
	Vienna, VA 22182
	703.123.4567 Phone
	703.123.4568 Fax
	joe.smith@acmewidgets.com
	www.acmewidgets.com
Consultant	Security Management International, LLC (SMI)
	Attn: Luke Bencie
	7600 Leesburg Pike
	East Building, Suite 340
	Falls Church, Virginia 22043
	703.962.1545 Phone
	703.997.8827 Fax
	luke.bencie@smiconsultancy.com
	www.smiconsultancy.com

Scope of Work   ACME Widgets, Ltd. (ACME) has employees who travel to hostile regions of the world, including countries such as Afghanistan, Iraq, and various nations in Africa. As most of these employees do not have prior military, federal law enforcement, or intelligence community training, ACME has wisely elected to enroll these employees in an Advanced Medical Training Course.

Security Management International (SMI) has developed an Advanced Medical Training Course designed to educate and prepare ACME employees on the potentially serious medical issues they may encounter overseas. SMI instructors with years of medical experience in hostile environments will deliver the course.

Course Schedule   The following is the tentative course content that can be provided to ACME:
- Trauma Preparedness
- Trauma Scenarios
- Medical/Emergency Equipment
- Emergency Travel Procedures/Resources
- Emergency Contact Forms
- AAABD:
  Area – Get off the X
  Arterial Bleed – Tourniquets
  Airway – Techniques/Resources
  Breathing – Chest Seal/Needle
  Decompression/Ventilations/CPR/AED
  Deformities – Severe injuries

Course Materials   Each student will be provided with the following:
- Copy of the lecture notes
- Medical checklists
- Hands-on experience with CPR mannequins and other training devices

Instructors   SMI will provide two instructors to teach each course. Both instructors have extensive overseas medical experience (in over 100 countries combined) working as intelligence professionals, diplomats and defense contractors. Their expertise is in emergency response, crisis management and other hostile situations, as well as operational tradecraft as it relates to counter-intelligence and espionage.

Measures of Success
ACME will know that employees have successfully completed the course when:
- Employees feel more prepared in their medical competency and response prior to traveling overseas
- Overseas medical threats are deterred by stronger planning
- Employee health vulnerabilities have been identified and mitigated
- Medical SOPs have been established and can be easily activated

Terms and Conditions
SMI's fees are always based on the project and never on time units. That way you are encouraged to call on us without worry of the "meter running," and we are free to suggest additional areas of focus without concern about increasing your investment.

SMI's fees for the following three training options are:

Option 1 – Two, 2-day "Advanced Medical Training Courses" (4 total days), for up to 25 students at the Acme offices: $XX,XXX

Option 2 – Two, 2-day "Advanced Medical Training Courses," plus two 4-hour "Medical Vaccination Courses" (6 total days): $XX,XXX

Option 3 – Two, 2-day "Advanced Medical Training Courses," plus two 4-hour "Medical Vaccination Courses," plus two 4-hour "CPR/AED Training for Office Personnel Courses" (8 total days): $XX,XXX

Payment Terms
50 percent is due on acceptance of this proposal and 50 percent on completion of the training. Alternatively, you may avail yourself of a 10 percent discount with payment in full on acceptance. If the project is canceled for any reason, SMI will retain the initial deposit.

ACCEPTANCE OF SERVICES AGREEMENT

Your signature below indicates acceptance of the option checked and your agreement with all the provisions and terms specified in this proposal. Alternatively, your deposit or full payment and indication of an option will also constitute that acceptance allowing us to begin the project together.

We accept (please check one):

Option 1 _____   Option 2 _____   Option 3 _____

And agree to the terms and conditions specified. We are providing a (please check one):

50% deposit _____

Full payment less a 10% discount _____

The total amount agreed upon for this project is _____ (please fill in total amount)

This agreement is made between SMI and ACME.

IN WITNESS WHEREOF, the parties hereto have signed this Agreement as of the date written above:

_____   _____

Name/Title   Date

ACME Widgets, Ltd.

_____   _____

Luke Bencie, President   Date

Security Management International, LLC

NOTE: The contract language above has been adapted from *Million Dollar Consulting Proposals: How to Write a Proposal That's Accepted Every Time*, by Alan Weiss. John Wiley and Sons, 2011.

Notice that we gave the client options for the types of services they would like to use. I learned this technique from Alan Weiss, who stressed that most people feel empowered by choices. And given a choice between three services of increasing price, clients will usually go with the middle option. It's the same thinking as why the second-least-expensive bottle of wine on a list is the one most commonly sold in a restaurant. People don't want to look cheap, but they also want to avoid paying top price if they can.

Social experiments aside, more often than not, I give clients only two choices – but I make sure I've already discussed those choices in detail, so I know which one's preferred. Offering two options allows negotiating room if the client suddenly experiences cold feet.

What's most important about the above proposal? The payment terms: 50 percent is due on acceptance and 50 percent on completion of the training. In the alternative, you might offer, as we do, a 10 percent discount with payment in full on acceptance.

As shown in the SMI contract above, be sure to include a sentence about retaining your deposit if the job is suddenly canceled. This happens more often than you might think; it's a way of protecting yourself.

If you're going to make it in this business, you need plenty of cash flow. So don't be shy. Ask for 50 percent up front. I'm happy to sacrifice 10 percent of my profits if I can get the money in hand immediately. I think most other consultants would. Give your clients an opportunity to pay in advance at a discounted rate, and you might be surprised at how many of them choose that option.

Conclusion

Let's face it, nobody likes writing proposals. They're a necessary element of the business, but more often than not they're also time-consuming and tedious. What's enjoyable is receiving a signed contract. Don't get bogged down in the murky world of RFPs; your business won't survive if you're constantly chasing them. Instead, build a relationship of trust with a prospective client *before* you send a proposal. This trust will render each proposal a simple formality between you and the client, instead of a bureaucratic exercise in paperwork. That's the best way to win contracts and grow your business.

FAQ

**36. What if a prospective client offers to award me a project
in return for a kickback?**

This is common in many parts of the world. If it happens to you, don't become alarmed. Politely but sternly inform the prospect that you cannot – and do not – operate that way. Period. If they still award you the project, it means they regard you as an ethical person. If not, you probably don't want the job. When in doubt, re-read the Foreign Corrupt Practices Act (FCPA).

37. Should I hire someone to help me to write proposals?

If you've never written a formal proposal before, you might want to enlist a professional to help with the first two or three. After that, you should be good to go on your own. Remember, the best proposal is the one that is more of a contract that you and the client have worked out after detailed discussions, not a document the prospect has never seen before.

**38. I just don't feel comfortable knowing how much to charge a
prospective client. What can I do to ensure to charge as much
as I can without creating sticker shock?**

That's a fair question. You'll learn this over time, as long as you work hard to understand the client's expectations. Be straightforward with them. Ask, "What would it be worth to you if I solve this problem and help you achieve your objectives?" Follow up with, "How much would it cost you if these problems do not get solved?" The answers should provide you with a strong sense of what they're willing to pay.

**39. Is it better to do firm-fixed-price proposals
or cost-plus proposals?**

It depends on how much the contract is worth and its duration. For smaller jobs, say, in the US$50,000-$100,000 range, I like to offer a firm fixed price for labor plus reimbursement for actual expenses. When the contracts reach the high six-figure or seven-figure range, and they extend beyond a six-month period, I typically build in a daily rate with a cost-plus structure.

40. How much detail should I go into in the proposal about my consulting methodologies and types of processes?

It depends on how much they ask for in the RFP. But know that whatever intellectual property you include in the proposal has a good chance of being recycled by someone else, particularly by your competitors, who might request to see other bidders' proposals. It happens from time to time. At the end of the day, you win a contract based on the following criteria: best price, best experience and best relationship. So, don't give away the secret sauce. You're the product, and your advice is the service.

Note from the Field
Somewhere over the Atlantic
1220 hours

I'm writing this from onboard a British Airways flight back from
London – my wife Viviane's favorite city. The two of us have just
concluded a couple days' worth of business meetings at some
very nice restaurants, including Jamie Oliver's Fifteen. Because
of our line of work, Viviane and I are constantly on airplanes.
That's why it's such a pleasure when we can travel together
for business. Not only do we get the chance to share more time,
but from a business standpoint Viviane is also my secret weapon when it comes to charming clients. Even though we're both
experienced professionals, I have a tendency to always talk
business, while Viviane has a more down-to-earth and personal
approach when meeting with clients. She also has a fantastic
memory for names and faces, an area in which I'm severely lacking. Together we make a great team.

9. Doing Business with 'Foreigners'

There are no foreign lands.
It is the traveler only who is foreign.
—Robert Louis Stevenson

DOING BUSINESS INTERNATIONALLY CAN BE INTIMIDATING. Most people don't like to veer too far away from their homes, their native countries and their national cultures. Dealing with someone who follows different ideals and an unfamiliar culture offers unique challenges, the most common being differences in language, business practices and religious customs..

This chapter offers easy-to-use advice on how to wade into unfamiliar international territory with some opportunity for success. It also offers cautions about the potential dangers of performing your services overseas.

Going global isn't for the faint of heart. You need to protect yourself, so you need to understand how the international security game is played and how the decision-makers conduct their business. Don't take my suggestions lightly. They might seem like common sense, but that doesn't mean they aren't critical to your success, safety or even survival.

I recently met with some German security engineers in Munich. I visited their impressive facility and was greeted hospitably by my point of contact. He walked me into their headquarters building, a stereotypically cold metal and glass structure, and into their stoic conference room, absent any photographs, plants or bright colors. Bland grays and whites constituted the room's theme. Seven distinguished looking German executives, all in their forties and fifties, stood at attention around the table. They wore European-cut wool suits and muted ties folded into extra-large knots around their necks. Their shirts were heavily starched. Their smiles were forced.

The conference table was lined with pitchers of water and juices, along with dozens of cans of various sodas and pots of coffee and tea. An assortment of cookies and crackers sat in baskets. Each place at the table featured a leather notebook complete with full-color brochures highlighting all of the company's services. In fact, so much stuff cluttered the table there was barely a hint of the polished mahogany surface.

Someone shoved business cards in front of our faces before pleasantries were even exchanged. Apparently, it was more important to share contact information than to greet us or ask if we had a pleasant trip.

A man named Dieter introduced himself and opened the meeting. He asked that we introduce ourselves around the table. No one had yet shaken my hand. For a second, I thought I might have walked into a legal deposition, and every word I uttered would be recorded and used against me later in a court of law.

Despite the initial stiffness, as the day progressed the atmosphere in the room gradually loosened. One reason: My Arab partners and I were world travelers. We all had experience conducting business with other cultures. More important, we had done our homework in advance and were well prepared to anticipate the idiosyncrasies of German businessmen. By the end of the day, we all had become friends and were joking about our mutually uncomfortable introductions. We enjoyed strong Bavarian beers that evening and shared more laughs. The relationship with our German friends has been positive ever since.

The moral of this story is this: Whenever you conduct international business, be sure to follow three rules:

+ Do Your Homework

+ Be Professional

+ Reputation Is Everything

Do Your Homework

Never go into a business meeting unprepared, particularly one with a potential international partner, client or competitor. This is especially true if you meet on their home turf. There's no excuse for you not gathering as much information as you can ahead of time about the people with whom you're meeting.

Say you're flying to Qatar in two weeks to meet with a company that has been expressing interest in your firm's vulnerability-assessment capabilities for oil pipelines. A similar company in Lebanon, to which you've previously provided consulting services, has referred you. You'll be traveling with a colleague who's an expert on critical-infrastructure protection. You have procured the necessary visas and letters of invitation, bought your airline tickets and packed your finest suit. You'll be staying at the Ritz Carlton in Doha, a five-star hotel, for which your hosts have graciously offered to pick up the tab.

What do you do next? Simple: prepare, prepare and then prepare some more.

Here's a checklist of what you'll need:

+ **Company background.** Via open-source intelligence and personal contacts, try to uncover what you can about the company's history, financials, leadership, legal issues, government involvement, locations, public and private investors.

+ **Company reputation.** Search for negative press, disgruntled employees and burned investors or partners.

+ **Clients.** This is the key. Who are the company's past and present customer and business partners? Is there anyone on the list you consider shady?

+ **Competition and concerns.** Who or what keeps this company awake at night?

+ **Country-specific business laws.** What are the laws for foreigners conducting business in this location and opening an office? Do foreign business owners require a local partner? What are the taxes? What are the banking laws?

+ **Culture.** Are there any cultural or religious restrictions that would hamper doing business in this country?

+ **Local customs and business practices.** Not knowing the local customs can make or break your meeting. Consider picking up a copy of the book *Kiss, Bow, or Shake Hands*. Otherwise, you could blow a business deal by unknowingly doing something considered rude or offensive.

+ **Geopolitical history.** You never want to be drawn into a sensitive political discussion with people you're just now meeting, because an errant remark could easily implode your deal. Learn everything you can about the history, geography and political polices of the country.

+ **Local phrases.** One of the advantages of speaking English is you usually don't need to learn an entire new language prior to your trip. But you must know how to communicate at least the following phrases in the local lingo:

Hello.

Good morning/afternoon/evening.

It is a pleasure to meet you.

How are you?

I am well. And you?

Goodbye.

Please.

Thank you.

Excuse me.

Where are the toilets?

+ **Smart questions.** You never want to appear empty, searching for the right words or with nothing to say. To avoid this awkwardness, prepare a list of smart questions that are either business related or non-business related that you can throw out during an uncomfortable silence.

+ **Your counterparts.** Learn as much as you can about their personal stories, and try to understand their motivations.

Being prepared will not only you make you appear more competent, but it will also improve the flow of the meeting, increasing your chances of success. But be careful what you reveal. You don't want your counterpart to think you have violated his or her privacy. This often conveys a lack of trust. Instead, keep your answers general and noncontroversial. But if, say, your Qatari colleague asks how you knew the last three Emirs of the country, you can respond this way:

> I thought it would be disrespectful if I didn't learn about your fine country before our meeting. I'm still a novice here, but I'm interested in discovering more about your history and traditions. Please excuse me if I ask seemingly uninformed questions.

In the 120 countries I've visited, humble responses such as this have helped me to disarm colleagues by getting them excited to talk about their national heritage. It isn't a ploy on my part but rather a show of respect. Plus, I do enjoy learning about other countries, especially from their proud and enthusiastic citizens.

Also, pay particular attention to learning each country's cultural taboos. For example, using your left hand to pass food in the Middle East is highly offensive, as is displaying the bottom of your shoe to someone. It won't matter if you have a degree from Harvard and look great in your custom-tailored Brioni suit. If you don't know the basic customs of a geographical region, your hosts will mock you as an amateur behind your back. Attempting to understand the culture – and learning those few phrases – will take you much farther than trying to impress people with your résumé.

I'll cover more of this in the next chapter.

Be Professional

Now that you've done your homework about the Qatari company, as well as studied up on the geopolitical and cultural issues of the region, you're ready to fly to Doha for your meeting.

The next step in doing in business with your new Qatari contacts is to be professional during your face-to-face meeting. I know it's a cliché but bear with me. I've been in dozens of boardrooms across the planet and have personally witnessed businesspeople – individuals who were hugely successful back in their home countries – completely sabotage themselves by improper interactions with their foreign counterparts. Their style and technique might have been great at home, but they ended up creating a disaster abroad. What are ordinary business exchanges in the United States can become career suicide in Japan.

By always being professional with foreigners, I mean adhering to the following international business protocols:

+ Be gracious with your compliments but avoid sounding phony.

+ Avoid being overbearing with the tone or inflection of your voice and the cadence of your dialog. Don't use wild hand gestures or display aggressive body language.

+ Avoid using sarcastic humor to break the ice unless you are certain it is relevant. If you feel the urge to be funny, light humor that can be easily interpreted – and universally appreciated – is better.

+ Avoid metaphors that could become lost in translation.

+ Always remember you're on their turf, so let them lead the discussion.

+ Know the local rules about asking personal questions. Some cultures will be in your face about your family, how much money you make or the size of your house, while others find these topics strictly *verboten*.

+ Avoid telling difficult-to-follow stories in order to make your point.

+ Avoid slang expressions.

+ Never engage in inappropriate conversation or contact with a female, particularly in the Muslim world.

+ Never refuse an offer of coffee or tea.

+ Avoid demonstrating signs of wealth by being too ostentatious.

+ Never talk down to someone.

+ Always dress professionally – the world's business uniform is a suit and tie – for meetings unless your cultural research informs you otherwise, for example, that overdressing can be interpreted as an insult.

+ Regardless of the recommended business attire, always have the shiniest shoes in the room.

+ Never abbreviate a person's name to make it easier for you to say – this is the kiss of death in some cultures. If a person's name is long, write it down ahead of time so you can visualize it. If you don't know how to pronounce it, ask politely.
+ Respect titles. In some parts of the world they mean everything. Even if the person with whom you're dealing isn't a peer, use their title as if they were a general, president or ambassador.
+ Never comment on any financial, political or social problems the country might be experiencing.
+ Never make a promise you cannot fulfill – ever.
+ The golden rule of being professional overseas is always listen twice as much as you speak.

Reputation is Everything

Picture this: You're 45 minutes into your meeting with the Qataris, and so far all of that time has been consumed by questions about the meal on your flight, recommendations for kicking jet lag and whether or not you like your hotel. It's 120 degrees Fahrenheit outside, and you're drinking your third cup of scalding hot tea with two Arab gentlemen in the whitest robes you've ever seen. You're sweating profusely in your dark wool Brooks Brothers suit, but on the outside you're well groomed and polished – much like your new shoes.

Instead of sitting in a typical corporate boardroom, such as the ones you've visited on Wall Street, you're planted on a puffy, beige leather couch that would more likely be found in a college student's dorm room. As you fight being swallowed up by this enormous piece of furniture, you realize you only have 15 minutes left to discuss business. You're trying to be as polite as possible, you've asked smart questions about the history of their country, and you've arrived prepared, knowing full well to expect this type of casual reception.

Still, you're worried you might not be able to say everything required to win the contract, so you deftly transition the conversation about the new Doha shopping mall into your sales pitch about protecting oil pipelines. Suddenly, your Qatari host cuts you off with a wave of his hand. He would like another refill of tea before you proceed. He presses a wireless buzzer, and a teenage tea boy scurries into the room with a fresh pot. Another five minutes pass by. Lighting a cigarette, your host tells you, "Okay, okay, now tell me about your services." You speak for about 90 seconds, until his cigarette is gone. He stops you again and says, "My friend, relax; save your sales pitch." You nervously ask if you've done something wrong. Your host responds with a big smile and informs you, "We already knew that you could deliver us a fine product. We just wanted to know that you were a good person. That is what is most important to us – trust. We like you and think we can do business with you. We will wire money to your bank right away so you can start next week."

You welcome the news and thank your hosts by shaking their hands and telling them you would be honored to work with them, as well. A multimillion-dollar security deal has just been completed. You can't believe it was that easy. Then you recall all the years of hundreds of phone calls, thousands of emails and countless time and money spent on research and preparation – all leading up to this moment. You were so close so many times before, but then the deal always seemed to fall through at the last minute. It took time, but your persistence finally paid off. You did it. You closed a big international security contract.

Patience and Persistence
Obviously in the story above, as they warn in the verbal fine print in commercials, results are not typical. It could take you months or most likely years to find yourself in that scenario. But it should be noted that when it comes to global security consulting, your reputation is far more important than your price, methodology, slick marketing materials, security credentials, family name or alma mater. In fact, you'll quickly discover that when you take your business overseas, particularly to areas where security concerns are paramount, your firm's identity will be based primarily on your reputation as the owner. Your key to successful growth will depend on referrals from prior customers – and not much else. So, place your highest

priority on building a stellar reputation for yourself and your company. Strive continually to be a person of exceptional character, someone who is recognized as ethical, competent and reliable. As Warren Buffet so famously stated: *It takes twenty years to build a good reputation and only five minutes to tear it down.*

The Dangers of Doing Foreign Business

I've painted a rosy picture of earning millions of dollars from one international meeting. Now let me impart some insight into the other reality of the global security consulting business: If one deal resembles the Qatari example, another 99 can be just plain nasty.

This isn't to say you'll be dealing with liars, cheats and criminals on a daily basis. On the contrary, it just means working in this business will rarely be easy. If you're lucky, you'll meet someone with unethical intentions perhaps only 10 percent of the time. But make no mistake; such people exist in this industry.

You must be careful with whom you do business.

After you've made the decision to take your security consultancy global, you'll require international contacts to help you open doors. If you compiled a successful previous career in the military, diplomatic corps, law enforcement or intelligence communities, or in defense contracting, many of your contacts are already well established. Use these connections to start. Reconnect with your international friends and colleagues, and use them as leverage to get your foot in the door with organizations within their country.

Some of your contacts no doubt will want a percentage of any deal you win as a result of their introductions. That's fine and customary. Just be sure to budget for it. If a friend provides me only with a useful introduction, I usually buy that friend a thank-you dinner or send a nice bottle of scotch. Only if a connection helps me win a contract do I make it a point to compensate that person. Depending on the size of the deal, it could be as little as 1 percent or as high as 10 percent.

This leads to a very important point: In order to conduct international business, you must fully understand and comply with the provisions of the Foreign Corrupt Practices Act.

FCPA

If you're an American, and you plan on performing security – or any type of business – overseas, you must fully understand and comply with the FCPA. If you aren't based in the United States, be assured that similar laws are on the books in your country or the country in which you plan to do business. Either way, I strongly advise you to read everything you can about what is, and is not, permissible about foreign security consulting transactions.

For example, according to the U.S. Department of Justice:

The Foreign Corrupt Practices Act of 1977, as amended, 15 U.S.C. §§ 78dd-1, et seq. ("FCPA"), was enacted for the purpose of making it unlawful for certain classes of persons and entities to make payments to foreign government officials to assist in obtaining or retaining business. Specifically, the anti-bribery provisions of the FCPA prohibit the willful use of the mails or any means of instrumentality of interstate commerce corruptly in furtherance of any offer, payment, promise to pay, or authorization of the payment of money or anything of value to any person, while knowing that all or a portion of such money or thing of value will be offered, given or promised, directly or indirectly, to a foreign official to influence the foreign official in his or her official capacity, induce the foreign official to do or omit to do an act in violation of his or her lawful duty, or to secure any improper advantage in order to assist in obtaining or retaining business for or with, or directing business to, any person.

Since 1977, the anti-bribery provisions of the FCPA have applied to all U.S. persons and certain foreign issuers of securities. With the enactment of certain amendments in 1998, the anti-bribery provisions of the FCPA now also apply to foreign firms and persons who cause, directly or through agents, an act in furtherance of such a corrupt payment to take place within the territory of the United States.

The FCPA also requires companies whose securities are listed in the United States to meet its accounting provisions. See 15 U.S.C. § 78m. These accounting provisions, which were designed to operate in tandem with the anti-bribery provisions of the FCPA, require corporations covered by the provisions to (a) make and keep books and records that accurately and fairly reflect the transactions of the corporation and (b) devise and maintain an adequate system of internal accounting controls.

Don't risk it. If you harbor any doubts or concerns about whether or not the international business in which you are engaging violates the FCPA, confer with a legal expert. You can also obtain information about this law from the U.S. Department of Justice website and the U.S. Department of Commerce's FCPA blog.

International Partners

As you begin to expand your security consulting practice into more exotic corners of the globe, you'll inevitably need to find new business partners in those areas. It's a common practice, but it requires vigilance. Not all countries operate under the same type of ethical business practices traditionally found in more developed nations. Corruption, corporate espionage and nefarious scams become more common when you start doing business in Africa, South America, Central Asia and Southeast Asia. You'll need to watch your back.

It's a sad fact that many unreliable and unethical businesspeople operate in this world. But it's been that way since the beginning of civilization. People abound who promise you the world and obtain your trust and then deliver nothing but pain and disappointment. Here are some words of caution against such individuals and how you can spot them before they can do you harm.

You can divide these characters into three categories:

+ Kooks

+ Cowboys

+ Conmen

Kooks. They're people who have no business being in the field of security. To them the word "security" means being able to carry guns. They're usually wannabes who secretly wish they were in the military, law enforcement or intelligence communities. They typically lack security training or experience, and they unmask themselves by outlandish behavior, such as displaying ridiculous logos on their websites – skulls, knives or guns – or using "death," "revenge" or "mercenaries" in their company names. Stay away from these characters, or they will sully your reputation as a legitimate global security consultant.

Cowboys. These individuals might possess even a fair share of previous military experience and are ready to take on any risk imaginable in the harshest of environments. But they also remind you of the characters from The A-Team TV series or the movie *The Expendables*. These hard chargers aren't necessarily bad people. In fact, they'd be the guys you'd most want to respond if you're ever kidnapped. Nevertheless, nine times out of ten they can be walking legal liabilities and thus bad business partners. In places such as Africa and Central Asia, they might have thriving operations. Strictly from a business standpoint, however, you need to understand the risks inherent in working with them.

Conmen. A problem in any industry, in the security world they seem to find themselves especially at home. When you start engaging in big-time international projects, these scoundrels will appear from nowhere. They usually claim to have access to princes, politicians or major players in particular countries. More often than not, they're just looking to capitalize on an association with your business by earning retainers or free airline tickets. But they're poison and will sink your business.

Here's a recent example of how one of these jackals tried to insinuate his way into my firm.

A friend of mine, who also happens to be vice president of international business development for a multibillion-dollar defense company, informed me he had recently met a gentleman from India who claimed to have direct access to the Saudi royal family.

Let me stop there for a moment. In the Middle East, or at least in the Gulf States, *everyone* claims to be related to, went to school with or somehow knows some wealthy royal family member from the Kingdom of Saudi Arabia. The fact that this person was from India and was talking about access in the KSA immediately raised a red flag with me.

My friend asked if I'd be interested in meeting with this

potential rainmaker over drinks the next time he was in Washington. I was wary but also curious, so I agreed.

We met in the bar of a popular D.C. restaurant after work. He walked in wearing a suit, and he was carrying *three* cell phones – something that raised my suspicions further. After ordering a couple glasses of wine and talking about the weather, I asked him how we might do business.

The gentleman claimed he was well connected in the kingdom and was friends with the Saudi minister of defense. He also claimed to own an apartment in New York City, two beautiful homes in Riyadh, and another in Mumbai. He boasted about how he could get me meetings with decision-makers and that he "only" did US$100 million deals. When I asked what his last $100 million deal was; he said it actually was only $20 million and refused to give further details because of confidentiality issues.

In Chapter 11, I'll discuss how in this business you must develop – forgive the crudity – a bullshit detector. At this point in the meeting, it was registering high alert. I informed the gentleman that I already had several good friends who were high-ranking officials in the Saudi government. I asked him what he could do for me that they could not. His answer was what I expected: vague and inconclusive. He muttered that he worked hard for his partners, knew the prince who will become the next king, knew people at the U.S. Embassy, and so on.

Realizing I was wasting my time, I allowed him to save face. I said I'd be happy to explore a partnership with him – if he could bring me a deal worth US$100 million. And if he helped me complete the deal, I'd pay him a commission. It was a standard offer, and I thought that would be the end of it.

But then he had the nerve to tell me he required US$18,000 per month salary, for a minimum of six months, $20,000 worth of business-class airline tickets to Saudi Arabia to "set up the meetings," plus 10 percent equity in my company. Appalled, I couldn't decide whether to laugh in his face or walk out in disgust. I laughed and asked why I should do any of those things. He responded that he was "the best" and "because he liked me he would drop his mandatory stake in my company to 1 percent.

At that point, my laughter turned to anger. It was one thing to waste my time; it was another to insult my intelligence. I told him, in choice words, that he was insane, that he knew nothing about business, and that he had wasted my time. I also reminded him that if he really could do everything he claimed, he would have been smarter to take a 10 percent commission from a US $100 million dollar sale instead of $18,000 a month and 1 percent equity in my company. Obviously, he was only looking to weasel his way into a few good months of paychecks, a free trip to Riyadh, and maybe some passive income if my company grew significantly.

This was a no-brainer, because the man was incompetent, transparently so. Other manipulative schemers might not be so easy to spot, however. Count on being approached by them, and never offer or promise anything unless you're certain the person with whom you're dealing is genuine.

Conclusion

Global security consulting is an exciting and glamorous profession. But it's also fraught with hazards. Whenever you leave the comfortable confines of your home, be prepared for the unexpected. It isn't easy, so you can never stop learning about the world. You need to read, travel and experience other cultures all the time. If you aren't prepared, you'll get burned.

Here's a bit of time-tested advice: If you find yourself in a poker game and you can't figure out who the sucker is – it's probably you.

FAQ

41. Why would a foreign client want to hire my security consulting firm if I am located halfway around the world?

The clients you want to have won't hesitate to pay for the best – and you want the best to be you. If a company or other organization only wants to pay for a low-cost, local security provider, they aren't the client you want.

42. I have a successful American security consulting firm. Should I still seek to expand into a foreign market?

You should only expand to those countries where you believe your services will be valued and the opportunity is there. You should also look for markets where you have a trusted partner who can broker contacts and develop business. There's no sense in entering a market only for the sake of being there.

43. What are your thoughts about performing security in the more dangerous parts of the world, such as the Middle East, Africa or Central Asia?

There are obviously big opportunities in hostile areas of the world. By the same token, you'll need to trust your partners absolutely in those situations, and always measure your risks versus potential gains before accepting a project. Never accept a job in a danger zone simply because the money is good.

44. How do I find a trusted partner in a foreign country?

You can't just jump into bed with the first individual who claims to have connections in a foreign country. You must do your homework. Request to see their security license, proof of insurance, references from past and current clients, and their annual sales. Perform as much due diligence as possible. I've even hired local investigators to run background checks. Also, be wary of strangers who reach out to you via LinkedIn or other social network sites, offering to represent you in faraway lands.

45. Working with governments from around the globe, what happens if you disagree with your client's politics, human rights issues or other moral concerns?

That's an excellent and important question. If you strongly disagree with the beliefs of your client, you must decide if taking their money is worth sacrificing your own ethics or morals. Obviously, with any international business, you might encounter dramatic cultural differences – some of which will shock, offend or even disgust you. Believe me, sometimes you sleep better at night by walking away from a big payday and knowing you didn't compromise yourself. The money is never worth it if you can't look yourself in the mirror the next day.

Note from the Field

Great Exhuma, Bahamas

0830 hours

I've always enjoyed the Bahamas. I used to travel here primarily for the marlin fishing in the Caribbean, but now I just enjoy the beaches and the scuba diving. This time, Viviane and I have rented a private villa, and I'm sitting at a wooden table on the back patio having my coffee. It's a windy day, and the waves are crashing hard in the blue surf.

As a global security consultant, my frequent-flyer miles are always plentiful. We flew here from Washington to escape a holiday snowstorm and recharge our batteries for four days and three nights.

If you want to make your living crisscrossing the globe – particularly when you have to visit some of the least inviting countries – take a getaway with your loved ones every chance you get, even if it's only a mini-vacation.

10. Do's and Don'ts of Global Travel
(Looking the Part and Getting There in Style)

> *The World is a book, and those who do not travel*
> *read only a page.*
> —Saint Augustine

WHEN I WORKED FOR THE GOVERNMENT, flying coach on 10-hour flights and sitting on the floor in dirty airports waiting for delayed layovers, I kept myself going by thinking about the day when I could travel the world in style. My imagination spared no expense: business-class reclining seats, attractive flight attendants, high-end waiting lounges with free drinks and welcome service. My imagination, however, doesn't pay the bills, and travel on my own dime comes at a premium.

I hope global security consulting sounds as exciting to you as it did to me at the start of my career. For some, it might be the idea of working in the harshest environments of Latin America, the Middle East or Africa that conjures up images of adventure and international intrigue, maybe even the type that James Bond is dispatched to resolve. For others, perhaps it involves frequenting the five-star hotels of Europe and Asia, offering wise counsel to eagerly receptive or even desperate senior business executives or government leaders.

Along with these tantalizing images, however, going global today exacts a high price – literally. So, before you max out your personal credit cards on your first international business trip, let me help you navigate your way through some of the typical financial pitfalls that await newly established global security consultants.

I've sat on both sides of the aisle when it comes to international travel – or should I say both sides of the cabin curtain. Like most low-level minions traveling on public funds, I started out in the cramped and often smelly confines of coach class, with its poor service, minimal room and no privacy. Through sheer persistence, I ratcheted my way up the frequent-flyer ladder. Even better, the government and then private employers started paying top dollar for me to head overseas in style.

The change was incredible: leg room, fine dining, meticulous attention to detail, all the things you'd find in a classy hotel but at 40,000 feet. I was hooked. Soon, as a very frequent flier, I achieved preferred status on all my favorite airlines and hotels. This led to first-class upgrades, as well as opulent suites at some of the world's finest hotels and even private car services to get there.

Here's a secret from the other side of the curtain: There's a massive difference between flying business class and flying first class. At one point, I became so spoiled that I would be disappointed if I couldn't get an upgrade to first class and had to return to the business-class cabin.

There were even times when the highlight of my trip was the first-class flight itself. Nothing compares to being pampered by Virgin Atlantic, Emirates or Singapore Airways. Your own private compartment folds into a comfortable bed complete with fitted sheets, fluffed ostrich-feather pillows and silk pajamas. The specially prepared gourmet meals and sommelier-chosen wines are worthy of five-star distinction. Attractive, consummately professional flight attendants provide you with the continuous attention befitting a king or queen – including foot massages. I send heartfelt thanks to Richard Branson for restoring the luxury and hipness of international air travel.

Then, when I decided to form my own company, I had to forsake my luxurious flights. I had to put aside those days of handmade martinis by the Virgin Atlantic bartender, the beachfront hotel suites in Abu Dhabi and the expense-account dinners in Hong Kong – at least temporarily. I returned to coach class and my humble beginnings. I went from the Ritz Carlton to budget hotels. My dinners at Michelin star-rated restaurants in Luxembourg became a McDonald's combo meal on the streets of Paris. I had to wash my undershirts in the bathroom sink and iron my clothes in the hotel room instead of sending my suits off with the valet for pressing or my shoes for shining. Meanwhile, the credit-card bills were piling up, and reality had officially sunk in.

Not that I'm complaining. I had made the decision and was living with the consequences, because I did have a dream and was determined to achieve it. If that meant giving up the high life, then that's what I had to do. And in doing so, I learned a valuable lesson.

Flying coach again was like returning to my childhood bedroom and finding that the bed had become too small. The room was the same, but I had changed. I was rapidly becoming a global security consultant, a foremost expert in my chosen profession. Soon, I was regularly placed on retainer by multinational CEOs and powerful government figures. The advice and services I offered were of tremendous value to clients on topics ranging from infrastructure safety and crisis response to employee security, competitive intelligence, product protection and enhanced market share. My advice could literally mean the difference between life and death.

Your experience will probably be the same. You might have retired as a senior leader at a government agency. You're probably an expert in counterterrorism, counterintelligence, infrastructure protection, crisis management or some other niche security field that has provided you with decades' worth of on-the-ground, practical experience. You owe it to yourself, and your clients, to be worthy of your background and help them solve their problems and achieve their goals. If your consulting services are truly that valuable, you've earned the right to look and act the part – and charge accordingly.

As stated previously, this is critical: Charge what you're worth. Many aspiring consultants have had difficulty transitioning from their government careers to private enterprise, because they neglect the importance of appearances in private industry. It isn't a dodge or a charade; it's looking the part and charging accordingly.

Think about it, if you were the CEO of an international corporation, would you hire someone to counsel you on security matters who bids for his coach airline tickets online, stays at cheap hotels and shows up wearing 10-year-old suits? In this business, perception is reality. You might not be able to afford the finest for a while, but finding a way to look the part, especially when you travel, is essential to global security consulting.

Your clients are going to be senior executives or government officials accustomed to conducting business in a certain way. If you want to appear as their equal – which as I discussed in Chapter 7 is imperative to selling your services – you must carry yourself in the same high regard.

The good news is the hard part is over. You've already accumulated a tremendous amount of security experience, whether in government or elsewhere. Now, all you have to do is translate that experience into the right international persona.

Please don't get me wrong; this doesn't mean being a bullshitter – something I'll cover in the next chapter. World-class executives and government leaders will see right through it. No, I mean polishing your act by genuinely expanding your tastes, increasing your reading list, learning new languages, taking academic courses and showing a greater interest in the geopolitics of the world around you. Security consulting often gets a bad rap as an industry for meatheads – knuckle-draggers is another common term. Your worth as a consultant, and your reflection on your peers, lies in actively contradicting that perception.

Traveling to an International Meeting

Something else I keep stressing: Always ask your client to cover your non-meal expenses, preferably business class. If a prospective overseas client contacts you and requests that you fly over to discuss your services, inform them you're in demand and would be willing to start with an initial teleconference. This might seem like a wasted opportunity, but your time is valuable, and not all client meetings are worthwhile.

Opting for a teleconference will allow you to determine if there's a fit between you and the prospective client and increase the chances they'll cover your travel for a follow-up face-to-face meeting. As I also discussed in Chapter 7, you'll need to use the teleconference to developed rapport. If you're successful, consider approaching the prospective client this way:

Mr. Amadi, I'm certain that I can assist your company in achieving its security goals and objectives. But please recognize that my time is of considerable value to me and my other clients. I am more than willing to fly to meet with you and your organization face-to-face to continue our discussions on this project, but in order to do so I would need to be compensated for my time and expenses. If you think your current security situation warrants these expenses – which according to our conversation appears to be the case – I would be available to travel to your location as early as next week.

If the client pushes back, saying the company is still in the interview phase and hasn't yet chosen a security consultant or that other consultants will travel to the client location on their own dime, I usually follow up with:

I understand that other security consultants would pay money just for the opportunity to take a meeting with you. Frankly, that's the difference between my consultancy and those others. We have already established our reputation, and we have earned the right to request compensation for our time.

If the client says that he cannot approve of the cost of the travel and labor fees, I might come back with:

Based on our initial meeting, I would consider it a privilege to work with your organization. Therefore, I'm willing to travel to your office and continue our discussion at no charge other than travel expenses. This would include business-class airfare and hotel accommodations only. If, after our meeting you decide to hire my firm, I will deduct the cost of those expenses from our agreement. If for some reason you decide not to hire my firm – which I don't anticipate once we've sat down and discussed your situation in depth – your cost would be only an airline ticket and hotel room. Is that acceptable?

If the client still objects, you can rightly wonder whether they're sincere about wanting to hire you. Some pushback on cost is common; a refusal to cover any costs is a bad sign. They might just be fishing for solutions like that local government did, as described in Chapter 8, bringing in a group of potential consultants and encouraging them to reveal their proposed solutions to the problem.

When to Fly on Spec

If your prospective client remains unwilling to pay your way to their city, but you consider the opportunity to meet with them too great to pass up, you're going to have to cover your own airfare. But you can capitalize on the situation, somewhat, by committing to one airline, preferably one that has a hub in your city, and staying with that airline – no matter the cost. Then apply for their credit card as your company business card in order to maximize your miles and upgrade opportunities.

I often fly American Airlines and their partner airline, British Airways, even if it costs US$300 more to fly on American than it does on, say, Delta. I do so because of the long-term benefits. By flying American only, I can reach their highest frequent-flyer status, something which allows me to:

+ Choose my seats earlier. If I have to fly coach, I can choose the emergency exit or bulkhead before other passengers have a chance to choose their seats.

+ Board the plane earlier. I can bypass the madding crowds and more easily find stowage for my carry-on.

+ Access the business lounge. I can get more work done and take advantage of the free food and drinks.

+ Avoid checked-baggage fees. This perk alone can save me US$50-$100 per flight.

+ Access possible free upgrades. This typically happens about every fourth flight.

In addition, my company credit card is also an American Airlines/Citi® Visa® card. When I purchase a ticket with it, I receive double frequent-flyer miles in my American account. Much of my company expenses go on this card, which usually exceed US$150,000 per year and are also applied on a mile-per-dollar basis to my frequent-flyer account. As my company has grown over the years, I've provided cards to my employees and temporary subcontractors, with their miles likewise accumulating on the SMI account.

The American Express Platinum® card is also of tremendous value to security consultants. It allows access to numerous business-class lounges across the world. It provides rental car insurance and an exceptional concierge service – which is better than a travel agency when it comes to international travel needs.

If I must fly overseas and have to pay out of my own pocket, I either use frequent-flier miles for the business-class ticket, or I buy a full-fare coach ticket and use miles to upgrade to business class, whichever is cheaper. I admit it; there's more to these upgrades than the need to sustain an image. In my Note from the Field on page 174, I commented that life is too short to be crammed into the cattle car that is coach, especially when you're moments from landing and signing a lucrative consulting agreement. You need to be at your best to perform international work, which means you must travel with limited stress in order to arrive refreshed. Your client's well-being depends on how alert you are – not to mention it's just plain fun.

When you reach the point where your security consulting services are in demand, you'll no longer need to pay your own way. If you're good enough, your clients and prospective clients will fly you, business class or better, to their locations. You can ask to make your own airline reservation, ensuring your preferred airline, and be reimbursed, or you can ask the client to make the reservation for you – all of which I described in detail back in Chapter 3.

CAUTION: No matter what you decide, if your client is paying, never cash in a business-class ticket for economy class in order to receive future airline credit. It's unprofessional and unethical. The same applies for the hotel room. Also, don't get in the habit of bringing your spouse or significant other with you on an introductory consulting trip. If the client finds out you're enjoying a mini-vacation on their dime, you've just sacrificed your credibility.

The Basics

Some of this next section might seem obvious, but in this business it doesn't pay to ignore even the simplest stuff. I've seen too many good businesspeople get burned by it.

One of my staffers likes to tell a story about a time he went camping. He was so focused on getting the major equipment together – the tent, cooler, saws and axes – that when he finally got to the site and started unpacking he realized he'd forgotten to pack a sleeping bag.

Don't lose sight of the travel tips I've listed here.

+ Be sure to arrive at your destination the day before your meeting to acclimate yourself to the time change. For flights that take you across six or more time zones, arrive two days early. In either case, go for a non-stop flight.

+ Before, during and after the flight, complete as much due diligence as possible about the prospective client and their security issues. Know their corporate or government structure, their annual sales and budget, their stock price, where they do business, what their security threats are and who their main competitors are. Get to know them and their needs beforehand. I covered more of this in Chapter 7.

+ If you're headed to a popular destination city, avoid the urge to regard your trip as a getaway instead of what it really is, a business sales call that should lead to a long-term contract and long-term referrals. If you've been traveling for work for a while, you already know that business trips and pleasure trips are two different beasts.

+ If you're new to business travel, heed this warning: Go easy on the in-flight drinks, and skip the sightseeing tours. Also, under no circumstances charge anything to your hotel bill other than the room itself. Nothing upsets a prospective or current client more than a consultant who charges room service, movie rentals, dry cleaning and a massage to the expense account. Such behavior is common around the world. Yet it still seems to shock some security consultants when their contracts aren't renewed.

+ Proper dress. It's always better to be overdressed than un-
  derdressed when meeting with clients. But if I'm flying from
  Washington to, say, London on a Monday morning for a meeting with a client on Tuesday morning, and with a return flight
  Tuesday night, I'm fine traveling in jeans with casual loafers
  and an oxford shirt under a sportcoat. Comfortable is important, but don't underestimate the power of looking stylishly
  comfortable. Airlines want your repeat business, and if they
  see you as a well dressed, card-carrying frequent flier, business suit or not you'll receive attentive service. Just make sure
  everything you wear looks clean, pressed and new.

+ Luggage. Use carry-on bags only. Any hotel worth its cost
  will gladly provide plenty of toiletries and other necessities
  on request, so take only what's necessary for your individual
  personal needs. In other words, you don't need to worry about
  whether your toothpaste is carry-on approved.

Regarding clothing and luggage, here's what I typically pack for
a one-night or two-night business trip:

+ One fitted dark suit. Brioni, Tom Ford or Brooks Brothers is my
  choice for meeting with clients; JoS. A. Bank is a good alternative if you're on a fixed budget. No matter what, make sure
  your clothes are tailored. I understand not having deep pockets, but at the very least your pants should fit right. Be sure
  to visit a tailor the next time you're in Southeast Asia, and get
  fitted for some suits at a low cost. I recommend Bobby Raja's in
  Bangkok.

+ One folded dress shirt. I have all my shirts folded and boxed by
  the drycleaner, because they're easier to pack and less wrin-
  kled on arrival.

+ One folded Oxford shirt. You can use a button-down Oxford,
  preferably with some color in it, with your suit for a more casual look if you join your client for dinner after the meeting.

+ One pair of dress pants. It's good to have them for unexpected
  follow-up meetings – or an unforeseen wardrobe disaster.

+ Two undershirts. Always wear an undershirt with white dress shirts; they prevent sweat stains and make your shirts look cleaner.

+ Two ties. More than any other item of clothing, people remember ties. You might have to return for a second meeting with your client, so always bring a backup tie. That way, you don't look like you only own one business ensemble.

+ Cufflinks. French-cuffed shirts never go out of style and will be appreciated by your European clients. Stick to classic links and avoid the gaudy or silly. You don't want to make your accessories the topic of conversation after the meeting.

+ Dress shoes. Shine, shine, shine! Nothing looks more unprofessional than obviously worn or cheap shoes. Personally, I judge people by their shoes as a first impression, and so do plenty of businessmen and women. Skimp on anything else if necessary but never on your shoes.

+ Three pairs of underwear. Never any fewer; your mother taught you better than that.

+ Three pairs of socks. Same deal.

+ Swim trunks or a bathing suit. Not necessarily for pleasure but possibly for exercise, something which should always be an important part of your routine. For short trips, it's easier to swim at the hotel than pack a pair of running shoes and running clothes.

+ Swim goggles and earplugs. A good investment if you only have time to do 15 minutes of laps in the pool. Plus, you don't want to show up at the meeting with chlorine eyes. The client might conclude you pulled an all-night bender.

+ Emergency medical kit. More than anything else on this list, don't forget or neglect this one when you're bound for a hazardous destination. See Appendix A on page 263 for a detailed list of essentials.

Along with my carry-on, I take my handcrafted Italian computer bag, which I can easily sling over my shoulder and which looks elegant and impressive. More important, the bag constitutes the heart of my consulting business on the road and contains the following:

+ MacBook Air with charger and other cables

+ International power converters
+ Smartphone
+ Leather notebook with notepad
+ Mount Blanc pen
+ Business-card holder with plenty of my cards
+ SMI marketing materials, such as company overview presentations and tri-folds of specific services we offer
+ Copy of my book *Among Enemies: Counter-Espionage for the Business Traveler*
+ Copy of the most recent magazine in which I've had an article published
+ *Among Enemies* challenge coins to give mostly to military people as tradition
+ Highlighters and other markers
+ Post-it notepads
+ Calculator – because I'm old school and find my fingers are too fat for my smartphone calculator app
+ Amazon Kindlefire
+ Yellow Card (proof of international vaccinations)
+ Photocopies of my passport
+ Extra passport photos

Other packing items or travel tips include:

+ Small printer. This is just in case I need to print a proposal or a contract or a nondisclosure agreement in a hurry.
+ Watches. Wearing a high-end timepiece says a lot about a person – particularly their business style. When I attend meetings or conferences in the more developed countries of the world, I wear my Omega Seamaster, which I've proudly owned for over 15 years and which Daniel Craig displays in his onscreen role as James Bond.

As a security professional, I often visit some of the planet's most dangerous places, such as Iraq, Afghanistan and much of Africa. These aren't the best locations for a tall white man to walk around with an expensive hunk of metal on his wrist. On those occasions,

I wear my Casio G-Shock – which I've also happily owned for 15 years and which you can find online for less than US$200. It's been a reliable companion whenever I've found myself traversing a hostile environment.

If you're looking for a hybrid of style and function, I recommend the Breitling Emergency chronograph with distress transmitter, though like the Omega it's a bit pricey.

+ Rental vehicles. I prefer to reserve a car in advance rather than take a taxi to my hotel. Over the years, I've discovered it doesn't cost much more than a cab and tends to be more reliable and less stressful. Plus, it's usually a cleaner vehicle. At the airport, the bilingual driver holds a sign with my name, or a cover name (see *Among Enemies* for more about travel security), along with a bottle of water and the local newspaper.

You can arrange the service easily via your hotel. Spend an extra US$50 to $100, and you'll be amazed at how much more smooth and enjoyable your arrival experience will be. Remember, everything you do as a global security consultant is geared toward enhancing your client's security situation. Time is money, and you're no amateur, so spend the extra money to save the time and trouble.

+ Hotels. I've found that the best thing to do on arrival at the hotel, after checking in and getting set up in the room, is take a walk, run or swim. Nothing beats fresh air to reset your internal clock to local time. Or, spend 10 minutes in a dry sauna followed by a massage. It will also do a body good. Just don't charge it to your client.

If I arrive late and need to grab some sleep before an early meeting the next day but find myself wide awake at midnight, I'll take a low dose of an over-the-counter sleeping pill. I'm cautious about taking sleep aids in full dosage, because most leave me groggy the next morning and can actually worsen my feeling sluggish.

Figure out which brand works best for you before your trip. Some pills can be addictive, while others can be dangerous if mixed with alcohol or other medications. I discovered this the hard way once on an airliner, when I passed out in the aisle on my way to the toilet. We can't be glamorous all the time.

+ Meeting prep. I like to obtain a local map from the concierge and identify the meeting site in advance. Sometimes, I'll even take a taxi to the location just to calculate the drive time and get a feel for the area. It's also good to budget extra time in case of heavy traffic the day of your meeting. You can reserve the private car again to take you to the meeting, just so you're not stressing over taxi availability, which is an issue in some cities. It always looks better if you arrive at a client's location in a Mercedes with a driver instead of a beat-up taxi. The latter is a bad show regardless of the country you're visiting – and it's even worse than showing up late.

+ Meeting etiquette. When you arrive at your client's building, project dignity and respect at all times. That means treating everyone with good manners – from the security guard at the front gate to the receptionist in the lobby to the person or group you're meeting. No matter what part of the world you're in, or the culture you're dealing with, you can never say "please" and "thank you" too much.

Incidentally, some languages don't have the exact equivalent of "please" in their vocabulary (such as Swedish). Make sure your knowledge of local culture, manners and sensitivities is up-to-date beforehand to avoid awkward or embarrassing situations. Again, *Kiss, Bow, or Shake Hands* is a great resource for this information.

One behavior I've noticed that's exhibited by brand new global security consultants is the tendency to slip back into a military mindset of ranks and hierarchies when they are around their clients or prospective clients. Remember, the client has hired you for your expertise. You are a consultant to them, not an employee or servant. Your advice is of tremendous value, so converse with your clients as their equal, at least in terms of your knowledge, skills and abilities. If you want to be a successful global security consultant, act and travel accordingly.

For example, if you meet with a client who's a senior government official, interact with him or her as a peer and not a subordinate. Go easy on the "Sir, yes sir" routine. Be respectful and remember the old mantra that generals like to talk with other generals.

FAQ

46. Should I avoid working in foreign countries where I don't speak the language?

It depends. Much of the world uses English as the language of business, which will greatly enhance your ability to perform your services. I've worked in numerous countries where I didn't speak the language, and I've never had an issue.

47. Everybody is talking about China these days. Should I be doing work over there?

China is certainly the place to be right now. But there, much of your security work will deal with intellectual property theft and due diligence rather than physical security. It's worth the investment, at least in terms of time, to try establishing contacts in that part of the world. On the other hand, there are riches in niches, so you don't necessarily have to follow the trends.

48. If I am going to be doing a lot of global travel, do you have any preferred airline programs you can recommend?

Everyone has a different philosophy on airline frequent-flyer programs. Some are loyal to one airline, while others seek only the best price for their trip. I've traditionally flown United, but that's because they have a hub at Washington Dulles Airport, near where I live, so it's easy for me to use them. For trips to South America I prefer American. But as I mentioned early in this chapter, my three favorite airlines, in terms of comfort and service, are Virgin Atlantic, Emirates and Singapore Airways.

49. What about hotel chains?

My hotel of choice is Hyatt, followed by the Hilton Conrad brand, because I've found their frequent-stay program easy to use, and their hotels are generally very clean with good restaurants. My wife prefers Marriott. But if you want to go first class, nothing beats the Four Seasons.

50. And credit cards?

American Express Platinum® will pay for itself if you plan to travel overseas extensively. Although it could cost up to US$500 per year for membership, the card provides you access to airport lounges and a concierge service that is second to none. Also, at this writing, you can buy a full-fare business-class ticket with the Platinum® card and receive a second ticket at no additional cost. When you start placing serious charges on your AMEX card, at least US$100,000 per year, they might invite you to apply for their exclusive Black Card program. You should also carry a Visa card as a backup, because some establishments don't accept AMEX.

Note from the Field

Athens

2200 hours

I'm sitting at the desk of my hotel room in Athens. I just enjoyed a nice sunset dinner atop the Hilton Hotel, which overlooks the Parthenon on the Athenian Acropolis. There's something inherently magical about watching the sun set over Greece's ancient ruins. It becomes easy to imagine the likes of Socrates, Plato and Aristotle enjoying the same view over 2,000 years ago. At these moments, I'm proud to have taken the gamble and struck out on my own as an entrepreneur.

If I can leave you with any parting words for this chapter, it would be these: You are a security consultant, not a security contractor. Know the difference. A consultant provides advice and services based on expertise in order to improve the situation of an organization. A contractor is a hired hand brought in to fill a gap temporarily. They both play critical roles, contractors don't command your fees. If you truly want to be a successful global security consultant, one who brings value to his or her clients, you must always remember to act, travel and even eat like one.

11. International Negotiation
(aka Learning to Decipher BS in Any Language)

> *You must never try to make all the money that's in*
> *a deal. Let the other fellow make some money, too,*
> *because if you have a reputation for always making*
> *all the money, you won't have many deals.*
>
> —J. Paul Getty

NUMBERS REPRESENT THE TRULY UNIVERSAL business language. No matter the dialect, no matter the inflection and no matter the monetary unit, the numbers don't lie, particularly when they're carefully studied. Profits and losses, cash-flow statements, annual growth percentages and balance sheets all translate easily across borders. If you're going to become a global security consultant, you'll need to understand the numbers – and be able to *negotiate* them *anywhere* with *anyone* around the planet.

Just as numbers constitute an international language, so does bullshit. Yes, you read that correctly. I'm talking about that unmistakable verbal diarrhea we've all encountered in business. And nowhere is this excrement more prominent than when a business deal is taking place between a citizen of one country and a citizen or citizens of another. In fact, the more passports are involved, the deeper the bullshit can pile up during negotiations.

If you are going to be a player on the global stage, you'll need to become fluent in the vital arts of number crunching and bullshit detection. Otherwise, you'll lose any chance of becoming profitable, and you'll be scratching your head about how it happened. And whatever the cause, you'll have no one to blame but yourself.

Pardon my continued profanity, but bullshit is the appropriate term. As I define it, it's when a deal sounds too good to be true. It's when the people telling you a story or giving you a sales pitch are acting far too confident. Chances are, they're stretching the truth like a rubber band and twisting facts with vague interpretations or gross exaggerations. Most of all, they're telling you what they think you want to hear.

In my travels, which include more than 100 countries, I have come to realize that the Middle East is the birthplace of this ancient art form. But don't think I'm bashing the merchant culture in that part of the world. On the contrary; I've have had plenty of wonderful business experiences and business partners throughout the Middle East. If I hadn't, I wouldn't spend so much time over there. My experiences have taught me, however, that the merchants of the Middle East have a tendency to wax fanciful when describing business opportunities. Yes, I've encountered similar performances in Southeast Asia and Latin America, as well as from Nigeria to India and from South Africa to Hong Kong, but for my money the real pros reside in the Middle East – and North Africa.

In other words, international negotiation can be most challenging and potentially costly. As a global security consultant, you'll be dealing across borders on a regular basis. Therefore you're going to need to distinguish fact from fiction quickly and unerringly. I've found the best way to accomplish this is to learn the most commonly used negotiating strategies and tactics, and this chapter will help you do just that. It also will show you how to achieve mutually agreeable results with your respectable foreign partners.

Properly armed and prepared, you'll be able to deal with these characters and protect your business interests, thereby maximizing your chances of achieving long-term international success.

What Is International Negotiation?

I define international negotiation as when an entity from one country or background presents an array of objectives to another entity or entities from one or more different countries with the aim of reaching a mutually acceptable and profitable agreement.

That's the long version. To put it bluntly, I regard a successful international negotiation as closing the deal without hurting myself or my business.

Why the harsh terms? Because, unfortunately, conducting

negotiations often involves aspects such as aggression, competition, unfairness, deception and outright theft. It can become a struggle for survival – not literally but often financially.

But successful international negotiation doesn't have to be a zero-sum game. In fact, done properly it can turn out quite the opposite. A successful international negotiator should strive to achieve a win-win situation for all parties involved. Such an outcome obviously requires compromise, but even more so it requires trust, creativity and an open mind.

Quite a few years ago, I was visiting the Old City in Jerusalem. For centuries, street vendors and shopkeepers have sold their wares to visiting tourists inside those walls, which are held as sacred by Judaism, Christianity and Islam alike. There, the art of negotiation has been passed down from generation to generation, from father to son to grandson and so forth. I've done deals with clients on five continents, but one of the toughest negotiators I ever ran across was a merchant in one of those little shops. I learned a valuable lesson from him.

I remember it was a particularly hot day, and I was walking through an alleyway along the same path Christ himself probably walked. Suddenly, a set of six wine glasses sitting on the shelf of a booth caught my eye. I had no burning desire to buy them; I just found them visually arresting. The old shopkeeper, noticing my interest, quickly pounced on me. With a big, toothless grin, he said, "I give you good price, one hundred and fifty dollars."

"No, thank you," I replied.

"Okay, how much you give me?"

"I am not interested, thank you."

Before I was able to take another step forward, the man had taken one of the glasses off the shelf and moved to block my path. He pulled a rag from his back pocket and began polishing off the dust.

"You see, very nice glass, from time of Jesus."

"Yes, very nice," I smiled uncomfortably. "But now I must go."

"No, no! I give you good price. How much?"

Thinking I could outsmart the man and insult him with a

ridiculously low quote, for the sake of letting me go I made an offer.

"Thirty dollars," I said smugly.

"Okay! Thirty dollars – deal!"

Damn! I thought to myself. *What am I going to do now?* I was just taking a stroll between business meetings; I didn't have an easy way to transport the glasses back to my hotel. *Damn!*

Then I made my second mistake: I told the man I had changed my mind; I didn't want the glasses after all. He immediately became enraged and loudly cursed me out in Arabic. Next thing I knew, a group of other merchants had surrounded us. They reminded me in rather aggressive fashion that a deal was a deal.

Feeling intimidated, I realized I couldn't back out. Thinking again that I had no way of carrying a sextet of wine glasses through the Old City, I told the man I would return for them later. Needless to say, I never went back. The merchant got thirty dollars and kept the wine glasses; I walked away thirty dollars poorer but a thousand dollars wiser.

Negotiating Rule Number 1: Never enter into a negotiation if you're not prepared to accept the results.

If I had relied on trust, creativity and open-mindedness, I never would have been taken that day.

ALTERNATIVE: I could have told the merchant I wanted the glasses packaged and brought to my hotel later that day, where I would have paid for them.

RESULT: I would have been out thirty dollars but would have the wine glasses I favored.

ALTERNATIVE: I could have looked for something else to buy that was more transportable.

RESULT: I could have saved money, left the market with my purchase and ended my encounter with the merchant without drawing the mob.

ALTERNATIVE: I could have given the man a ten-dollar deposit and told him I would return later.

RESULT: I would have been out ten dollars instead of thirty.

PREFERRED ALTERNATIVE: I could have refused to give him a price in the first place, kept on smiling politely and backed away at the first opportunity.

RESULT: Avoiding the confrontation and – as it turned out – paying a ransom.

Instead, I was caught off guard, and the result was, on that day in Jerusalem, the old man played me like a fiddle. It reminds me of that hilarious British comedy *Bedazzled,* which was made in 1967 in England and 2000 in Hollywood. In both versions, the Devil offers a schnook seven wishes. But each time the schnook makes a wish, the Devil outsmarts him, resulting in more and more ridiculous situations and eventually the loss of his soul. I mention the plot of that movie to introduce…

Negotiating Rule Number 2: Never agree to a deal unless you've figured out all potential loopholes.

The Middle East might be the birthplace of aggressive negotiations, while Japan is home to a more subtle and noncommittal but just as tricky approach. Negotiating with a Japanese businessman can be long and, at times, tedious. Always maintaining a sense of formality and respect in their negotiations, the Japanese are pros at weighing the risks versus gains and holding out for an agreement that suits them.

One benefit of dealing with the Japanese is that they strive to achieve business relationships that will last for many years. It's critical to present the correct professional demeanor to ensure they will want to conduct business with you over time. This starkly contrasts with Russian businessmen, who will often throw absurd demands onto the bargaining table, trying to frame the negotiations more to their advantage. It's also typical for Russians to become more vocal at the table and at times even get up and walk away. These examples show why it's so important to understand the culture with which you're dealing – and to understand their form of bullshit.

You'll Need a BS Detector

So, how do you detect bullshit? I've heard many people claim they know it when they hear it. I agree, but there are certain characteristics that seem to be common among bullshitters, and you'd do well to learn them and keep an ear out for them:

+ The bullshitter always seems "this close" to achieving something spectacular.
+ He's a consummate name-dropper.
+ He claims to have money, but it's currently tied up in escrow or not readily accessible.
+ He rarely misses an opportunity to top your story with a better one of his own.
+ He always has an incredible deal for you – and only you.
+ He's always pushing his potential over his experience and performance.
+ His stories sound like they're from a Hollywood movie script.
+ His favorite word is "I."

And yes, there are female bullshitters, but this is primarily a masculine domain.

Any of it sound familiar? There's a phrase going around that suits it to a tee: déjà moo.

It's no crime to spew bullshit. Truth be told, in some parts of the world exaggeration is expected as part of everyday business – you'll find this out quickly if you ever do business with an Argentinean. Customary or not, bullshitting insults the intelligence of the listener and leaves a bad impression on those looking to engage in respectable business dealings. Across most of the globe, bullshitting is deemed arrogant and offensive – it's the kiss of death if you ever try to hard-sell a Japanese businessman.

Of course, it's your prerogative in your sales presentations to embellish your résumé or claim to know important people to whom you might have spoken only in a formal reception line. But my aim here is to help you become successful in this chosen line of work. So my advice is: Cut the crap.

As I mentioned, I've traveled to more than 100 countries. Everywhere I've gone, the more successful business people I've met, as a rule, are reserved and conduct themselves in a quiet, dignified manner. The flashy, big-mouthed individuals who throw their money and status around are decidedly in the minority at the top rungs of the ladder of commerce.

Therefore, never assume the person doing all the talking during an international negotiation is necessarily the most powerful decision-maker in the room. The person who always concerns me most at the negotiation table is the one who listens intently, clearly understands everything being said, and only speaks to ask the occasional, incisive question. He might not always be the decision-maker, but he probably exerts the greatest influence on the outcome.

Again using the Japanese example, their businesspeople are notorious for taking copious notes during negotiations, only to review them later in front of you and make statements such as, "I have studied your argument carefully, and I am afraid this will not work for us," or, "I have made the calculations, and unfortunately the numbers are not acceptable."

How to Conduct an International Negotiation

The best way to open a negotiation with someone from another country is to avoid taking a rigid, hard-line position. Don't jump into the numbers or attempt to posture for advantage. If you do, you'll immediately create an atmosphere of suspicion and defensiveness.

Instead, begin by discussing what a great opportunity the meeting presents for both (or all) of you. Suggest creative options before you talk about price. Be cordial with everyone and focus, at least at first, on how you can do the deal together. You goal should be to develop a long-term business relationship. Think of your first deal as a precursor to a much bigger deal that could happen in the future. In other words, if you've been thinking that this deal is of the one-and-done variety, you might want to reconsider why you're even doing business with this person or entity in the first place.

It might sound like obvious advice, but avoid doing business with assholes – again, forgive the crudity. Always keep in mind the prospect of building a lasting relationship with your negotiating counterpart. Otherwise, reevaluate.

Based on personal experience, discussions with colleagues and wisdom derived from other resources, here are my 10 Most Useful Tips for how to pull off an effective international negotiation:

1. Do your homework.
2. Listen more than you speak.
3. Be polite.
4. Be flexible.
5. Ask probing questions.
6. Trust but verify.
7. Keep (most of) your thoughts to yourself.
8. Control the negotiation.
9. Come prepared.
10. Be creative.

Each of these steps is critical to achieving a win-win negotiation in an international context. Here are more detailed descriptions:

1. Do your homework. In any negotiation, particularly an international one, you must conduct research on your prospective partners as well as the deal itself. You must uncover as many details as possible, because knowledge is power, and within knowledge resides confidence.

Start by examining the history of any previous deals the partners have done, including their possible constraints:

+ How long did previous negotiations take?
+ How much money was involved?
+ What negotiating style was used?
+ Was ego evident in completing the deal?
+ Were there personal situations, such as divorce, that impacted the negotiations?
+ More basic, what's in this new deal for them?
+ Are there cultural sensitivities or issues involved?

You should also research industry trends and market forecasts to help understand the terms under which the deal was set. This broader perspective might also provide clues about your prospective partner's thought processes and the underlying reason why he is considering doing business with you.

Never walk into an international negotiation blindly. Otherwise, remember what happened to me with the wine glasses. You could likewise find yourself being snookered.

2. Listen more than you speak. Some people speak when they should listen; that's a potential kiss of death in international negotiation. There seems to be a misconception that the person who talks the most in a negotiation is somehow winning. Don't fall for it. I always try to listen more than I speak, because I can only give away my position by talking. By listening, I have a better chance of understanding the other person's motivations and objectives. Plus, the less I say, the more I keep the other side guessing. I learned that lesson most vividly the day I bid thirty dollars for wine glasses.

3. **Be polite.** Don't feel bad if you hate the thought of negotiating. Few people truly enjoy the process. But it's necessary for doing business, particularly overseas. And if that's the case, you want to do everything you can, within reason, to put your counterparts at ease, and the best way is to show good manners.

Sure, a firm handshake, a smile and making eye contact are essential for creating a good first impression. But here's something you might not have heard. At first meeting, if someone hands you a business card, don't glance at it and stuff it in your pocket – and never in the back pocket of your pants. Certain cultures regard such a response as disrespectful and insulting.

As I mentioned earlier, accept the card with both hands; take a moment to read it carefully; perhaps extend a compliment such as, "I see your office is located in the free trade zone of Dubai – a convenient location and a smart business decision," and place it either in your shirt pocket or the breast-level pocket of your suitcoat. Sound trivial? It isn't. It suggests you will value your dealings with this person. It conveys respect and thoughtfulness.

If you want to learn more about the important nuances and points of etiquette in international negotiation, you should consider taking a diplomatic protocol course.

How your prospective international partners regard you will guide their decisions now and in the future. Besides, doing business is always better when you like the people you're dealing with. Life's too short for you to work with a mistrusted partner. It's always better to discuss your expectations sooner rather than later.

It demonstrates respect and encourages cooperation.

Anytime you don't trust the person sitting across the negotiating table from you, politely excuse yourself and leave. You don't need the headaches such a relationship inevitably will create.

4. Be flexible. To put it another way, bend but don't break. I don't necessarily mean you need to make unnecessary concessions, particularly on pricing matters. But being flexible means you're willing to consider alternatives and unconventional options in lieu of digging your heels in on price.

A word of caution: It's important for *both* sides to be flexible. If you sense you're the only one giving ground, be aware that your counterparts might be trying to take advantage of you. Be flexible, but insist – politely – on reciprocity.

5. Ask probing questions. Just as I outlined in the chapter on sales, you need to learn how to ask the right questions to discover your partner's Needs, Wants, Wounds, Authority and Money (NWWAM).

There's nothing wrong with asking someone why they are behaving in a particular way.

For example, "Mr. Hadid, I understand that no one wants to sacrifice profit, but perhaps you can tell me why you will not lower your margin on this particular deal just a few points."

Or, "Please, help me to understand why you want to keep that clause in the agreement."

Or, "Why is that issue is so important to you?"

Of course, the other side might not give you an honest answer. But it's your responsibility to employ your BS detector. The important thing to remember is if you're wondering, ask.

6. Trust but verify. This phrase was made famous by President Ronald Reagan referring to the relationship between the United States and Soviet Union during the Cold War. Certainly you want to be friendly and respectful to your negotiating partners – and you hope they will extend you the same courtesy. Just be sure you're not being played for a fool.

During an international negotiation, never take someone at their word without evidence to back it up – though sometimes there is no such evidence, and you'll have to rely on faith. Soviet leader Mikhail Gorbachev once related how he and President Reagan had reached an impasse during their first summit meeting. He said Reagan suddenly stood up from his chair, extended his hand, and said, "Hi, my name is Ron. Can we start over?" This led both men to break out in laughter, and from that point forward the two became lifelong friends and together changed the world.

The story also proves that you should never underestimate the power of your gut instinct.

7. Keep (most of) your thoughts to yourself. Poor negotiators have a tendency to come to the bargaining table and lay out everything they know and want right then and there. Clear communication is a vital part of negotiation, but there's no sense assuming that the other side knows everything you and your team are thinking.

Remember the scene in *The Godfather* when Sollozzo is pitching his deal to cooperate in the drug trade, and Sonny Corleone butts in with the surprised comment: *Are you telling me the Tattaglias will guarantee our investment?* Later on, Vito chastises his son: *Never tell anyone outside the family what you're thinking again.*

Vito was right, because Sonny's careless comment precipitated an attack on the don's life.

The Godfather is fiction, but that scene demonstrated wisdom. Never share everything with your counterparts; be honest, but provide only what is absolutely necessary. This is true even if you have obtained non-disclosure agreements and non-circumvention agreements. You are under no obligation to provide your thinking on all matters. It's a safe bet the other negotiators will be acting that way.

8. Control the negotiation. I don't mean talking incessantly or using an aggressive tone with others. You can listen twice as much as you talk and still fully guide the conversation.

The way to control a negotiation is to ask the other participants a combination of direct and open-ended questions. If someone begins to ramble with an answer, you can politely reel them back in with a direct yes/no question.

For example, "Ms. Whitcomb, I want to clarify something. You did say 10 percent, correct?" This allows for a break in the action and provides a chance for others to join in the discussion, or for you to ask another question.

You can also use the technique if someone else tries to control the conversation. That person might try to monopolize the time by laying out expectations and demands for everyone else at the table. The way to counteract it is to interrupt them, politely, with a question demonstrating that although you're listening, you're nevertheless the person directing the discussion – even if no formal moderator has been assigned. I call this the adult-in-the-room technique.

For example, "Mr. Polande, please allow me to interrupt you for a moment. You have gone on for quite some time, and I would like to hear the opinions of the others at the table. Could we please hear someone else's ideas for getting this deal done?"

Incidentally, the best way to cut someone off without offending them is by beginning your interjection with their name, even if you have to say it repeatedly. For example, "Mr. Polande, excuse me for a moment," instead of "Excuse me for a moment, Mr. Polande." If they continue rambling, just keep repeating their name, "Mr. Polande … Mr. Polande … Mr. Polande…" Trust me, it works.

9. Come prepared. Call it a variation on the Boy Scout motto. Arriving prepared to a negotiation is different than doing your homework. It means what you bring with you and what your overall strategy will entail.

On the television show The Apprentice, starring real-estate mogul Donald Trump, you might have noticed George H. Ross, Trump's attorney for over 30 years, offering his insights from time to time. Mr. Ross published an exceptional book on negotiation, *Trump-Style Negotiation: Powerful Strategies and Tactics for Mastering Every Deal*. The key takeaway I gleaned from Ross's expertise is the idea that you can create what he calls the "aura of legitimacy" by arriving with your own documentation, i.e., contract agreement forms, to begin your discussion.

By preparing documentation that will finalize the terms of the negotiation on your side of the table, you have demonstrated preparation, willingness and enthusiasm for completing the deal. This will serve you in a number of ways:

+ You set the tone and timeline of the negotiation with your documents. You might even intimidate others into believing you've fully researched all viable options of the deal already; thus they should trust your conclusions.

+ You've encouraged the other side to go along with you, because you've done all of the groundwork.

+ Your documentation will keep people on the record and discourage them from reneging on an agreement.

+ By controlling the documentation, you also control the conversation.

+ You've demonstrated you'll be no pushover at the negotiating table.

When I wrote my last book, *Among Enemies: Counter-Espionage for the Business Traveler*, I sent a copy to George Ross. I enclosed a note informing him that I enjoyed *Trump-Style Negotiation* and had used some of the strategies he recommended within my own business. Within a couple of weeks, Mr. Ross sent a personal note thanking me and wishing me luck. It was a class act from a wildly successful businessman whose time is obviously in great demand and a gesture from someone who has never forgotten where he came from.

10. **Be creative.** Hard-and-fast rules can often derail a negotiation before it begins. For example, I know a German executive who has worked at the same company for 30 years and has become resistant to change. More often than not, he's unflinching in his bargaining position for no other reason than he has always done business a certain way.

I'm not picking on my German colleagues, who are among the finest businesspeople on the planet. In fact, many positive stereotypes such as promptness, efficiency and discipline appropriately apply to their business culture.

I've also negotiated with a person from Brazil – a Paulista, meaning a person from São Paulo – who suddenly placed a strange array of new bargaining options on the table. These were items I'd never considered before and which weren't even directly involved with the initial discussion. Yet they somehow found merit by all involved.

Creativity can often become the leverage that gets a stuck deal back on track.

In this particular case, my Paulista wanted to increase the prices he was charging me for the use of his fleet of armored vehicles. Because of the rise in local fuel costs, and the fluctuation between the U.S. dollar and the Brazilian real, he wanted me to pay 20 percent more on every job.

At the time, my margins already were slim, and I didn't want to forfeit even one more dime of profit. I also didn't want to go back to my clients and inform them I had to raise my prices. We were at an impasse.

Because we had enjoyed a business relationship built on mutual trust and respect, my partner and I were able to find a creative solution that solved both our problems – we proposed creative options that we could both live with.

I agreed to a 5-percent rate increase instead of 20 percent. But I also promised to make a 50-percent down payment before he performed any job. It meant I would have to start asking my clients for a down payment as well, but it turned out to be one of the best business decisions I ever made. It put money in my pocket quicker and helped stop clients from contracting my services and then reneging at the last minute.

In return, my partner would have to provide an armored vehicle and driver, at no charge, anytime I flew down to Brazil. Because I traveled there several times a year, this more than made up for my concession. It was a win-win. It provided cash on hand much sooner for my partner and me, he received a 5-percent increase in fees, and I saved money on in-country transportation. It happened because we both compromised, and from then on we enjoyed a successful business relationship.

Five Hard-and-Fast Negotiation Rules
to Keep You Out of Trouble

Dealing with international partners can sometimes seem daunting. You could find yourself in a conference room far from home, sitting down with several foreign individuals in dark suits who want nothing more than to take advantage of you and your business. When – not if – you find yourself in this type of predicament, keep in mind the following five rules to prevent you from saying or doing something stupid that could jeopardize your business:

Rule 1: Don't say "yes" too quickly. Seeming too eager could paint you as a sucker. No matter how much you need the job, don't suggest that's what you're thinking. There's nothing wrong with pondering the deal for a little while. It has worked wonders for the Japanese.

Rule 2: Don't make the first major concession. Never be the first to blink – unless it's something you were willing to give away in the first place, and it will help free the negotiation from deadlock.

Rule 3: Do the math. Avoid giving away small fiscal concessions that could eat up your profits over the long run. Be cautious whenever the person across from you says, "All we are asking is that you give up a few dollars on XYZ product/service." Over time, those few dollars could cost you big money. But you won't know for sure until you do your own math and verify their numbers.

Rule 4: Remain skeptical. Smile politely but analyze every word you hear. Always ask yourself why your counterpart seems willing to concede on a particular point and not another.

Rule 5: Control the clock. Don't allow the person across the table from you use the threat of time running out to pressure you into making a huge concession. That's another recipe for potential disaster. On the other hand, there's nothing wrong with you turning the tables and setting a time limit on your offer. Negotiating is an art, not a science. If you're confident enough in your product and your people, you can afford to make the other guy sweat a little.

Knowing When to Walk Away

As the song goes, you have to know when to hold 'em, know when to fold 'em, know when to walk away, know when to run. Easily said, but withdrawing from the negotiating table can be a tough thing to do. Many of us get so involved with a deal we find it difficult to quit when irregularities in the project begin appearing.

Even when we begin to catch on to our potential partner's grandiose claims, we still think of the sacrifices already incurred and hope that, by seeing the deal through, the rewards will outweigh the shortcomings. Even if we smell a rat – or our BS detector starts ringing – we might still choose to look the other way.

This is dangerous. As Warren Buffett once said, "The difference between successful people and very successful people is that very successful people say 'no' to almost everything." You must know when to kill a deal and walk away from the negotiating table.

I recently had to walk away, even though it pained me to do so. I had negotiated an agreement involving a large commission from any investment capital or sales revenue I could generate for an international high-tech startup company. I believed strongly in the technology the company had developed, but I really didn't care much for one of the company's main partners. He had a sleazy demeanor that reeked of bullshit. He was not someone I would trust, much less do business with. Yet, I opted to push ahead anyway, because I was so impressed by the product.

In an attempt to find investment money, I brought in some of my friends from the Middle East to review the technology. One gentleman in particular, for whom I had great trust and respect, flew for several hours just to sit in on a two-hour meeting. He would fly back that same day. The technology demonstration went very well. Everything worked, and the potential of the system was evident to everyone in the room. However, the sleazy partner laid on the bullshit way too thick and insulted my guest with one absurd claim after another. On the drive back to the airport, my friend told me, "Luke, I can get you seed money for this technology; however, that one partner can in no way be involved with the deal. I will not have him anywhere near my people. Either he goes, or I go."

Suddenly, I was in a corner. I didn't have rights to the technology, so my bargaining power with the owners was limited. I also knew that even if I revealed my friend's concerns, they would have found a way to make it look like the one partner was not involved, but he would still be pulling strings from behind the scenes.

Truth be told, I shared my friend's qualms about the deal. I suggested we both move on. It was more important for me to tell him, "We each have concerns, and I do not want to take your money and jeopardize our friendship and our future business dealings. I am willing to walk away if you are."

So we did. As a result, I sacrificed a short-term profit – albeit very respectable as part of a seven-figure deal – in return for a more credible long-term opportunity. The technology company went on to moderate success, but I never once questioned my decision – nor has my friend, with whom I've done much larger deals since that day. Sometimes you can't be afraid to walk away. Just don't think it will be easy.

Bottom Line

When you start to succeed in your security business, you will gain more attention from people who want to do business with you. This isn't because people think you're such a great guy/gal to work with. Rather, it's because they see you as a vehicle to make money.

This is by no means a bad thing; your goal is also to make money. Just be sure to pay attention to people's motives.

In global security consulting, it's easy for a potential opportunity to transform itself into a nightmare rather quickly. The more successful you become, the more bullshit artists will show up on your doorstep. You must constantly keep your eye open for opportunities, but you also need to be watching your backside. One of the easiest ways to do this is to become more skeptical. Learn to say "Prove it," and assign milestones to your international contracts. Always ask for substantiation, demand that timelines be followed, monitor those timelines, keep an eye on your partners and vendors, and don't allow details to slip through the cracks.

Above all, trust but verify.

As your business progresses, international negotiation will become routine. But you must always be prepared for it. Like many other acquired skills, negotiating proficiency is perishable. You must practice in order to keep sharp.

FAQ

51. If I don't have much negotiating experience, do you have any advice to bring me quickly up to speed?

Remember the old joke about how to get to Carnegie Hall? This is similar. There are plenty of good books on negotiation available, but the only way to get good at it is by performing – over and over. But to start, I'd recommend taking a course from a reputable outfit, such as the Karrass seminars that have been advertised in airline magazines for decades.

51. If a potential client has a limited budget, is it a good idea to offer to perform a short-term pilot program at a discounted rate just to get my foot in the door?

No. More often than not, avoid pitching pilot programs. They shortchange both you and the client. If your potential partner isn't willing to allow you to perform your services to the best of your abilities, a test program is usually a waste of time.

53. What do I do if the client wants to hold me to a specific ROI guarantee? In other words, what if they expect a tenfold return or they're not paying?

Your job as a consultant is to improve the client's situation to make life easier. But sometimes a client will demand unrealistic goals as part of the contract, so even though you do improve their situation, they don't have to pay you. If the client insists on certain benchmarks in the proposal, then counter with performance bonuses for achieving the benchmarks.

54. Is it better to present a serious demeanor or a friendly one at the bargaining table?

It depends on the subject being negotiated. Unless you're a diplomat painstakingly creating a delicate peace agreement, or a lawyer hammering out the details of a divorce settlement between two vindictive spouses, always opt for a friendly tone. I do, because negotiating should be fun. Be yourself, use the tactics and strategies outlined above, and seek a win-win solution. When the negotiations are concluded, both parties should say to themselves, "I'd like to deal with this person again."

55. What if the negotiator tells me to take it or leave it?

If someone gives you an ultimatum, you have two choices: Walk away or change the dialogue. Tell your counterpart, "I don't agree with the terms you're offering, but I still want to do business with you. Let's find another way to restructure the deal in a way that satisfies us both." If he or she opposes this idea, you should walk away. It probably won't be worth doing business with this person in the long run.

Note from the Field
Island of Borneo
2235 hours

Thirteen time zones removed from my home in Northern Virginia, I'm sleeping tonight in a beachfront hotel in Bandar Seri Begawan, Brunei. As I lie in bed, my windows are open, and I am enjoying the sounds of a strong tropical downpour. A family of monkeys is howling excitedly in the trees. The waves of the South China Sea are crashing hard on the rocks below my balcony, all of which I can only hear and not see, because complete darkness has engulfed this tiny kingdom. Never in my wildest dreams would I have thought I would be here. It's just another reason why global security consulting is such a great profession. No matter where you are in the development of your practice, keep pushing forward. Hard work does pay off.

12. Now It's Time to Deliver

*You know what my father used to say? Being with a
client is like being in a marriage. Sometimes you get
into it for the wrong reasons and eventually they hit
you in the face.*

—Roger Sterling, Mad Men

IF YOU'RE A FAN OF THE POPULAR TELEVISION SHOW cited above, you've probably heard the main character Don Draper, among others on the show, utter the phrase: *The day you sign a client is the day you start losing them.* I hate to reinforce Mr. Draper's cynicism, but the truth is you can't always please every customer. Believe me, I've tried.

It might seem like an odd note on which to start this chapter, but please hear me out. To get this far you've successfully identified, contacted and inspired confidence in a prospective client. You've talked up your services, shown how you can save your new client money and gotten the signature on the dotted line to make it official. You've celebrated accordingly and obtained a 50-percent payment up front.

That was the easy part. Now you have to manage your relationship with the client and deliver what you promised. If winning business is like dating, then Roger Sterling is right: Serving a client is like a marriage. And as anyone who's been married knows, the two are vastly different.

In the international security business, things will not always go your way. Think about the challenges facing you. In some instances, you're hired to maintain order when your client has been directly threatened, many times forcing you to operate in a hostile environment. It's by no means easy. We're not being paid to provide traditional consulting services such as financial audits, employee

satisfaction surveys or management strategy sessions. We're performing international due diligence to prevent a company from walking
into a bad deal. We're assessing critical infrastructure to thwart a
potential terrorist attack. We're securing corporate intellectual property from computer hackers and foreign intelligence services. We're
investigating suspicious incidents or protecting the lives of employees and their families. Any errors on our part can be devastating
to a company and will likely result in losses far more serious than
bookkeeping irregularities.

Global security consultants are paid to minimize threats. But
they're never 100 percent successful. Every now and then, a client's adversaries will catch a lucky break in their attempts to harm,
embarrass, outwit, or otherwise disrupt the client's emotional or
physical state. When this occurs, the consultant shoulders the blame
and often the liability. To say the least, this leads to hard feelings
between the client and the consultant.

But if you stay in this business long enough, you won't be able
to avoid it. In these times, this has become an unfortunate-but-true
statement: Government (or a security company) needs to be successful 100 percent of the time, while a terrorist group needs to be
successful only 1 percent of the time.

In every case, you must constantly strive to provide your client
with the finest, most professional service possible. But you must
also recognize that perfection, be it ever the goal, is not possible in
our field. Looking back on every global security job I've performed,
there was always something I know I could have done better.

How do you deal with this ever-present risk of error? You must
establish metrics and conduct after-action reviews for every job.
They're crucial to the development of your business. Perhaps more
important, you must manage client expectations as a routine part of
your relationship.

If you screw up a job – which, if you're diligent and lucky
should not happen often – the best thing to do is own up to it,
immediately and straightforwardly. Clients always appreciate it
more when, instead of making up excuses, you say something like
this:

I know we failed to meet your expectations and desired goals. I agree with that assessment, and I'll do everything in my power to make it right immediately.

Don't offer to renegotiate the price of the contract. Likewise, don't offer discounts on future jobs. And by no means try to start again from scratch. This is the time to demonstrate how competent and task-oriented you are. You need to act quickly to solve the client's problem, to minimize the headaches as quickly as possible. *That's* the best type of apology.

How to Do It
Everything you've read so far has dealt with establishing your global security consulting business and winning new clients. Assuming you've set yourself up on solid ground and have sold yourself effectively, you're still left with the most important task of all: actually doing the job.

I'm asked about this a lot. "How do I do it?" If that's what you're thinking, good for you! It means you understand that delivering on your promises to international clients will be a difficult and complex process.

Moreover, if you've been following this text closely, you know there's no magic bullet or secret sauce in this business. The term "security" is so all encompassing that the field has sprouted too many diverse niches, so a set of boilerplate instructions or templates will never fit every situation. Even this book, which I think anyone with a reasonable background can use to break into the field, can't be universally applied. Likewise, if you try to work from canned materials, your clients will soon realize you're not offering a unique service. Many security consultants hide behind methodologies and matrices, because they have low self-esteem and don't know how to deliver outside that tight box. If so, say goodbye to your value as a consultant.

I can't just give you a business plan and send you on your way. But there are some guidelines you might find instructive as you try to meet client needs. I call them my Fast Five – immediate steps you can use when beginning any global security work:

Step One: Confirm the requirements and establish measurements of effectiveness.

As soon as a client has hired you, start to manage their expectations. You never want to dedicate yourself to a consulting project only to find out at the end that you didn't do what the client was expecting. That's business poison. You must make sure you're both on the same page from the start. How?

+ Don't take anything for granted.

+ Put everything in writing.

+ Carefully walk the client through his or her list of expectations.

+ Establish up front how you're going to conduct the project, how long it's going to take, what your client will be responsible for – because the client usually has a role to play, too – and what your deliverables will include.

+ Be realistic and honest about what the outcomes will be.

+ Never over-promise, but do over-deliver.

+ Establish measurements of effectiveness, or benchmarks, to help both sides comprehend more easily how the project is progressing.

+ Set realistic timelines.

+ Prepare a Plan B, and be sure to discuss how it can be used if the project doesn't progress as expected.

In all these cases, it's much better to discuss them before starting a project rather than even mid-way. Put yourself in your client's shoes. If someone has paid you up front, and then three months into the project you announce, "This isn't working; we need to change tactics," it's a much easier pill to swallow if you've already discussed the possibility of changing tactics or strategy. Don't try to force a solution down the client's throat if you both know your current plan isn't working.

Likewise, don't worry that you're bothering a client by asking questions or providing updates – within reason. Communication is always the best way to ensure your relationships and projects run smoothly. And establishing benchmarks is the best way to ensure effective communication.

Step Two: Get moving. Sometimes the best way to begin a project is to just do it.

As soon as you sign the contract, and you understand the client's expectations, take immediate action. Don't wait or tell the client you'll begin on such and such date, several weeks from now. Begin today.

That doesn't mean you must jump right on a plane. There are several tasks you could and should be doing. They include:

+ Request documents from the client, such as employee data records, threat reporting, emergency response plans, previous consulting reports, investigation information, and diagrams and blueprints.

+ Conduct open-source research on the client, competitors, area of operations and interest, and so forth.

+ Introduce the client to the key members of your staff assigned to the project.

+ Interview employees or other people related to the project.

+ Observe the client's day-to-day operations.

+ Perform a security advance of the location and assets in question.

+ Establish a liaison program with the key individuals who will be needed during the project.

I generally advocate productivity over activity, but it's also important to establish early momentum. Show the client that the check you've already cashed was not issued in vain. Be proactive and move with purpose – or urgency if necessary.

Step 3: Ask smart questions then shut up and listen.

I can't stress this enough. This rule should apply not only when you are selling your services but also as soon as you've won the contract. It's a basic truth about any type of consulting business: You must be able to know the right questions to ask.

As a security consultant, you are hired to identify problems and prescribe solutions, much like a doctor diagnoses an illness and prescribes medication. The only way you can identify a problem is to listen to what the client has to say about it. In order to guide the client into giving you the vital information, you must first be able to ask smart questions. As long as you're serving the client, your responsibility to ask penetrating questions never expires.

What is a smart question? It depends on the situation, but most of the time a smart question is an open-ended one. Questions with yes or no answers are usually not as effective as questions that encourage the client to describe or assess their take on a particular situation.

It's always important to get to the Who, What, Where, When, Why and How of any issue, but you can ask those questions in a way that elicits more detailed answers:

+ Whom do you believe is responsible and why?
+ What do you assess the problem to be and why?
+ Do you think there might be another underlying issue and, if so, why?
+ Who shares this belief and why?
+ Who does not share this belief and why?
+ When do you expect the next incident to take place and why?
+ What are the repercussions if this happens and why?
+ What are the repercussions if this does not happen and why?
+ Where do you think the next incident will take place and why?
+ How do you think the next incident will happen and why?

I hope you noticed the pattern in my questions: Never underestimate the power of Why. We learned this as children, but as we grow up we can begin to feel ashamed about it. Chalk it up to pride or foolishness. Either way, if you don't know something, it's okay to ask.

As a highly paid security consultant, your success rests with asking the right questions. But sometimes the simplest questions are the hardest to answer. Nevertheless, they can be the ones that trigger both diagnoses and prescriptions for the problems at hand. The most comforting and successful doctor is the one who begins with "Tell me where it hurts" and follows up accordingly.

Something else: Don't try to solve a client's problem within the first 20 minutes, no matter how long you have worked with this client. The client is looking for a speedy solution – which you should be striving to provide – but your thoroughness is what will make you effective. The more security you're required to provide, the greater your potential liability. Don't sacrifice time for a sloppy performance.

Take in all of the information, but don't be afraid to ask follow-on questions. Often, by persisting with questions, you can help your client reach the right conclusions. That's okay, and it doesn't devalue your role at all. Some clients hire a consultant to help push them over the hump of procrastination or inaction; others need to reach a conclusion on their own to see its merit.

Whatever the motivation, your greatest success will always come from listening to your clients. The more you speak, the more opportunity you create for putting your foot in your mouth. You don't need to solve all of the client's security problems during a one-hour meeting. Incidentally, I recommend that you charge US$500-2000 per hour for a security consultation and assessment, which is why you must grasp the concept of value-based fees.

Step 4: Document, Document, Document!

This is another big one. You must document *everything* you do for a client. Even if it seems trivial, document it. This can not only protect you legally, but it also demonstrates the time and effort you have committed to the client. It's also useful when situations such as scope-creep arise or when you need to renegotiate the original contract.

The best way to document your work is to create a project folder. I prefer the ones with a 5-tab divider. In it, record your time, expenses, email correspondence, project notes, timelines, measurements of effectiveness and miscellaneous paperwork. Keeping folders is also a great way to chronicle your experiences and develop your consulting skills. This shouldn't consume a large amount of your time. The more you document at first, the more proficient you will become, and future consulting projects will become easier for you.

Despite this electronic age, use an actual manila folder, in addition to an electronic copy that can be deleted, stolen or misplaced in the black hole that is personal computing. It might sound time consuming, but in the end it will keep you better organized and better focused on the project at hand. It will also allow you to subcontract your work more easily or bring others up to speed much more quickly.

When I meet with my clients, I often bring the project folder containing these documents with me. It serves not only as a source of reference but also psychological reinforcement. I can show my client that, yes, I have in fact been deeply engaged in the project and I'm carrying the proof. The folder also makes it more difficult for the client to hesitate about making the final payment.

Back to the Boy Scouts motto: Be prepared.

Last, avoid the trap of procrastinating your documentation. Too many times it's easy to say to yourself, "I'll get to it later." When later does come, you might have forgotten some things.

It's worse if you're managing more than one project simultaneously. If you allow your project-folder entries to fall behind, it will become even easier for things to fall through the cracks – an email here, a receipt there. Build enough time into your daily schedule to update your project folders. You'll be glad you did if your client ever challenges you about something at a later date. Besides, the process will keep you well-focused on the projects at hand and more engaged with them. As a result, you'll be better able to respond to client inquiries or crises at a moment's notice.

If you're just too busy to update your project folders, it probably means your business is doing well and it's time to hire a personal assistant to do it for you. That's progress.

Step 5: Play the 'What If?' Game.

Forgive me for bringing this up again, but I learned something while playing football that was reinforced even more when I started doing intelligence work overseas: Always ask yourself, "What if?"

What if this defender blitzes on this play?

What if the kicker tries to run the ball?

What if the guy I'm supposed to meet in the middle of the night on this remote Afghan road is setting me up?

One situation might be more important than the other, depending on how big a college football fan you are, but each question points you in the same direction: Always consider every possible scenario – good or bad.

Anticipating various outcomes will not only protect your assets as a security consultant, but it will also help you determine how to proceed with a client's problem:

+ What if the car gets a flat tire?

+ What if someone blocks the road?

+ What if the client has a heart attack in the car?

+ What if the car gets rear ended by another vehicle?

+ What if someone shoots at our vehicle?

+ What if we hit a dog crossing the road?

+ What if the road starts to flood?

+ What if an IED detonates?

As you can see, you can play the What if? game indefinitely – and sometimes literally. You can run through 50 scenarios, and then something completely unimagined occurs during an actual situation. The point isn't to ask so many questions that you panic and get caught up in some absurd logical extreme. It's that you always have well-considered contingency plans, at least three of them per scenario. The more you discuss and practice these contingencies, the more effective you will be with your job, and the more effective you will be in unplanned scenarios.

This reminds me of a line from the opening scene in the movie *Ronin*, in which Robert DeNiro, playing a former CIA officer, is supposed to meet a contact in a bar for the first time. Before going in, DeNiro's character hides a gun in the alley behind the bar. When he retrieves the gun later in front of the contact, he remarks: *I never walk into a place without a plan to walk out.*

Before walking into any global security situation, always be sure you have a plan to get yourself and your client safely out.

Delivering Your Services

In this business, your deliverables might consist of a physical service, such as secure executive protection or armored transport. Or, it might be a written report containing valuable information or intelligence useful to your client. What matters most is that you deliver.

Presenting your deliverables is important, but always take care not to lose sight of the client's final objective. Too many consultants become hung up on pretty reports, with fancy charts and pictures, but they never solve the client's underlying problem.

I confess I've personally spent way too much time and money delivering the perfect report to a client. Let's face it: We all want to do and look our best, and sometimes a sexy report is the easiest way to wow a client. Just be conscious that artwork doesn't replace substance. Discerning clients will know that.

When it comes to final reports, size doesn't always matter. Don't get hung up on the idea that you need to write a 200-page report to satisfy the client's problem – or justify your consulting fee. You want to be thorough, but clarity should always be your first consideration.

If you have a tendency to write page after page or feel the need to bulk up your report with charts and graphs, be sure to include an executive summary. Clients in this business are extremely busy people. You might have labored on the report for weeks, but the client should see answers to his or her questions and proposed solutions to the problems at hand right up front. Later, and time permitting, the client can pore over the details you've laid out in the body of the text.

The hallmark of many strategic management firms is to overwhelm clients with their PowerPoint presentations, aka decks, throwing in the latest two-by-two matrices, moon charts or cascading graphs. A competent global security consultant, on the other hand, should be able to lay out proposed solutions succinctly and with commonsense language. At SMI, we often present only a CARVER matrix or what's called a Pair-Wise-Comparison chart (see Appendix B on page 264) to qualify and quantify our findings and recommendations. We stick to the basics, and our clients never suspect us of peddling fluff. Don't over-rely on graphics. If you can't describe the gist of your solution in a couple of paragraphs, written or spoken, maybe you haven't yet fully grasped the problem.

The report might be a point of pride for you, but to a senior executive or high-ranking official it's just another memo. It doesn't mean your effort has been wasted; it's that the style in which you present it is of less importance than the *order* of information.

When it comes to deliverables, the rule of thumb is to under-promise and over-deliver. When you've completed your project, you'll want to see a big wide smile on your client's face. If so, you've successfully executed Step One. You've managed the client's expectations. The more you can control what your client anticipates – though you need to be careful you don't shatter confidence in you – the more likely you'll have made an outstanding impression by the time the final payment is due.

As I stressed in Chapter 6, referrals are the essence of your business, and the best time to ask is at the end of a successful project. Referrals keep you honest. If you're always thinking, *Is this work good enough to guarantee me a recommendation or two?* then you should succeed nine times out of ten.

Dealing with Difficult Clients

Some clients are impossible to please. No matter what you do, they will not be satisfied. You think you've provided them an outstanding deliverable, yet they argue it's incomplete. Often, such clients are the little guys, the smaller accounts who are always complaining about price and demanding discounts. They contact you insistently with ridiculous requests or complain about irrelevant subjects.

Trust me; they're out there. Interesting, but the big accounts are usually less demanding. As long as you perform, the big-name players will gladly pay on time and continue to use your services. We should all be so lucky to confine our clients to the Fortune 500.

I've lost a lot of sleep over the little guys. They're the best and worst things that will happen to your business. They're often the first to risk working with you, the most vocal in their early support and referrals, and the most committed to maintaining the relationship. But companies and individuals that must be dealt with for fear of losing guaranteed revenue can also be nightmares. They're the biggest offenders of scope-creep – the term applied to clients that sneak in additional tasks without paying for them. They can be relentless drains on your time.

How can you keep your more demanding clients happy? Simple, get rid of them. Unless an account is worth substantial annual revenue – say, over US$100,000 per year – consider refusing their business. Yes, $100,000 sounds like a lot of money – and it is – but when broken down over the 1-year or 2-year lifetime of a contract, when you have to pay employees, insurance, taxes and other expenses, it can actually cost you money. It's never worth your time or dignity to put up with the headaches of clients that consider you beneath them or who think they can push you around.

I've written in previous chapters about the need to present yourself as an equal to prospects and clients. But that works both ways. If a client fails to treat you as an equal, it's time to seek business elsewhere. This might sound arrogant or pretentious. But know that I'm a firm believer in the adage "Pride goeth before a fall." I never want to present myself as being better than my clients. I never forget who is working for whom. But I also believe respect should be a two-way street, no matter how much the client is paying me.

As an alternative, if a demanding client represents substantial value to your business, you could hire extra people to shoulder the burden of their demands. It could be worth sacrificing some profit from the account to gain more sleep at night. The client will like having even more personal attention through dedicated project managers, and you can allow the phone to ring at someone else's desk. But until you can afford the support staff, consider cutting the problem accounts loose. As I've mentioned repeatedly, life's too short – in this case to put up with difficult people.

Postscript

I never tell subject-matter experts how to operate in their area of expertise. If you earn your living as a bomb tech, I'm not going to tell you how to defuse a bomb. If you specialize in North Korean nuclear issues, I won't tell you how to do whatever North Korea nuclear analysts do. My goal in this chapter has not been – and really can't be – presenting a blueprint for how each security shop should operate. Instead, my objective has been to show you how to begin and follow through on a security-related consulting project: how to get organized, how to stay focused and how to stay out of trouble. At this point in your life, you should already be an expert in your chosen field. My job is to help you turn that expertise into a sustainable career.

A lot of businesses, SMI included, like to boast, "We have been in business for X years and we still maintain our very first client." Those are the success stories of people who approached every job from the outset with professionalism and dedication. Testimonials, however, don't tell you how to retain clients. You constantly must deliver on what you promise. Make sure you have the infrastructure and policies in place to hit the ground running. Make sure you maintain an open line of communication with each of your clients. Make sure you let each client know what to expect and when to expect it. Make sure you rectify problems or shortcomings without hesitation. Make sure you hear before you speak. Make sure you don't waste your client's time in reports, meetings or billable hours. Make sure you don't waste your own time. And above all, make sure you provide your clients with what they desire most: solutions. That's what global security consulting is all about.

FAQ

56. How can I be sure I am delivering the best customer service?

Simple: Ask your customers. Have them complete a survey at the end of each project to tell you what you could have done better. Customer service is something that can always be improved. You might also consider booking a suite at the Four Seasons for a weekend to see what customer service is all about.

57. If I know I can solve my client's problem right away, should I stretch out my time to increase my profit?

No, it's quite the opposite. The sooner you can solve your client's problems, the more valuable you will become. Plus, it isn't ethical to bill your clients unnecessarily.

58. If a client is paying me US$50,000 for a due-diligence report, how long should that report be?

Page length is something only university professors care about. In the real world, the value of the information is far more important than a bunch of charts and graphs that only add bulk to a text. The client isn't paying you to report what's already known. You're paid to uncover what's been unknown. My due-diligence reports typically range from 5 pages to 30 pages.

59. If my client isn't satisfied with my work, should I offer a discount?

We only offer a discount if someone on our team has been negligent. We always guarantee our work. But if a client tries to renegotiate the contract after services have been rendered, I resist. If a client wants to quibble about price, I might offer a discount on the next job or agree to provide some additional services to justify the current price. I very rarely lower the amount in a contract that's been signed

60. To be honest, I'm a bit intimidated by my client. Who am I to tell this CSO, COO or CEO how to run his or her business?

It's natural to be nervous with a big-name client. Just don't let it affect your confidence in your expertise. When in doubt, adhere to the four C's – confidence, character, consistency and commitment. Those attributes will serve you well in front of even the toughest client.

Note from the Field

Beirut

1500 hours

I just returned from having lunch with a good friend at the beautiful restaurant Indigo on the Roof, which overlooks the blue waters of the Mediterranean and is located at the Le Gray Hotel. Whenever I'm in Lebanon for business, I never miss a chance to catch up with my good buddy Reed. He's a U.S. Naval Academy graduate who has vast experience in the nuclear security field. For the past two decades, he has made his living as a business development middleman – aka a rainmaker – throughout the Middle East and North Africa. Besides discussing college football, we both like to hear each other's opinions on the various international deals we're constantly developing.

It's always a good idea to bounce ideas off a trusted colleague from time to time. Such open discussions can often prevent you from wading into a bad situation or discredit the rumor mill about potential opportunities. It never hurts to have a fresh pair of eyes take an objective look at one of your pending deals. Just make sure those eyes are looking out for you.

Afterword

It's not how you start; it's how you finish.

—Chuck Bencie

SO, YOU'RE FINALLY READY TO OPEN THE DOORS on your new global security consultancy. You've read all the books – with this one kept near your desk as a convenient reference – and made all the necessary preparations. Now it's time to launch your business. It's game time. Therefore, allow me to offer some final words of encouragement and advice.

For your pre-launch pep talk, here's something that Nick Saban, my coach at Michigan State, once told our Spartans football team during the week leading up to a game against our rival, the University of Michigan Wolverines, a game we won despite being heavy underdogs.

Saban told the story of Julius Caesar's invasion of England at the White Cliffs of Dover. Anyone familiar with history knows that Rome's invasion was more of a temporary incursion in 53 B.C. And anyone really familiar with history knows the story is similar to something the Spanish explorer Cortez did some 1500 years later. But to Saban, the tale provided a motivational lesson he thought his team would need.

Caesar had dispatched his naval armada to conquer England, a country defended by skilled and undefeated soldiers. Although the Roman legions required roughly 800 ships, they were still greatly outnumbered by the powerful English army. To make matters worse, as the Romans approached the coast, the English were seen eagerly lining up for battle atop the steep cliffs – vertical rock walls that were considered unclimbable.

Caesar directed his commanders to anchor downshore from the cliffs and establish a beachhead. Although his men disembarked and constructed their camp successfully, they knew they faced a determined army above them. Fearing that his troops would not be inspired to advance, Caesar gave the order "Burn the boats," thus preventing any chance of retreat. Defeat was no longer an option; it was victory or death. The Romans had no choice but to succeed – which they did. Historians might dispute the story, but the message remains valid: Perseverance pays, and sometimes you must burn your own boats before great things can happen.

As an entrepreneur, you will inevitably find yourself looking up at what appears to be an insurmountable obstacle at some point during the evolution of your business. It could be competing against a larger, more established company for a contract, trying to satisfy an overly demanding client, or desperately needing to close a deal in order to pay the rent. You will no doubt encounter more challenges as a business owner than you ever did as someone else's employee.

When I was starting out, there were many months in which I never took a paycheck. I had to pay an employee or vendor instead. For the first couple years, my wife and I had to give up dining at fancy restaurants in favor of eating at home. Instead of going out to lunch, I brown-bagged it at my desk. Money was scarce, and I needed to be smart with every purchase. I had exhausted my savings – I had burned my boats – and had no choice but to prevail. It wasn't easy, and there were many nights that my stomach required that vaunted speedy relief from Alka-Seltzer.

I'm not trying to discourage you. Provided you're doing the right things every day, showing measurable if incremental improvement, you will succeed. You have to commit yourself to getting better each day. You have to make that one additional, uncomfortable phone call to a prospective client. You have to send out that one extra news release. You have to reexamine your processes to find areas where you can streamline your efforts and be more efficient. You have to maintain neatly balanced books. You can never stop improving.

Throughout my life, I've had my share of ups and downs. We

all have. But you must keep pushing forward. In these pages, I've laid out my ideas, suggestions and opinions to help you build a global security consultancy. Now, let me leave you with something that has served me well for over 25 years. It might be helpful when your practice undergoes challenges of its own.

It's a simple poem you might already know. My dad shared it with me when I was a teenager. If you're ever struggling with your business, it might be the equivalent of Nick Saban's story to keep you forging ahead.

Don't Quit

When things go wrong, as they sometimes will,
When the road you're trudging seems all uphill,
When the funds are low and the debts are high,
And you want to smile, but you have to sigh,
When care is pressing you down a bit,
Rest if you must; but don't you quit.

Life is queer with its twists and turns,
As everyone of us sometimes learns,
And many a failure turns about
When he might have won had he stuck it out;
Don't give up, though the pace seems slow;
You might succeed with another blow.

Often the goal is nearer than
It seems to a faint and faltering man,
Often the struggler has given up
When he might have captured the victor's cup.
And he learned too late, when the night slipped down,
How close he was to the golden crown.

Success is failure turned inside out;
The silver tint of the clouds of doubt;
And you never can tell how close you are,
It may be near when it seems afar;
So stick to the fight when you're hardest hit;
It's when things seem worst that you mustn't quit.

— Anonymous

I don't pretend to hold all the answers. I can only offer you my personal experiences as a guide to help you establish your own identity. I hope you've found this book to be valuable on your journey to establish your own global security consulting practice. The real key to success will be your passion and commitment to your business. Always try to remember why you chose this field in the first place. For the past five years, I've never once said to myself, "I wish I didn't have to go to work today." Instead, it's usually, "I can't wait to get in the office this morning!" For me, that's the perfect job. I hope you'll find that same enjoyment.

When you're up and running, feel free to drop me a note and let me know how you're doing. Who knows? We might end up doing business together.

Until then, I wish you good luck and great prosperity.

Acknowledgments

After my first book, *Among Enemies: Counter-Espionage for the Business Traveler*, took me 18 months to write, I thought it would be some time before I would try being an author again. But as the book became more popular, I began to field numerous questions from friends and colleagues who wanted to know how to start their own security consulting business. Before I knew it, I was up at 6 o'clock each morning typing away once more. Now that I've completed my second act, I need to thank the following people:

My unbelievably dedicated and understanding wife, Viviane, who once again put up with my crazy travel and work schedule. Her patience and countless hours listening to my chapter ideas make her a saint. She is my best friend, my most trusted adviser and love of my life. We have come a long way since stapling proposals together on the floor of our old one-bedroom apartment.

To my publisher Phil Berardelli and his outstanding team at Mountain Lake Press, thank you once again for allowing me the freedom to share my ideas and observations with what I hope will become a large and loyal readership.

To all the employees, subcontractors, vendors and friends with whom SMI has had the privilege to work over these past years, you have made our firm what it is today. I could not have done it without your unselfish contributions.

To our SMI clients, who took the chance on a small firm when we were just starting out, thank you for believing in us. We hope we can always provide you with the superior service you so rightly deserve.

Last but not least, to my parents, for their unconditional love and support all these years. My mother continues to teach me about business, and my father continues to teach me about life. Thank you both from the bottom of my heart!

Appendix A

Emergency Medical Kit Contents

As a global security consultant, you might have to travel to some of the harsher locales on the planet, such as West Africa or the poorly resourced "Stan" countries (Afghanistan, Pakistan, Uzbekistan, etc). On one occasion I had to be medevaced out of Nepal because of health issues, and I almost suffered brain damage in Ghana because of dehydration. Obviously, in this business you must learn to become your own doctor. Now, I always carry an ample medical kit with the following items:

+ Antibiotics – There are some nasty bugs out there, you need something that can kill them in your body fast. I prefer doxycycline for daily use and ciprofloxacin when I'm seriously infected – but always check with your doctor about side effects.
+ Anti-diarrheal – Dehydration from diarrhea kills millions of people worldwide each year in the underdeveloped countries. Pack plenty of Imodium as well as Gatorade powder to replace your electrolytes.
+ Anti-malarial – Also one of the biggest killers in the world, it's usually treated with a quinine derivative. I pack mefloquine, but chloroquine is the most widely used, and doxycycline can double. Again, check with your doctor.
+ Pepto-Bismol or Alka-Seltzer to keep your stomach together.
+ Israeli bandage – This all-purpose bandage can take care of severe cuts or lacerations.
+ Tourniquet – just in case you become seriously wounded.
+ Triangle bandages – They're easy to pack and incredibly useful.
+ Alcohol wipes/hand bottles – There are a lot of sharp things in the world; you don't need an infection.
+ Gauze pads/large bandages – When you are cut, you need to keep your wounds sterile and covered.
+Duct tape – It's always more useful than athletic/medical tape alone.
+ Medicated wipes (Tucks® or Preparation H® make good ones) – You would trade away your car for one of these if you suffer severe diarrhea (or "become bitten by the cobra," as they say) on one of your trips. I always over-pack them.

You should also consider investing in Medevac insurance.

Appendix B

Sample charts

SMI's CARVER Matrix

Facility:												
Date:												
Prepared by:												
Asset	Description	Design Basis Threat	Criticality	Accessability	Recoverability	Vulnerability	Effect	Recognizability	Risk	Pa
Intake	2MGD	Physical destruction	3	5	2	4	3	3	20	0.67
									0	0.00
									0	0.00
									0	0.00
									0	0.00
									0	0.00
									0	0.00

SMI's Pair-Wise-Comparison Matrix*

Adversary	Active Shooter	Theft	Assault	Hacker	Arsonist	Vandal	Ranking	Pair-Wise Ranking
Active Shooter							0.00	Pair-Wise Ranking
Theft	6.00						6.00	1 – Much Lower Than
Assault	6.00	6.00					12.00	2 – Lower Than
Hacker	6.00	6.00	6.00				18.00	3 – The Same As
Arsonist	6.00	6.00	6.00	6.00			24.00	4 – Greater Than
Vandal	6.00	6.00	6.00	6.00	6.00		30.00	5 – Much Greater Than

*introduced to SMI by Sandia National Laboratories

Recommended Reading

Accounting for Dummies: 5th Edition, by John A. Tracy. Hoboken, New Jersey: John A. Wiley & Sons, 2013

The Art of the Start: The Time-Tested, Battle-Hardened Guide for Anyone Starting Anything, by Guy Kawasaki. New York: Penguin, 2004

The Art of War, by Sun Tzu (Thomas Cleary translation). Boston: Shambhala Publications, 1988

The Art of Woo: Using Strategic Persuasion to Sell Your Ideas, by G. Richard Shell and Mario Moussa. New York: Penguin, 2007

Blue Ocean Strategy: How to Create Uncontested Market Space and Make Competition Irrelevant, by W. Chan Kim and Renée Mauborgne. Boston: Harvard Business School, 2005

Confessions of an Economic Hit Man, by John Perkins. New York: Plume, 2005

The Craft of Intelligence: America's Legendary Spy Master on the Fundamentals of Intelligence Gathering for a Free World, by Allen W. Dulles. Guilford: Lyons Press, 2006

The Effective Executive: The Definitive Guide to Getting the Right Things Done, by Peter Drucker. New York: HarperCollins, 2002

The E-Myth Revisited: Why Most Small Businesses Don't Work and What to Do about It, by Michael E. Gerber. New York: HarperCollins, 2004

Enchantment: The Art of Changing Hearts, Minds, and Actions, by Guy Kawasaki. New York: Penguin, 2001

The Essential Deming: Leadership Principles from the Father of Quality, by W. Edwards Deming, Joyce Orsinig. McGraw-Hill, 2013

The Firm: The Story of McKinsey and Its Secret Influence on American Business, by Duff McDonald. New York: Simon & Schuster, 2013

Good to Great: Why Some Companies Make the Leap ... and Others Don't, by Jim Collins. New York: Harper-Collins, 2001

Guerrilla Marketing for Consultants: Breakthrough Tactics for Winning Profitable Clients, by Jay Conrad Levinson. Hoboken: Jay Wiley & Sons, Inc, 2005

How to Win Friends and Influence People, by Dale Carnegie. New York: Simon & Schuster, 1981

Kiss, Bow, or Shake Hands, by Terri Morrison, Wayne A. Conaway, and George A. Borden. Avon: Adams Media Corp, 2006

The Lords of Strategy: The Secret History of the New Corporate World, by Walter Kiechel III. Boston: Harvard Business Press, 2010

The Magic of Thinking Big, by David J. Schwartz. New York: Fireside Press, 1987

McKinsey's Marvin Bower: Vision, Leadership, & the Creation of Management Consulting, by Elizabeth Hass Edershem. New York: John Wiley & Sons, 2004

Million Dollar Consulting: The Professional's Guide to Growing a Practice, by Alan Weiss. McGraw-Hill, 2009

Never Eat Alone: And Other Secrets to Success, One Relationship at a Time, by Keith Ferrazzi with Tahl Raz. Random House, 2005

The Tipping Point: How Little Things Make a Big Difference, by Malcolm Gladwell. Little, Brown and Company, 2002

To Sell is Human: The Surprising Truth About Persuading, Convincing, and Influencing Others, by Daniel H. Pink. Edinburgh: Canongate Books, 2013

Trump Style Negotiation: Powerful Strategies and Tactics for Mastering Every Deal, by George H. Ross. Hoboken: Wiley, 2008

Trust Me, I'm Lying: Confessions of a Media Manipulator, by Ryan Holiday. New York: Penguin, 2012

The Ultimate Sales Machine: Turbocharge Your Business with Relentless Focus on 12 Key Strategies, by Chet Holmes. London: Penguin, 2008

What Got You Here Won't Get You There: How Successful People Become Even More Successful, by Marshall Goldsmith. New York: Hyperion, 2007

What the CEO Wants You to Know: Using Business Acumen to Understand How Your Company Really Works, by Ram Charan. New York: Crown Business, 2001

Win: The Key Principles to Take Your Business from Ordinary to Extraordinary, by Frank I Luntz. New York: Hyperion, 2011.

The Winner Within: A Life Plan for Team Players, by Pat Riley. New York: Berkley Books, 1987

Winning, by Jack Welch. New York: HarperCollins, 2005

Wooden on Leadership: How to Create a Winning Organization, by John Wooden. New York: McGraw-Hill, 2005

Index